Spirit Wind

Spirit Wind

The Doctrine of the Holy Spirit in Global Theology
—A Chinese Perspective

EDITED BY
Peter L. H. Tie
AND
Justin T. T. Tan

☙PICKWICK *Publications* • Eugene, Oregon

SPIRIT WIND
The Doctrine of the Holy Spirit in Global Theology—A Chinese Perspective

Copyright © 2021 Wipf and Stock Publishers. All rights reserved. Except for brief quotations in critical publications or reviews, no part of this book may be reproduced in any manner without prior written permission from the publisher. Write: Permissions, Wipf and Stock Publishers, 199 W. 8th Ave., Suite 3, Eugene, OR 97401.

Pickwick Publications
An Imprint of Wipf and Stock Publishers
199 W. 8th Ave., Suite 3
Eugene, OR 97401

www.wipfandstock.com

PAPERBACK ISBN: 978-1-5326-3273-0
HARDCOVER ISBN: 978-1-5326-3275-4
EBOOK ISBN: 978-1-5326-3274-7

Cataloguing-in-Publication data:

Names: Tie, Peter L., editor. | Tan, Justin T. T., editor.

Title: Spirit wind : the doctrine of the Holy Spirit in global theology—a Chinese perspective / edited by Peter L. H. Tie and Justin T. T. Tan.

Description: Eugene, OR : Pickwick Publications, 2021 | Includes bibliographical references.

Identifiers: ISBN 978-1-5326-3273-0 (paperback) | ISBN 978-1-5326-3275-4 (hardcover) | ISBN 978-1-5326-3274-7 (ebook)

Subjects: LCSH: Holy Spirit. | Theology. | China.

Classification: BT121.3 .T54 2021 (print) | BT121.3 .T54 (ebook)

Scripture quotations marked (NIV) are taken from the Holy Bible, New International Version®, NIV®. Copyright © 1973, 1978, 1984, 2011 by Biblica, Inc.™ Used by permission of Zondervan. All rights reserved worldwide. www.zondervan.com The "NIV" and "New International Version" are trademarks registered in the United States Patent and Trademark Office by Biblica, Inc.™

12/29/20

Contents

Acknowledgments | vii
Contributors | ix
List of Abbreviations | xi

Biblical-Theological Perspective

1. Spirit, Scripture, Saints, and Seminary: Toward a Reappropriation of "Spirit Illumination" in "Scripture Interpretation" for Seminarians | 3
   —Peter L. H. Tie

2. From "the Spirit of the Lord *Clothed* Gideon" to "*Put On* the New Man" | 37
   —Kwang-Chi Liu

3. You Have Made All Things Beautiful in Their Time: Reflections on the Spirit of Beauty | 66
   —Justin T. T. Tan

Historical-Theological Perspective

4. *Charismata* in the Early Church | 81
   —Samuel H. H. Chiow

5. Montanism: Precursor of the Contemporary Charismatic Movement? Feminist Aspirations? | 101
   —Esther Yue L. Ng

6. The Holy Spirit: Retrieving the Patristic Pneumatology of the Fourth Century | 128
   —Loe Joo Tan

Cultural/Pastoral-Theological Perspective

7. The Logos and Pneuma of Creation: A Cross-Cultural Reading of Romans 8 and the Inspirited World | 147
   —K. K. Yeo

8. An Analysis of the Conceptual Metaphor The Holy Spirit is Fire in Selected Mandarin Christian Songs | 162
   —Kai-Wen Karen Yuan

9. Renewing Global Christianity: An Asian American Pentecostal Perspective on the Way | 190
   —Amos Yong

Acknowledgments

THE CHURCH'S UNDERSTANDING OF the person and work of the Holy Spirit has continued to be a fascinating area of investigation, and recently, the globalization of theology has given rise to multi-faceted research from the majority World. Indeed, the research into the ministry and person of the Holy Spirit has affected all aspects of the theological enterprise, and it has manifested itself as wide-ranging as the Holy Spirit is majestic. Theologians from the majority World, with their unique cultural background, have now begun to contribute to the widening flow of the theological stream.

The present volume is but another input to that theological stream. It is not meant to provide a comprehensive study of the doctrine of the Holy Spirit, but is intended to help God's people acknowledge and perceive the continuous works of the Holy Spirit about which we often feel unapproachable and inconceivable.

Spirit Wind was initially a project for the 20th Anniversary of Melbourne School of Theology's [MST] Chinese Department (Melbourne, Australia). Being a Chinese Theological Department, Justin Tan, who was then the vice-principal of the College, and Peter Tie, who was the Theology lecturer there, were assigned the task to showcase what the Chinese Theology is contributing to the global theological enterprise.

Peter went about contacting Chinese theologians globally, and the responses were overwhelming. When Peter moved to Christian Witness Theological Seminary [CWTS] in USA, the project was delayed for various reasons. The publication of this volume would not have been possible without the collaborative effort of the following four significant groups of people:

First, we are thankful for each and every author who has demonstrated not only his or her academic excellence but also Christ-like passion to delve into the mysterious and sovereign works of the Holy Spirit in order to help God's people understand and appreciate their faith more intimately. Their chapter contributions are invaluable for further theological conversations within the Orient and the West.

Second, we are grateful for the people who are involved in the tedious processes of translating, proofreading, and/or editing. Their commitment and perseverance are to be commended. Without them, the manuscript would not have been successfully completed. They deserve to be mentioned by name (alphabetically by surname):

Dr. Andrew Brown (MST, Old Testament lecturer);

Jane Chang (CWTS, Associate Librarian);

Dr. Kevin Chen (CWTS, Old Testament professor);

Wu Kiat Foo (MST, M.Th. candidate in Old Testament);

Anastasia Tie (Biola University, BA student majoring in English: Writing).

Third, we are also grateful for Wipf and Stock Publisher (Pickwick) for being patient with us and flexible with the manuscript submission date. For various reasons, we have had to keep postponing the project, but the publisher has shown us grace and understanding. Thank you, again.

Finally, from Peter, he would like to thank his family's ongoing partnership and prayerful support; they are one of the main reasons that he is able to accomplish this project. Big hugs to his loving family! And from Justin, he could not have done this without Peter! It is Peter's labor that has made this publication possible. The wonderful faculty and staff at MST and CWTS (and all the students past and present) have been for us a God-given support throughout.

While as editors, we do not endorse every perspective proposed in this book, we *do* pray that every chapter may serve as an instrument of motivating believers to love God—the Father in Christ through the Spirit—more humbly and serve him more passionately.

Peter L. H. Tie, San Jose, California

Justin T. T. Tan, Melbourne, Australia

Contributors

(by surname)

Samuel H. H. Chiow (PhD, Saint Louis University)
Professor of Church History and Theology
China Evangelical Seminary, Taiwan

Kwang-Chi Liu (PhD, Southern Baptist Theological Seminary)
Associate Professor of Old Testament
Taiwan Baptist Christian Seminary, Taiwan

Esther Yue L. Ng (PhD, University of Aberdeen)
Adjunct Senior Professor
Christian Witness Theological Seminary, USA

Justin T. T. Tan (PhD, University of London)
Director and Senior Lecturer
Centre for the Study of Chinese Christianity, Melbourne School of Theology, Australia
Senior Research Fellow, Australia College of Theology

Loe Joo Tan (PhD, University of St Andrews)
Lecturer in Systematic and Historical Theology
Trinity Theological College, Singapore

Peter L. H. Tie (PhD, Southwestern Baptist Theological Seminary)
Associate Professor of Theology
Christian Witness Theological Seminary, USA

K. K. Yeo (PhD, Northwestern University)
Harry R. Kendall Professor of New Testament
Garrett-Evangelical Theological Seminary, USA
Affiliate Faculty, Department of Asian Languages and Cultures, Northwestern University, USA

Amos Yong (PhD, Boston University)
Professor of Theology and Mission
Fuller Theological Seminary, USA

Kai-Wen Karen Yuan (PhD, University of Aberdeen)
Assistant Professor of Old Testament
Taiwan Baptist Christian Seminary, Taiwan

Abbreviations

ANF	Alexander Roberts and James Donaldson. *The Ante-Nicene Fathers.* 1885–87. 10 vols. Reprint, Peabody, MA: Hendrickson, 1994.
BDAG	Walter Bauer, et al. *Greek-English Lexicon of the New Testament and Other Early Christian Literature.* 3rd ed. Chicago: University of Chicago Press, 2000.
BDB	Francis Brown, et al. *Hebrew and English Lexicon of the Old Testament.* New York: Oxford University Press, 2001.
HALOT	Ludwig Köhler, et al. *Hebrew and Aramaic Lexicon of the Old Testament.* 2 vols. Leiden: Brill, 2001.
NIDOTTE	Willem A. VanGemeren, ed. *New International Dictionary of Old Testament Theology and Exegesis.* 5 vols. Grand Rapids: Zondervan, 1997.
NPNF	Philip Schaff, ed. *A Select Library of Ninece and Post-Nicene Fathers of the Christian Church.* 14 vols. Grand Rapids: Eerdmans, 1956.
TDNT	Gerhard Kittel and Gerhard Friedrich, eds. *Theological Dictionary of the New Testament.* 10 vols. Translated by Geoffrey W. Bromiley. Grand Rapids: Eerdmans, 1964–76.
TWOT	Gleason L. Archer, et al., eds. *Theological Wordbook of the Old Testament.* 2 vols. Chicago: Moody, 1980.

Biblical-Theological Perspective

1

Spirit, Scripture, Saints, and Seminary

Toward a Reappropriation of "Spirit Illumination"
in "Scripture Interpretation" for Seminarians

Peter L. H. Tie

Introduction

Defining biblical infallibility and/or inerrancy may help clarify the question of the authoritative nature of Scripture,[1] but it still may not satisfactorily answer the related questions of the use of Scripture. Scripture, though completely trustworthy and truthful, does not necessarily guarantee correct interpretation and application of Scripture by Christians or theologians.[2] They acknowledge that the Bible's trustworthiness is rooted in

---

1. The trustworthiness and truthfulness of Scripture is historically captured in the concept of "infallibility," and more recently and controversially, in the notion of "inerrancy." Erickson defines succinctly that biblical inerrancy simply refers to the Christian Scripture as "fully truthful in all of its teachings" (Erickson, *Christian Theology*, 189). The International Council on Biblical Inerrancy [ICBI] produced the "Chicago Statement on Biblical Inerrancy" (CSBI) in 1978. An overview of the background and statement may be found at http://www.bible-researcher.com/chicago1.html. Further clarification of the CSBI may be found at http://www.bible-researcher.com/chicago2.html.

2. Hence, the ICBI subsequently produced two more statements to provide guidelines for proper interpretation and application, namely on biblical hermeneutics (1982) and biblical application (1986), within the boundary of biblical inerrancy. Both articles are found at http://library.dts.edu/Pages/TL/Special/ICBI.shtml.

divine inspiration (*theopneustos*), i.e., the Holy Spirit is the ultimate Author of Scripture, yet the Spirit designated and used human authors to inscribe the words. This is commonly called "concursive inspiration," namely the co-operative authorship of God and humans.[3] Thus, the Bible is God's word in human words.[4] Dockery stresses, "Scripture cannot rightly be understood unless we take into consideration that it has dual-sided authorship . . . What must be affirmed is that the Bible is entirely and completely the Word of God and the words of the human authors (Acts 4:25)."[5] Dockery adequately highlights the divine-human authorship of Scripture and identifies its crucial implications for proper interpretation of Scripture.

Theoretically, the concept of "divine and human authorship" seems rather simple to grasp.[6] To accept the *divine aspect* of inspiration is to affirm the Bible as the word of the eternal God who "speaks eternal truth that is applicable to readers of all times, beyond the original recipients."[7] To embrace the *human aspect* of authorship is to acknowledge the Bible as the words "from godly men to specific communities addressing problems and situations within certain contexts and cultures."[8] Dockery concludes unambiguously that "inspiration applies to all of canonical Scripture (including the process, purpose, and ultimately the product) and assert[s] that by the concursive action of God the Scriptures are, in their entirety, both the work of the Spirit and the work of human authors."[9] Point taken. A firm commitment to this dual authorship is indispensable for biblical interpretation. To disregard one or the other is to plunge oneself into great peril.

Acknowledging the dual authorship of Scripture suggests, on the one hand, Christians should rely on the Spirit's illumination to understand Scripture;[10] on the other hand, they are responsible to interpret Scripture

---

3. Dockery, "People of the Book," 24–25.

4. Cole expresses the same idea of inspiration with dual authorship: "Scripture is God's word in human words. There is a joint authorship. Scripture can be seen as the product over time of divine providence (government or *gubernatio*) and *concursus* (joint action, human and divine)" (Cole, *He Who Gives Life*, 107).

5. Dockery, *Christian Scripture*, 38. Dockery rightly observes, "It is our belief that the divine-human tension is the most crucial issue in contemporary discussions concerning Christian Scripture" (37).

6. For a recent and succinct discussion on some important implications of dual authorship—freedom (or free will) of the divine and human agents, "accommodation" of the divine knowledge, and the limitation of human authorship/understanding—see Feinberg, *Light in a Dark Place*, 201–5.

7. Dockery, *Christian Scripture*, 38.

8. Dockery, *Christian Scripture*, 38.

9. Dockery, "People of the Book," 26.

10. Webster defines the illumination of the Spirit thusly: "the Spirit's work of so

using the proper hermeneutical tools. Ideally, keeping the two—illumination and interpretation—in proper balance is the goal of biblical interpretation. A more relevant question in this chapter is whether believers, especially theologians and seminarians who are called to teach Scripture, have preserved the intimate connection between the Spirit and Scripture for better understanding of God's word and will.

The initial step of this chapter is to assess the issue concerning whether Christians and/or theologians keep a proper balance between the divine (illuminating factor) and human (interpretive methods) aspects in the interpretive process, that is, if "concursive inspiration" or "dual authorship" is faithfully acknowledged and executed in practice. This writer will briefly analyze a common situation in Chinese churches, in particular, as to why some discourage seminary training in biblical or theological understanding (hint: too academic, not spiritual enough!). Then, I will investigate a handful of substantial textbooks on biblical hermeneutics used in evangelical seminaries to see if they give "sufficient seriousness" to both the "divine and human" aspects in interpretation. An initial survey suggests a significant imbalance, i.e., overemphasizing the human aspect over the divine aspect, throughout the selected textbooks. Put concisely, the divine aspect of "Spirit illumination" seems to be proportionately deemphasized in seminary studies. Finally, I will offer a tentative proposal to counteract the imbalance of the human endeavor and Spirit illumination in the hope of fostering a more biblically balanced hermeneutical principle and practice. In this section, I will also attempt to include the relevant hermeneutical writings from those selected textbooks while interacting with other hermeneutical works on the illumination of the Spirit. By providing a broad overview of the "Spirit illumination" aspect in relation to interpretation, the ultimate goal is not only to help the seminarians grasp solidly the theological understanding of Scripture, but also to grow continuously in spiritual discernment/maturity as disciples and churches of Christ.[11]

---

enlightening the church's reading and contemplation of the words of the prophets, evangelists and apostles that regenerate intelligence comes to know the mind of God" (Webster, "Illumination," 326).

11. It is noteworthy that "[r]ather than being exclusively, or even primarily, a scholarly pursuit, interpretation is required of every believer. While it is true that God has given to the church certain individuals who are to serve as teachers and pastors (Eph 4:11), he expects *every* believer to progress toward spiritual maturity (Col 1:28–29). For this reason, we all should assume responsibility for our spiritual growth and make every effort to grow in our ability to handle God's Word accurately and with increasing skill (2 Pet 3:17–18)" (Köstenberger and Patterson, *Invitation to Biblical Interpretation*, 63).

A Brief Observation of a Seminary Situation on Scripture and the Spirit

Something that is not uncommon among Asian (particularly Chinese churches) and Western churches is that some Christians strongly discourage seminary studies. Most of us do not encounter these people in the higher theological institutions (since they deter believers from theological studies and are determined to avoid seminaries themselves), but we do meet them in the local churches. They are by no means less genuine in their beliefs or less disciplined in their Christian walk. In fact, they could be the most fervent Christians in the churches.

One of the most obvious reasons for discouraging seminary training is related to the "liberal" teachings of many theological institutions.[12] Chinese believers who have read John Sung's life testimony (宋尚節, 1901–44) receive an impression that theological education, as in Sung's experience at Union Theological Seminary (New York), hardly uses the Bible whilst training ministers in the Christian faith.[13] It is true that seminarians read many more exegetical, theological, historical, and philosophical works than the Bible alone. Stephen Holmes, a British Baptist theologian and Senior Lecturer in Systematic Theology at the University of St Andrews, also acknowledges that "[t]here is an idea around in the churches that studying theology is the surest way to destroy faith."[14]

Another reason for rejecting seminary education is scriptural in nature, that is, all true believers have received the divine anointing, i.e., the Holy Spirit; therefore, they can and will learn from the Spirit himself without any intermediary. This theological conviction is often based on First John 2:27, "As for you, the anointing you received from him remains in you, and you do not need anyone to teach you. But as his anointing teaches you about all things and as that anointing is real, not counterfeit—just as it has taught you, remain in him."[15] As the argument goes, since the Spirit

---

12. A quick browse on the Internet for seminaries or divinity schools will disclose that some of them are considered "liberal" in their core beliefs from an evangelical vantage point. For example, The Association of Theological Schools in the United States and Canada (see www.ats.edu) have over 270 member institutions, and a handful of them are distinctly "liberal" in core beliefs (e.g., on Trinity, Christology).

13. 于中旻 (JAMES C. M. YU), 〈宋尚節〉, lines 91–109. For recent news about Union Seminary's chapel where its students confessed to plants, see https://utsnyc.edu/worship-at-union/. Union Seminary promotes interfaith training for social justice; see https://utsnyc.edu/about/.

14. Holmes, "John Webster Dies at 60," line 14.

15. Unless noted otherwise, this writer uses the New International Version (NIV, 2011).

is the Teacher who can teach his people directly and individually through Scripture, learning at seminaries implicitly denies the promise, presence, and power of the Spirit.[16] On the other hand, rigorous academic training frequently results in a common criticism: "Seminary studies do increase my theological knowledge but, unfortunately, extinguish my spiritual passion." Thus, the question is both cogent and urgent: "Why should we risk our faith and fervor in theological education at a seminary while we have the Spirit of Truth who can teach us directly and personally?"

From a theological perspective, the reasoning against seminary education seems to reveal an undeniable presupposition underlying the argument, namely, the privatized notion of the universal Christian priesthood. Christian priesthood is often (mis)understood as every Christian's "free and direct access" to God based on the principle of "soul competency,"[17] which is often aided and fuelled by the idea of individualism.[18] Consequently, if every Christian has direct access to the Spirit's teaching and knowledge, why do we still need to attend seminary? If this argument is valid and consistently implemented, then no Christian should bother going to church to listen to a pastor's sermon or attend a more in-depth Bible study. I suspect no reasonable Christian would agree to this sort of action or conclusion. Duvall and Hays correctly warn, "When it comes to biblical interpretation, having the Holy Spirit does not mean that the Spirit is all you need."[19] The fact that Christians are indwelt and illuminated by the Holy Spirit does not exclude human agents from continuing the tasks of preaching and teaching, whether to believers or nonbelievers. A case in point, Paul urged his younger co-workers, Timothy and Titus, to ensure their own and other elders' faithful preaching and teaching of the word to the churches (1 Tim 3:2; 4:16; 5:17; Titus 1:9).

From a more practical perspective, we hear the common church complaint that "Seminary training has not adequately equipped future pastors to carry out their work effectively." What went wrong? This complaint could be expressed concisely in a twofold manner, that is, seminary is "too academically infused but practically insufficient!" or "intellectually driven, spiritually deficient!" Put differently, seminary basically contributes to the separation of head and heart, or disconnection between theology and practice,[20] rather

---

16. Similarly, some may ask, "If we have the Spirit, . . . why do we need to worry about proper [interpretive] procedures?" (Duvall and Hays, *Grasping God's Word*, 225).

17. Hobbs, *You are Chosen*, 4, 18; Tie, *Restore Unity*, 38.

18. See Stanglin, *Letter and Spirit*, 3.

19. Duvall and Hays, *Grasping God's Word*, 229.

20. The compartmentalization or departmentalization in biblical, theological, historical, and practical/pastoral theology since the nineteenth century in North America

than encouraging the proper combination of truth and love.[21] Consequently, the common experience of disconnection between Scripture interpretation and Spirit illumination ensues, though often unintentionally.

This writer, as a theological educator, does not believe that the problem lies with the academics per se nor the accrediting institutions striving to excel in academic standards. Rather, it is more an issue of how intentionally and persistently seminaries integrate the two seemingly separate aspects—knowledge and practice, theology and life, Scripture and ministry—into a coherent whole. Specifically, seminarians are to learn or maintain a healthy balance between Scripture interpretation and Spirit illumination throughout their seminary studies, and thereafter. Nevertheless, striving for a proper balance is much easier said than done. Part of the problem lies with what they typically encounter in their reading at seminaries.

Now, I would like to sample some of the major textbooks on biblical interpretation to evaluate if they maintain a "proper" balance between interpretation and illumination.

A Brief Survey of Some Seminary Textbooks on Basic Biblical Hermeneutics

Biblical scholars, church pastors, and seminary students, by means of exegesis or hermeneutics, endeavor to ascertain the original meanings of Scripture and ultimately apply their significance (and/or abiding principles) to Christian living or church life today. Introductory textbooks on biblical hermeneutics used in evangelical seminaries usually introduce literary criticisms, interpretive methods, syntactical studies, background studies, genre classifications, etc.—most of which are grammatical, historical, and literary tools—in order to help interpreters discover the original meanings intended by the authors, and eventually, the theological principles used for pastoral applications.[22] All these exegetical or interpretive tools are not particularly "divine" for they can be used and are used by all practitioners, Christians and non-Christians alike. Phrased differently, anyone can determine the original meanings of the human authors of the Bible without

---

has led to a myriad of courses, which in turn results in a lack of integration between academic theories and pastoral practices (Vallet, *Stewards of the Gospel*, 187).

21. Theilicke unambiguously and emphatically calls the real conflict between truth and love "the disease of theologians," whereas the possession of theological knowledge (by a seminarian or theologian) could be used to support one's spiritual superiority over those who have no theological training but do have personal relationship with Christ. Put precisely, pride in truth kills love for others (Theilicke, *Little Exercise*, 16–20).

22. Duvall and Hays, *Grasping God's Word*, 230.

any particular aid or illumination from the divine Spirit.[23] Nevertheless, as further noted, while human literary methods are indispensable for sound interpretation, "rationalistic scholarship alone cannot fully discover truth in the Bible."[24] This precisely touches on the Spirit's indispensable role in the understanding of God's word.

What makes biblical hermeneutics distinct from other literary studies is the recognition of the "divine" aspect of Scripture, namely, the Holy Spirit's active role in the final product of the canon, the continuing process of illumination, and the ongoing proclamation from the Bible. Stated differently, the Holy Spirit is the divine Author who is not only crucial in the work of inspiration but also in the whole process (i.e., inspiration, inscripturation, illumination, and internalization[25]) of Scripture. Dockery is definitely correct in encouraging Christian exegetes to take both divine and human authorships seriously, but what does it actually look like to take both authorships *equally seriously*? This writer takes it to mean that the concept "concursive inspiration" not only remains a hermeneutical presupposition, but also impacts the interpretive process.[26] If the dual authorship of the Bible is to be consistently applied to biblical inerrancy and interpretation, then it is not unrealistic to expect a "reasonable" amount of treatment on the "divine" (generally speaking) or "Spirit" (specifically speaking) element in textbooks of biblical interpretation. This should not be taken to mean that one must give an equal amount of pages to both human and Spirit aspects in the textbooks. Nevertheless, a simple chart (below) appears to indicate

23. It has been noted that "many non-Christians can apply sound hermeneutics to understand the meaning of Scripture . . ." (Klein et al., *Introduction to Biblical Interpretation*, 635). Quarles summarizes adequately that higher criticism "stresses the human rather than the divine authorship of the Bible (though it does not necessarily deny divine inspiration) and seeks to discover the message that the original human author intended to communicate through the text to his original readers. Because of the human element in the origin of the Bible, practitioners of the historical critical method believe that it is appropriate to interpret the Bible like any other ancient document. The interpreter must seek to understand the language of the text and its historical background in order to discover its original meaning" (Quarles, "Higher Criticism," 63).

24. Klein et al., *Introduction to Biblical Interpretation*, 18.

25 "Inscripturation" refers to the writing down of the revealed truth. "Internalization" refers to the inward or inner work of the Holy Spirit in the hearts of believers, bearing witness to the truthfulness and authority of Scripture (Dockery, "People of the Book," 27).

26. Speaking of inspiration in biblical interpretation for theological education, Vallet cites the work of Brueggemann that in every biblical text "'God's wind blows through and past all our critical and confessional categories of reading and understanding.' That 'powerful and enlivening force' does not simply ordain the text as Scripture but also affects 'its transmission and interpretation among us'" (Vallet, *Stewards of the Gospel*, 72, 75). See also Brueggemann, "Biblical Authority," 14.

that a significantly disproportionate amount of attention is given to the human factor over the Spirit aspect. As Joel B. Green also notes, "Predictably, . . . academic manuals for biblical interpretation, irrespective of whether these were written with the university department of religion studies or the seminary in mind, render the work of biblical study mostly, if not entirely, in anthropological than pneumatological terms."[27] Undeniably, the latter needs to be adequately emphasized in biblical interpretation if we really claim to uphold the "concursive authorship" of the Bible.

In view of the aforementioned, this writer has conducted a brief survey of selected books on biblical interpretation commonly used in evangelical seminaries. The basic idea is to shed light on whether the authors who hold to the "concursive authorship" apply their presupposition consistently throughout their interpretive process. Specifically, this writer intends to assess if the authors have provided sufficient and significant guidelines for the "Spirit" aspect of hermeneutics.[28]

The survey involves counting the total pages devoted to "Anthropological Aspect" [AnA][29] and "Pneumatological Aspect" [PnA],[30] in view of the total number of pages [T.N.P.] for each textbook.[31] The selected textbooks are:

---

27. Green, "Spiritual Hermeneutics," 156–57. Keener's monograph attempts to counterbalance the disproportion of the Spirit- and human-aspect in biblical interpretation. See Keener, *Spirit Hermeneutics*, 11. Keener expresses a similar sentiment about the disproportion in this way: "I have little patience for [hermeneutical] approaches that claim to be 'of the Spirit' yet ignore the concreteness of the settings in which the Spirit inspired the biblical writings, settings that help explain the particularities in the shape of such writings" (2).

28. Köstenberger and Patterson, *Invitation to Biblical Interpretation*, 69. The following selection is based on the conditions that these are commonly used, evangelically oriented, and/or recently published/republished hermeneutics. Those that deny the divine/dual authorship of Scripture are beyond the purpose and scope of this chapter. This writer does not consider Keener's *Spirit Hermeneutics* (2016) an introductory textbook in a seminary course on hermeneutics; therefore, it is not part of this survey. Keener's writing clearly demonstrates he is well aware of the urgent need for pneumatic sensitivity in biblical interpretation (14). Meanwhile, however, he recognizes this book is an advanced hermeneutic, supplementing (not supplanting) the basics of biblical interpretation (2).

29. "Anthropological aspect" in interpretation includes the basic exegetical methods and tools used to determine the original meanings of the Bible (e.g., word meanings, syntactical studies, genre classification, background studies, etc.).

30. "Pneumatological aspect" in interpretation involves the themes directly or indirectly related to the Spirit's involvement and illumination in the inspiration, interpretative, and/or application process (e.g., inspiration, illumination, prayer, the Spirit's role).

31. Not including Table of Contents, Abbreviations, Preface, Scripture Index, Names Index, Subject index, and Appendix (unless it is related to the pneumatic aspect on interpretation).

Duvall and Hays, *Grasping God's Word*, 2012 [GGW][32]

Fee and Stuart, *How to Read the Bible for All Its Worth*, 2014 [HTR][33]

Klein et al., *Introduction to Biblical Interpretation*, 2017 [InBI][34]

Köstenberger and Patterson, *Invitation to Biblical Interpretation*, 2011 [IvBI][35]

Osborne, *The Hermeneutical Spiral*, 2006 [HS][36]

---

32. Duvall and Hays, *Grasping God's Word*. Pneumatological Aspect [PnA] includes: "The Role of the Holy Spirit," 225–33 (7 pages); and Appendix 1, "Inspiration and Canon," 443–54 (11 pages). The total number of pages [TNP] includes Appendix 1, "Inspiration and Canon" (443–54).

33. Fee and Stuart, *How to Read*. Pneumatological Aspect [PnA] includes: "The Nature of Scripture, 25–27 (3 pages), and "The Second Task: Hermeneutics," 33–35 (3 pages). Interestingly, Fee, who is an expert in NT Pneumatology (e.g., Fee's *God's Empowering Presence: The Holy Spirit in the Letters of Paul*), does not seem to place the importance of Spirit illumination in *How to Read the Bible for All Its Worth*, although he emphasizes the inspiration aspect. In the least, this indicates he was not intentional in helping interpreters grasp the vital connection between Spirit illumination and human interpretation.

34. Klein et al., *Introduction to Biblical Interpretation*. Pneumatological Aspect [PnA] includes: "Eternal Relevance—the Divine Factor," 59–61 (3 pages); "Qualifications of the Interpreter," including "A Reasoned Faith in the God Who Reveals," "Willingness to Obey Its Message," "Illumination of the Holy Spirit," "Membership in the Church," and "Willingness to Employ Appropriate Methods," 202–10 (9 pages); and "Presuppositions for Correct Interpretations," including "Presuppositions about the Nature of the Bible," "Presuppositions about Methodology," "Presuppositions about the Ultimate Goal of Hermeneutics," 210–26 (17 pages). In addition to the above pages, see other pages that also mention the guidance of the Spirit (255–58, 597), the illumination of the Spirit (41–42, 93–94), praying to and relying on the Spirit (635–36), role of the Spirit (39), and the witness of the Spirit (94)—13 pages in total.

35. Köstenberger and Patterson, *Invitation to Biblical Interpretation*. Pneumatological Aspect [PnA] includes: "Characteristics Required of the Biblical Interpreter," 62–65 (4 pages), and "Figure of Speech and the Inexpressible," 669–72 (4 pages). Other places that mention inspiration (69, 214, 494, 579, 610)—5 pages in total. While the authors touch on inspiration in general, there is no "illumination" listed in Subject Index.

36. Osborne, *Hermeneutical Spiral*. Pneumatological Aspect [PnA] includes: "The Inspiration and Authority of Scripture," 25–26 (2 pages); "Expository Preaching," 29–30 (2 pages); "Inspiration/revelation," 386–87 (2 pages); "The Place of the Holy Spirit," 435–37 (3 pages); "A Devotional Experience," 437–39 (3 pages); and "A Biblical Theology of Preaching, 439–40 (2 pages).

Textbooks	AnA	PnA	T.N.P
GGW	413 pages (95.8%)	18 Pages (4.2%)	431 pages
HTR	247 pages (97.6%)	6 pages (2.4%)	253 pages
InBI	556 pages (93%)	42 pages (7%)	598 pages
IvBI	742 pages (98.3%)	13 pages (1.7%)	755 pages
HS	486 (97.2%)	14 pages (2.8%)	500 pages

The brief survey seems to suggest a disproportionate amount of attention given to the human element in biblical interpretation, despite the serious call to emphasize the dual character of Scripture. Before coming too quickly to a conclusion, a word of caution and some observations are in place:

First, the number of pages may not convey a correct impression, but the dearth of them *does* imply that the seminary training in Scripture interpretation relies more on academic exercise than pneumatic discipline. To put this in perspective, no author aforementioned denies the fact that the Holy Spirit plays the undeniably ultimate role in the true interpretation of Scripture, though with various degrees of emphasis in integration. As Fee and Stuart adequately assert, as generally agreed by others, the Spirit is the one who inspired the original intent; therefore, his role is indispensable in the rediscovery of the original intent (meaning) and reapplication of the meaning in our current context.[37] The central question is: In addition to Spirit inspiration, *how* does Spirit illumination play an indispensable role in interpretation?

Second, an overeager emphasis on the "Spirit aspect" in interpretation may lead to overstepping the boundary of "how" the Spirit illuminates in the process of believers' interpretation. In accord with Fee and Stuart, Dockery undoubtedly affirms "the Spirit's work of illumination that enables believers to interpret the biblical text in its original context in such a way as to understand the biblical author's meanings, as well as its canonical significance for our contemporary world."[38] While acknowledging the vital role of the Spirit in understanding the original meanings and their significance for today, we must not naively assume that the illumination of the Holy Spirit will automatically begin to operate as soon as the biblical interpreters engage in the human elements of interpretation.[39] Admittedly, no theologian or exegete is

---

37. Fee and Stuart, *How to Read*, 34.
38. James and Dockery, *Beyond the Impasse?*, 225.
39. Duvall and Hays have made a similar observation that "when it comes to biblical

able to hold the Spirit captive so as to produce one's desired result. Rather, as Webster states correctly, the "workings of the Spirit in illumination, as in all things, are mysterious, exceeding creaturely capacity."[40] As much as we want to acknowledge the vital role of the Spirit, we have to confess that we are apt to employ the "human factor" (i.e., critical methods) but inadequate to appropriate the "divine factor" in the task of interpretation and theologization. In fact, conservative biblical scholars and theological experts, whether in the Orient or the West, unanimously acknowledge that we may still draw erroneous observations or conclusions, even though we use the interpretive methods adequately and appreciate the Spirit illumination duly.

Having surveyed and commented on the selected hermeneutic textbooks, one may now perceive that interpreters must maintain a delicate balance between the *absolute necessity* of the Spirit's illumination in biblical interpretation and the *absolute freedom* of the Spirit in illuminating human interpreters. With this in mind, I would like to provide an initial proposal to incorporate the "pneumatological" factor with the "anthropological" aspect in terms of product-canonicity, process-community, and purpose-communication.

A Theological Task of Illumination and Interpretation: Spirit-Saints in Product, Process, and Purpose

Webster states insightfully, "A theology of illumination avoids both hermeneutical naturalism in which the actings of the mind, unmoved from outside, claim sufficiency for themselves, and hermeneutical immediacy in which seizure by the Spirit breaks off the exercise of intelligence and interpretation becomes rapture."[41] Webster's statement precisely captures the two extreme attitudes—the sufficiency of human mind without the Spirit's illumination and the efficacy of the Spirit without the human mind and effort in interpretation—that occur not only among Western Christians but also Asian Christians (esp. Chinese). The mysterious role of the Spirit in illumination and the mindful role of saints in interpretation are not mutually exclusive.

---

interpretation, having the Holy Spirit does not mean that the Spirit is all you need. The Spirit does not make valid interpretation automatic" (Duvall and Hays, *Grasping God's Word*, 229).

40. Webster, "Illumination," 326.
41. Webster, "Illumination," 337.

This writer intends to demonstrate that the Spirit's work of illumination is not only vital in the present act of interpretation-understanding, but also active in the past process of inspiration and canonization, as well as in act of communication and ultimate glorification. "Spirit illumination" should be more properly considered as a comprehensive concept. In the following, I attempt to capture the effective and enduring work of "Spirit illumination" in close relation to the Scripture and saints past and present, as deduced into three interrelated themes of canonicity, community, and communication, with the hope that these could be adequately applied to theological students today for a more faithful Scripture interpretation.

Product of "Spirit Illumination": Canonicity

A proper understanding of the Spirit's crucial role in inspiration and canonicity directly affects how one approaches "Spirit illumination" and "seminarian interpretation."[42] Concerning Spirit-inspiration (*theopneustos*), by keeping the uniquely cultural, educational, and personal experiences of each of the biblical authors, the Spirit sovereignly enabled the human authors' understanding (i.e., illuminating them) and superintended them to write down what they intended to say (that is, to their particular audience dealing with their specific issues in their historical contexts), corresponding to what the Spirit intended to say. This dual intention indicates dual authorship, and vice versa. Furthermore, the final product of the canon (and its canonicity) presupposes the Spirit's inspiration in the chosen prophets, apostles, and their close associates, as well as the providential work of the Spirit through the church in the later centuries that resulted in the present canonical form of Scripture.[43] How did the Spirit help the church to recognize the canonical books? Frame states, "By *illumining* and persuading the church concerning the true canonical books, He [the Spirit] has helped the church to distinguish between false and true."[44] In short, the Spirit's work of illumination plays a *decisive* role that directs the *decision* of the church; hence, a dual action of decision determines the product of the biblical canon.

---

42. This specific notion is similar to what Allison observes in general that one's understanding of the nature of Scriptures (i.e., canonicity, inspiration, authority, sufficiency, perspicuity, etc.), as defined in the doctrine of Scripture, directly affects one's interpretation of Scripture, "therefore, its interpretation is and must be ruled by its nature as the Word of God" (Allison, "Theological Interpretation," 29).

43. Cole, *He Who Gives Life*, 107. This writer considers the sixty-six books of Scripture as the Spirit-inspired canon, whereas the apocryphal (pseudepicryphal) writings are historically helpful and spiritually edifying in a limited sense.

44. Frame, "Spirit and the Scriptures," 229; emphasis added.

The dual intention (concerning inspiration) and the dual decision (concerning canon) affirm crucial works of the Spirit's illumination and affect one's biblical interpretation. Osborne states fittingly, "The goal of evangelical hermeneutics is quite simple—to discover the intention of the Author/author (Author=the Spirit who inspires; author=the inspired human author)."[45] Stated otherwise, in order to grasp the Spirit's intent, one must first and foremost work diligently to ascertain the intents of the human authors by using proper historical, cultural, and literary tools.[46] Logically, one begins with determining the primary meaning of a statement, passage, section, or book by a particular author. This involves all the basic steps that theological students learn in their Hermeneutics course, such as word studies, syntax, historical background, and genre, to name a few. The next major move is to make a holistic interaction and integration of all biblical books as the inspired and unified canon to discern the Spirit's ultimate intent, that is, "the absolute truths of Scripture."[47]

The theological concept *sensus plenior* ("the fuller sense") teaches that there is a deeper and fuller meaning (or significance), beyond the original intention of human authors, and yet intended by the ultimate Author of Scripture, the Spirit himself who progressively revealed and providentially oversaw the final canon.[48] *Sensus plenior* is fundamental for biblical exegetes (or exegetical interpretation), and it is certainly crucial and beneficial for systematic theologians (or theological construction) because it helps go beyond the literal and literary (or grammatical-historical) sense of the OT and NT without doing violence to the ultimate intention of the unified canon as inspired by

---

45. Osborne, *Hermeneutical Spiral*, 24.

46. Osborne is convinced that "[t]hough inspired of God, it was written in human language and within human cultures. By the very nature of language the Bible's univocal truths are couched in analogical language, that is, the absolute truths of Scripture were encased in the human languages and cultures of the ancient Hebrews and Greeks, and we must understand those cultures in order to interpret the biblical texts properly" (Osborne, *Hermeneutical Spiral*, 23).

47. Osborne, *Hermeneutical Spiral*, 23. On the other hand, as adequately explained by Melick ("Can We Understand the Bible?," 90–91, 110–16), it is certainly possible to read the Bible devotionally (that is, without using any interpretive tools) and understand the message, based on the principle of "perspicuity" and the Bible's "self-correcting mechanism" (90); the latter "involves the unity of Scripture [that is, canonicity], the consistency of its message, and the Holy Spirit who guides devout readers to the truth" (90n3). The central question is: If one may be able to fully grasp the messages in the Bible through devotional reading, why do we have to belabor the obvious by employing hermeneutical tools? Hopefully, the rest of this chapter may provide an adequate response to the question, whether directly or indirectly.

48. Moo, "Problem of *Sensus Plenior*," 201–4.

the Spirit. Formulating the doctrine of the Trinity is a case in point.[49] While *sensus plenior* may encounter the issues of marginalizing the original human intent and providing no specific approach to interpretation, Barker lists four challenges for those who reject *sensus plenior* outright: "(1) the manner in which Jesus and the NT authors interpret the OT, (2) how the OT can function as God's current word to the new covenant community, (3) how there could be any communicative intent at the canonical level, and (4) whether God can be understood to share the communicative intent of the human author in every case."[50] Without acknowledging *sensus plenior*, one is destined to see Scripture only as the word *to them then*, not *to us now*, as well. To omit the concept of *sensus plenior* is to abandon the Spirit's timeless theological truths. Stated positively, *sensus plenior* is closely related to the "theological interpretation of Scripture" [TIS] or "theological exegesis."[51]

Undeniably, present interpreters no longer have direct access to the minds of human authors in order to ascertain the meanings of "uncertain" passages. The idea of going beyond the primary meaning of the human author to seek a fuller understanding of the Spirit could sometimes suggest departure from the principle of *sola scriptura*.[52] Consequently, one could read unscripturally founded doctrine into the Bible,[53] such as Immaculate

---

49. The term "Trinity" cannot be found in the Bible but it is the "master concept" that unifies "several strands of biblical evidence" (such as, the oneness of God in the *shema*; the name of one God in the Father, Son, and Spirit; and the biblical distinction of the three beings) and faithfully captures the overall sense of Scripture as a whole canon (Cole, *He Who Gives Life*, 64–65).

50. Barker, "Speech Act Theory," 230; see also 228, 239.

51. See Brown, "Problems of the *Sensus Plenior*," 462, 464–66; LaSor, "Prophecy, Inspiration, and *Sensus Plenior*," 50, 52, 54; Vanhoozer, *First Theology*, 213. Allison succinctly explains that TIS is not a theological system (or confessional theology) imposed on scriptural texts, but to go beyond historical, literary, or sociological interpretation in order to "detect divine action as affirmed in and through those texts . . . TIS is a family of interpretative approaches that privileges theological readings of the Bible in due recognition of the theological nature of Scripture, its ultimate theological message, and/or the theological interests of its readers" (Allison, "Theological Interpretation," 29). Keener acknowledges, "Today . . . many biblical scholars and theologians have sought rapprochement through theological interpretation of the Bible," rather than holding to a dichotomy that biblical scholars discover Scripture's past meaning and theologians seek Scripture's present significance (Keener, *Spirit Hermeneutics*, 15). In a more succinct statement, TIS "seeks to help theology to be more biblical, and biblical studies more theological (Treier and Anizor, "Theological Interpretation," 4).

52. Vanhoozer argues, "There is no contradiction between acknowledging the [continuous] work of the Spirit in biblical interpretation and affirming *sola scriptura*. For God's communicative action in and through Scripture is triune, involving both Word and Spirit" (Vanhoozer, *First Theology*, 11).

53. LaSor, "Prophecy, Inspiration, and *Sensus Plenior*," 59.

Conception or Assumption of Mary.[54] This is clear evidence of ecclesiastic traditions hovering forcefully over scriptural truths. Nevertheless, theological hermeneutics urges the interpreters to attempt to understand the primary intents of the human authors in their own contexts by employing the proper interpretive means, including the original languages, cultural backgrounds, geographical layouts, and living conditions of the time.[55] After discovering the primary meanings of these authors and their *particular passages*, theological interpretation continues with grasping the ultimate significance in relation to the *whole canon*. The latter is called the theological understanding of the whole Bible. As LaSor rightly notes, "If it is a deeper meaning, intended by God but not clearly intended by the human author, then we cannot discover it by using grammatico-historical exegetical methods."[56] Therefore, understanding of the Spirit-intended meaning necessitates the Spirit's work of illumination,[57] which nonetheless necessarily and concomitantly involves human effort in theological interpretation.

Vanhoozer argues that the Bible should be read and interpreted like other books, but the reading must not be without the "Spirit of understanding" who alone "can convict us of hermeneutic sin—interpretive violence that distorts the text—and *illumine* our eyes so that we see the Logos that is 'really present' in the letter" of Scripture.[58] Reading the Bible like read-

---

54. A recent example, see Levering, *Mary's Bodily Assumption*. For Levering, the faith in Mary's Assumption is rooted in "the role of typological reasoning in the New Testament's portrait of the mother of Jesus Christ and in our understanding of her mission; the Church's authority as interpreter of divine revelation under the guidance of the Holy Spirit; and the fittingness of the Assumption of Mary within God's carefully orchestrated plan for salvation. Rather than focusing on the historical development of the doctrine . . . " (locs. 89–92 of 5092), Levering argues that the doctrine of Mary's Assumption is not a historical event per se, but it is "scriptural" in the sense that the Holy Spirit illumines the church to interpret Scripture so as to help the church to believe this as biblical truth.

55. Dockery, "Study and Interpretation," 48.

56. LaSor, "Prophecy, Inspiration, and *Sensus Plenior*," 54;

57. Dockery, "Study and Interpretation," 49; LaSor, "Prophecy, Inspiration, and *Sensus Plenior*," 50, 52, 54.

58. Vanhoozer, *First Theology*, 208; emphasis added. Allison notes the advocates of TIS oppose "reading the Bible 'like any other book'" (Allison, "Theological Interpretation," 29). Nevertheless, as noted by Vanhoozer, who is one of the main advocates of TIS, the Bible has to be read "like any other book" but with a theological qualification: "Theology undergirds our theories of language and interpretation. The Bible should be interpreted 'like any other book,' but every other book should be interpreted with norms that we have derived from a reflection on how to read Scripture. I stake my claim that the Bible should be read like any other book, and that every other book should be read like the Bible, within a Christian worldview" that goes along with the "Spirit of understanding" (Vanhoozer, *First Theology*, 208).

ing other books suggests human elements of interpretation, namely, the interpreter uses the same proper tools as other readers use to determine the original meaning of a text because "a text has only a single meaning, the meaning it had for the original author."[59] The rediscovery of the original meaning of the human author as the end of interpretation, however, seems to fall short of the ultimate purpose of the Spirit who inspires the whole canon. The Spirit of understanding illuminates our further understanding of the Spirit's intention as imparted in the canon as a whole.

To put this in perspective and practice, the Spirit's illumination of the Spirit's intention in the whole canon does not vitiate "hard work and proper principles of hermeneutics."[60] This is precisely the issue facing those overemphasizing the role of the Spirit and overlooking Christians' unfinished labor in studying the Bible. Theological students ought to recognize the continuous endeavor expected in order to properly understand Scripture in its specific parts and as a canonical whole. On the other hand, for those who rely excessively on hermeneutical techniques in order to determine the original meanings of the human authors, "perhaps it is not surprising," as Green observes, "that those who are inducted into these [hermeneutical] interests and protocols find themselves more and more reading about the Bible (rather than immersing themselves in the text of Scripture itself), and less and less sure of the immediacy of the Bible's message for their lives and the life of the church."[61]

Hermeneutical teachings and techniques pervade seminaries, but unfortunately "[a]cademic study of the Bible has not concerned itself with how those who study the Bible might hear God's own voice speaking in and through Scripture."[62] As we try to listen to the "voices" of the human authors, we neglect the "voice" of the Spirit speaking in and through the whole canon. No wonder there is much feedback from seminarians concerning the "dryness" of scripture interpretation, in addition to the complexity of the process of interpretation. "Interpreting Scripture theologically," says Vanhoozer, "involves more than dealing with biblical words, more even than rules for textual interpretation. Interpreters must have receptive spirits as well, a possibility that depends on the work of the Holy Spirit."[63] By properly appropriating the human factors and appropriately recognizing the Spirit's ultimate intention, interpreters aim at uncovering the "Word in the

---

59. Vanhoozer, *First Theology*, 209.
60. Dockery, "Study and Interpretation," 49.
61. Green, "Spiritual Hermeneutics," 154.
62. Green, "Spiritual Hermeneutics," 154.
63. Vanhoozer, *First Theology*, 11.

words,"⁶⁴ that is, the divine word in human words. Studying Scripture is not only about reading Scripture, but also immersing ourselves in the scriptural texts by listening *prayerfully, personally,* and *purposefully* to the Author's voice through the whole canon. Now, we move from the whole canon to the whole community as we continue with the theme of the illuminative process of the Spirit in the interpretative process of the saints.

Process through "Spirit Illumination": Community

How exactly does the Spirit continuously use the entire canon to convey his intent? First and foremost, the unspoken misconception is: when a Christian or seminarian employs hermeneutical methods, tools, or steps correctly in biblical interpretation, the Holy Spirit will "automatically" guide him or her in the whole process to the "right" conclusions.⁶⁵ While the Spirit holds absolute authority in determining whom, when, and what to understand about God's words, the Spirit continuously enables his people to know him more, particularly those who earnestly seek to understand Scripture, namely, the obedient individual, faithful community, and disciplined seminary/theological institution. These three parts work collaboratively for a deeper understanding of Scripture.

Individually and subjectively, the Spirit's illumination entails ongoing obedience of the interpreter. Accurate reading of Scripture requires not only the correct use of "scholarly tools," but also ongoing discipline in "Christian virtue."⁶⁶ Understanding the Spirit's intention ultimately leads to responding to the word. "There is a Word in the words, to which the reader is responsible,"⁶⁷ namely, the obedient response to the divine word in human words. Green is emphatic about the Spirit's active preparation by "inculcating in us dispositions and postures of invitation, openness, and availability."⁶⁸ In the meantime, interpreters of Scripture must continuously exercise "[a]n integrated life of devotion to God our willingness to participate in a repentance-oriented

---

64. Vanhoozer, *First Theology*, 212.

65. Duvall and Hays similarly state, "When it comes to biblical interpretation, having the Holy Spirit does not mean that the Spirit is all you need. The Spirit does not make valid interpretation automatic" (Duvall and Hays, *Grasping God's Word*, 229).

66. Vanhoozer, *First Theology*, 210. See also Hauerwas, *Unleashing the Scripture*, 9, 17.

67. Vanhoozer, *First Theology*, 212.

68. Green, "Spiritual Hermeneutics," 171.

reading of Scripture—these dispositions and concomitant practices are fruit of the work of the Spirit in our lives."[69]

On the one hand, "A person who is spiritually minded may get more out of the Scriptures, simply because he or she puts more into the study of them and is listening more keenly for God's word"; on the other hand, one must take the wise warning that this "person does not have any additional new revelation."[70] Inspiration by the Spirit that results in the final canon necessitates illumination by the Spirit, and yet the illumination does not give any new revelation but does offer the earnest and obedient interpreter a *fuller* and *renewed* understanding of the revelation. If, however, an interpreter becomes uncontrolled or unruly in his or her understanding and teaching of Scripture or doctrines, the church, as the disciplined community of Christ, has to restore order and purity of the word. Vanhoozer rightly points out, "Far from being a charter for every individual interpreter to read in a way that is right in his or her own eyes, the royal priesthood [i.e., the church] is an ordered and disciplined community that exists largely to interpret Scripture, binding and losing certain doctrines and those who hold them in order to preserve its integrity as a local embassy of the kingdom of God."[71]

As one might discern here, the Spirit's illumination in understanding Scripture involves not merely individual obedient Christians but also disciplined local communities because "biblical interpretation is a communal exercise," namely, "[r]eading Scripture ought to take place in the context of the local church."[72] Although a local church is not "the whole church," it is "wholly the church" that is "authorized [by Christ] to make binding interpretive judgments about the meaning of Scripture."[73] Even a local church makes mistakes, doctrinally and ethically. It is, therefore, not just a matter of caution but also an obligation for a local church to interpret Scripture in collaboration with other local churches.[74]

What is, then, the role of seminaries or theological institutions in the interpretive community? To interpret the word accurately and to know God truly is what the seminary does as well. Why do we need the seminary when we have churches that interpret, teach, and preach Scripture? On the one hand, seminary studies, for some Chinese Christians, are similar to Sunday

---

69. Green, "Spiritual Hermeneutics," 171.

70. LaSor, "Prophecy, Inspiration, and *Sensus Plenior*," 59.

71. Vanhoozer, *Biblical Authority*, 174.

72. Vanhoozer, *Biblical Authority*, 175; see also Dockery, "Study and Interpretation," 49–50.

73. Vanhoozer, *Biblical Authority*, 176.

74. Vanhoozer, *Biblical Authority*, 176.

School classes at local churches, though more intentional and intense in the former. Green states even more emphatically, "At the end of the day, though, theological work with Scripture—listening to what the Spirit is saying to the church in and through Scripture—finds its home in the church and not in the university [or seminary]. Listening for God's address in Scripture is an ecclesial practice that, ultimately, does not and cannot depend on academic accreditation."[75] On the other hand, Kesley believes that the goal of a theological school is to be a community of God's people studying to understand God more truly, even though the subject, *theos* or God himself, cannot be studied directly and scientifically. "Therefore, it is more accurate to say that what distinguishes a theological school is that it is a community that studies those matters which are believed to *lead* to true understanding of God."[76] Although his answer is accurate, one cannot help but ask, again, "What is the fundamental difference between Sunday Schools and theological schools?" Since the church holds corporate authority to Scripture interpretation under the illumination of the Spirit, the interpretive function of theological schools seems redundant.

Is there a distinct function of the seminary that justifies its existence? Here is my attempt to address the question: the fusion of individual saints, the church, and the seminary. Some specially called individuals are sent by the local churches in order to *learn to read* Scripture with other specially called community of believers at a seminary.[77] Eventually, they all *learn to lead* with Scripture in local churches. In this sense, the seminary and the church are not two distinct Christian communities; rather, they forge an intimate collaboration and connection. Again, the church sends the believers to the seminary to *learn* Scripture reading; in turn, the seminary sends the believers to the church to *lead* Scripture reading. Consequently, the churches will not lack able teachers of the Word and the seminary will not lack arduous students of the word.

Furthermore, one of the main goals of theological schools or seminaries is to help the students construct solid biblical and theological principles, so as to prepare them to apply those theories in personal, familial, ecclesial, and social contexts. In order to rightly derive principles based on Scripture and rightly apply these principles into practice, the seminary plays the crucial role

75. Green, "Spiritual Hermeneutics," 155.

76. Kelsey, cited in Vallet, *Stewards of the Gospel*, 187.

77. Studying with the community of God includes learning from the historically past members of the community "whose knowledge of Scripture, devotion, and piety, whose wisdom and trust in God, would put us to shame"; this community of the deceased is part of the integrally interpretive community (Stanglin, *Letter and Spirit of Biblical Interpretation*, 4).

of empowering seminarians to acquire the critical and charitable capability[78] (capacity-ability) of "theological *habitus*," i.e., having theological discernment and making theological judgment.[79] It is this theological *habitus* or discernment that is not usually taught in the church context.

Training in theological habit or discernment is more than knowing how to construct theological principles or propositions. Vanhoozer proposes a "well-versed propositionalism" where studying Scripture involves both cognitive/content and affective/attitudinal aspects.[80] Concisely, the purpose of reading Scripture is to shape our holistic worldview, form our affections, and train us in discipleship so that both our *knowledge* of God and *love* for God may mature.[81] While knowing theological content is essential, "knowing how to think theologically comes by habit and imitation, not by the mere acquisition of isolated facts."[82] As one reads Scripture in various literary forms, the person attempts to participate with imagination and affection in what the biblical authors witnessed.[83] This disciplined and well-rounded reading of Scripture will eventually enhance one's personal theological judgment to make wise distinctions and decisions in a particular situation.[84] Additionally, one's theological judgment is never merely a human exercise but it also necessarily involves the Spirit's ongoing work in the interpreter.[85] Vanhoozer rightly notes, "Good theological judgment is largely a matter of being apprenticed to what Scripture says (and how it says it)—of having *one's capacity for judging formed and transformed by the Spirit* via the ensembles of canonical discourse that constitute the Old and New Testaments."[86] Theological judgment (or discernment) is, therefore, akin to theological interpretation of Scripture,[87] as well as closely connected to the Spirit's work of illumination.

In summary, one's obedience and earnestness in devotional reading of Scripture is integral to personal growth in Christian disposition, the result

---

78. For a recent and excellent discussion on doing theology critically and charitably, see Anizor, *How to Read Theology*.

79. Vallet, *Stewards of the Gospel*, 187–88.

80. Vanhoozer, "Love's Wisdom," 264.

81. Vanhoozer, "Love's Wisdom," 264–65.

82. Aquino, cited in Vanhoozer, "Love's Wisdom," 264.

83. Vanhoozer, "Love's Wisdom," 264–65.

84. Vanhoozer, "Love's Wisdom," 265.

85. Vanhoozer states, "A well-versed propositionalism plays an important role in the pedagogy of Word and *Spirit* that shapes readers into wise participations in the drama of redemption" (Vanhoozer, "Love's Wisdom," 265; emphasis added).

86. Vanhoozer, "Love's Wisdom," 267; emphasis added.

87. Vanhoozer, "Love's Wisdom," 261.

of the Spirit's illuminating work in the word—yet one may go further, to the next level of communal reading of Scripture. Communal reading as a church is imperative to faithfully seek and do God's will as a whole so as to fulfill the ambassadorial role of God's kingdom community[88]—yet some may go even further, to the next stage of learning Scripture in seminaries. The arduous interpretive effort in theological institutions is indispensable because its training equips a specially called community of Scripture leaders to lead Scripture reading with solid, Spirit-informed judgment in their communities of faith. Nevertheless, this circle of Scripture reading should not be seen as an exclusive community; rather, the Spirit-led communal study of Scripture should result in effective communication of the word within and beyond the church community.

Purpose of "Spirit Illumination": Communication

The purpose of Spirit illumination (as well as Spirit-inspiration) is to *communicate* God's will/intention so that people may understand and respond to the divine messages.[89] Communication is always reciprocal—one delivering a message and the other(s) responding to the message, and without one there is a communication breakdown. Nevertheless, the Spirit who inspired Scripture never fails in his communicating, as Isaiah 55:11 testifies, "[S]o is my word that goes out from my mouth: It will not return to me empty, but will accomplish what I desire and achieve the purpose for which I sent it." The Spirit communicates effectively and purposefully.

Keener reminds that the Spirit can be active on the so-called anthropological level of exegesis.[90] This means that "Spirit illumination" is integral to and integrated into "saint interpretation" from the initial reading to the eventual response to the message. Traditional hermeneutical presupposition

---

88. Vanhoozer argues, "the Bible is best read in the context of a community of disciplined readers, not because there is no meaning in the Bible apart from its reception by the Spirit-led community, but because the church is the place where the Spirit cultivates righteousness and the willingness to hear the Word" (*Is There a Meaning?*, 413–14). This statement does not necessarily deny that the seminary is another disciplined (perhaps more so) community context where the seminarians are more eager to allow the Spirit to cultivate righteousness and willingness to submit to God's calling and word.

89. Duvall and Hays, *Grasping God's Word*, 226. Vanhoozer argues articulately, "The Spirit's role in bringing about understanding is to witness what is other than himself (meaning accomplished) and to bring its significance to bear on the reader (meaning applied)" (*Is There a Meaning?*, 413).

90. Keener, *Spirit Hermeneutics*, 12–13. "Still, the Spirit can be active even on the level of exegesis, most often through the clear functioning of our cognitive faculties in exploring and embracing the text" (12).

often indicates that the interpreter is relatively capable of carrying out grammatical, historical, and/or literary exegesis on his or her own to discover the meaning of the particular text with *minimal* help from the Spirit. Duvall and Hays state, "At the level of cognitive understanding, the Spirit appears to play a minimal role"; and "When it comes to biblical interpretation, the Spirit appears to work *little* in the cognitive dimension, *more* in the area of discern truth, and *most* in the area of application."[91] While there is no way to determine the exact amount of the Spirit's involvement in non-Christians' cognitive understanding,[92] it is rather speculative to reason that the Spirit is "minimally" involved in the level of Christian cognitive understanding. If true understanding of Scripture involves the whole person (mind, emotion, actions, etc.) and if sin truly affects the whole person (cognition, emotion, and body, even of a Christian), then the interpreter has no way to come to a true understanding unless the Spirit works actively on all levels to bring persuasion and conviction to one's cognition, emotions, and actions. The presupposition that the Spirit is *always minimally* involved on the cognitive level suggests that Christian interpreters do not have to rely

---

91. Duvall and Hays, *Grasping God's Word*, 227, 228; emphasis original. Other authors have been trying to maintain a balance between the Spirit's role on an interpreter's application of Scripture and the person's reliance on the Spirit in the hermeneutic effort: "[E]verything we have taught in this book falls short of the intended goal if interpreters do not simultaneously pray and rely on the Holy Spirit to guide them in the hermeneutical task . . . Many non-Christians can apply sound hermeneutics to understand the meaning of Scripture; without the Spirit, however, they refuse to apply it adequately to their lives" (Klein et al., *Introduction to Biblical Interpretation*, 635).

92. Since the unbelieving interpreter did not end up believing, it could be retrospectively argued (or by means of cause-effect) that there had been minimal or no work of the Spirit on any levels of human interpretation (cognitive level, truth-discerning level, or application level, based on the classification by Duvall and Hays, *Grasping God's Word*, 228). This writer, however, is hesitant to "quantify" the amount of the Spirit's illuminating work on any level, for doing so is to limit the free sovereignty of the Spirit, resulting in holding him captive to human interpretive power. Rather, this writer contends that even on the human cognitive level the Spirit can be as active as he is working on other levels. For example, when an unbelieving interpreter, after interpreting Scripture, comes to an intellectual and historical conclusion that Jesus is the Christ, who physically rose from the dead, it is already a demonstration of the Spirit's enablement in the person's proper cognitive function to help him "know" the message. If, for instance, the person is unwilling to accept or embrace the "illumined" conclusion, it should not be assumed the Spirit works "minimally" in that person. Rather, it is the person's unwilling or rebellious heart that rejects the Spirit's work in the person's mind through the word. The Spirit in his sovereignty may continue to illuminate (persuade or convict) the person to ultimate submission. It is not for us to determine how (much/often) the Spirit should do his work. In short, to designate more illuminating power to the "area of application" (or action) is to neglect the Spirit's illuminating work in the human cognitive function. This sort of implication would be more than unfortunate, if not theologically damaging.

as much on the Spirit while applying hermeneutical principles. This unintentionally and unfortunately creates what we have often seen in seminary studies, namely, seminary students taking hermeneutical exercises as less "spiritual" or "Spirit-illumined" than "devotional reading" of Scripture. This writer contends that Spirit illumination is not merely about enabling interpreters to understand the messages in Scripture and to respond as such, but also about enabling the proper functioning of their cognitive faculties while they use the interpretative principles. With this in mind, I shall return to the theme of Spirit illumination and communication, as elaborated in a threefold aspect: response-with-words, response-with-actions, and response-with-words-and-actions.

The first desired result of Spirit illumination is the response-with-words, namely, personal praying. Praying is communicating, that is, orally responding to the messages communicated and understood through the Spirit's illuminating work. Since Scripture is Spirit-inspired writing, the Christian interpreter must place himself in constant "communication with the Spirit. Prayer is the medium of communication. And therefore it is necessary for the right understanding of the Bible."[93] As often observed, prayer virtually always goes with devotional reading and much less with exegetical reading. The latter seems to be less "spiritual" because, as some may reason, more discipline in human thinking implies less exercise in prayer. Thus, as some may conclude: more thinking (use of human mind) implies "less spiritual," and more praying (use of human spirit) implies "more spiritual." This is an unnecessary and unfortunate dichotomy. Both devotion and diligent readings, however, can be faithful and spiritual, by having them both merged rather than split asunder.[94]

Realistically in seminary contexts, more often than not, seminarians who try to take control of the hermeneutical principles leave no room for devotional reading because the latter is often seen as mutually exclusive from diligent interpretation.[95] Consequently, there is a distinct separation of reading Scripture for devotional purposes (i.e., no sound interpretation allowed!) and studying Scripture for academic, preaching, or teaching purposes (i.e., only sound interpretation allowed!), as if devotional reading of Scripture should not involve one's active mind, or interpretative activity hinders one's spiritual growth. This is, obviously, a false distinction. Rather than

---

93. Lightfoot, cited in Keener, *Spirit Hermeneutics*, 14.

94. As Duvall and Hays also note, God "gave us minds, and he expects us to use them when it comes to Bible study. He wants us to think clearly and reason soundly. He wants us to study the Scriptures diligently and faithfully. Since God created us to think, [Bible] study is 'Spiritual' (i.e., in line with the Spirit's will)" (*Grasping God's Word*, 229).

95. Keener, *Spirit Hermeneutics*, 14.

one or the other, seminarians should take care to navigate the dual terrain of devotional and interpretive readings so as to strike a healthy balance that reconciles and fosters both their spirituality and understanding. Hence, it is necessary for seminarians to begin engaging in the Spirit through prayer as soon as one starts reading Scripture devotionally and interpretively, as well as throughout the whole process of studying.

Practically and traditionally, one does not have to always read Scripture with in-depth analysis.[96] More significantly, however, one does not have to always read Scripture "devotionally" without interpretive effort, as if the hermeneutical approach would interrupt the spiritual communication between the Spirit and the interpreter, or hinder the spiritual growth of the interpreter. The root problem does not lie as much with the "devotional" or "diligent" approach as with the disassociation of the head and the heart. The integration of both devotion and interpretation should be considered as an on-going process, or more appropriately, a "spiral": one should always begin reading the passage(s) prayerfully (as practiced in *lectio divina*) and continue to read the passage(s) as one applies the interpretive methods. As one does in-depth interpretation, one may pause to pray, meditate, and/or contemplate. This becomes a spiritual-hermeneutical spiral, rather than a dissociated function either for the heart (by devotion) or for the head (through interpretation).

The second desired result of the Spirit's communication through illumination is the response-with-actions. Keener reminds what interpreters often forget, namely, that "[d]uring and once we have done responsible exegesis, how may we expect the Spirit to apply the text to our [personal] lives and communities?"[97] Concisely, readers who *believe in* Scripture as Spirit-inspired must read it in a way to *live out* Scripture, personally and communally. The response-with-actions involves not just outward deeds, but also, more significantly, inner attitudes. The interpreter must, on the one hand, painstakingly and continuously put off pride, laziness, stubbornness, and on the other hand, readily and progressively put on willing, teachable, diligent, repentant, and submissive attitudes.[98] We naturally

---

96. The traditional practice of *lectio divina*, "holy reading" or "prayerful reading" (including remaining silent, reading, meditating, praying, and contemplating), is usually seen as a "complement" to the interpretive study of Scripture. See Duvall and Hays, *Grasping God's Word*, 231.

97. Keener, *Spirit Hermeneutics*, 3.

98. Duvall and Hays, *Grasping God's Word*, 233. Wright and Martin emphasize a twofold aspect of one's spiritual encountering with God in Scripture: 1) the Spirit's enlivening act of giving insights and understanding [i.e., illumination]; 2) the act-attitude of the Scripture reader (or hearer), namely, his or her "active participation in the life of the church, repentance, humility, piety, personal application, obedience, and

think that one should cultivate these attitudes during "devotional" reading, when in fact, interpretive reading expects even more of these inner postures. One of the reasons for the neglect of these attitudes during the interpretive process is that seminarians expect to or are expected to use their minds to think, reason, and discern, without placing an adequate emphasis on the spiritual attitudes during diligent Bible interpretation.[99] Furthermore, most seminarians aim at achieving the academic goals that supposedly produce minimal or no spiritual value to them. Consequently, they hear more the voices of men (from commentaries) than the voice of God spoken through Scripture from the Spirit.

Applying interpretive tools in Scripture reading is tedious, but it does not necessarily mean that the Spirit is not actively involved in the process. As an illustration, the process of learning a musical instrument requires one's tedious effort in the beginning, and yet gradually the person enjoys the sound and beauty of the music. Similarly, learning to use the techniques of hermeneutics may seem to be a tedious and demanding process. The result, however, of continuous and diligent learning is the person's deep appreciation of and conviction concerning the beauty and voice (such as God's commands or promises) of Spirit-inspired Scripture.[100] To continue the music analogy, some children learn musical instruments very diligently but without a willing spirit (the common reason being that they have no choice because the parents expect them to do so!). Eventually, they do grasp these musical skills but are unable to truly appreciate the sound of music; or worse, some lose their interest in (or even give up) music altogether. Similarly, some are diligent in using hermeneutical tools (they don't have much choice because the professors expect them to do so, or they will suffer academically!), but ultimately they are unable to truly appreciate the powerful and beautiful voice of God through Scripture. The main reason is that they lack the willingness to yield to the Spirit. In simpler terms, they neglect the attitudes of their hearts—the matter of the heart is the heart of the matter in biblical interpretation.[101]

---

persevering faith and love" (Wright and Martin, *Encountering the Living God*, 243).

99. The brief survey of the textbooks of biblical interpretation in the earlier section has adequately demonstrated the disproportional emphasis.

100. Duvall and Hays, *Grasping God's Word*, 225.

101. Vanhoozer states, "The Spirit's illumination of our minds is . . . dependent on his prior transformation of our hearts" (*Is There a Meaning?*, 413). While it is true that the changing of one's heart is prior to changing of one's head (or mind), this writer sees heart transformation as part of Spirit's illumination, that is, Spirit illumination is an umbrella term for Spirit's works (i.e., to convict, to enlighten, and to sanctify).

The attitude of the heart is the crucial domain of the Spirit's illuminating work. The Spirit teaches and cultivates proper attitudes in the heart in order to bring about spiritual maturity. As rightly noted by Duvall and Hays, "spiritual maturity affects our ability to hear the voice of the Spirit (the divine Author) in the Scriptures."[102] Maturity is a process that requires the interpreter's ongoing humility or prayerful submission, and even this very attitude requires the Spirit's illumination.[103] The illuminating work of the Spirit in Christian maturity may involve the following fourfold aspect. First, the Spirit *convinces* the reader's heart that Scripture is truly the Spirit-inspired word of God in human words.[104] From the very beginning, it is imperative for the reader to possess a proper attitude of fear and humility approaching Scripture. Second, the Spirit *convicts* the heart of the interpreter towards repentance of "hermeneutic sin," namely, the act of "interpretive violence" to the text by forcing into Scripture one's own sense (i.e., prejudiced, ideological, stereotypical, mistaken, and/or unscriptural presuppositions) that distorts the true sense of the text.[105] The interpreter who reads with this conviction will continue to grow in his or her affective qualities, such as teachableness.[106] Third, the Spirit not only restores the "foundational sense" (heart and head made right) of the reader but also *communicates* the "fuller sense" of the text, so that the reader is able to discern theological insights and principles in view of the canonical wholeness, whether in the form of command, promise, exhortation, or assertion.[107] Fourth, the Spirit *conforms* the reader's heart and head to a fuller meaning of the text so as to bear on the reader to receive with understanding and to reapply the principles into his or her life wisely and effectively.[108]

The third result of Spirit illumination in communication is the response-with-words-and-actions. Vanhoozer stresses that reading and

102. Duvall and Hays, *Grasping God's Word*, 230.

103. In Eph 1:17–19 and Col 1:9–12, Paul showed that prayer, Spirit, and enlightening/understanding are intimately connected to each other.

104. Vanhoozer, *Is There a Meaning?*, 413. A skeptical interpreter will very likely misunderstand the fuller sense of the text because of the fundamental matter, i.e., distrust in God's Spirit-inspired word, a matter of the heart.

105. Vanhoozer, *Is There a Meaning?*, 413.

106. Vanhoozer, *Is There a Meaning?*, 413.

107. Vanhoozer, *Is There a Meaning?*, 413. Duvall and Hays, *Grasping God's Word*, 230. This is the part which most theologians consider as the Spirit's work of illumination. For this writer, illumination involves the whole reading and interpretive process—convincing, convicting, communicating, and confirming.

108. This fourfold aspect of Spirit illumination (convincing, convicting, communicating, conforming) is based on Vanhoozer, *Is There a Meaning?*, 413, in conjunction with Duvall and Hays, *Grasping God's Word*, 230.

knowing what Scripture says or signifies is "not the end of understanding [because] understanding includes a moment of appropriation," that is, "the Bible includes many types of communicative acts and calls for a variety of responses and appropriation."[109] As mentioned above, transformation in personal prayer, attitude, and action are parts of the response expected through reading Scripture. Through Scripture's speech-act, the Spirit calls for another crucial communicative response that involves both words and actions, namely, preaching. The following focuses on two aspects of preaching, specifically, the preparation process of sermons and the theological nature of sermons, especially in view of a seminary context.

First, the preparation process. Osborne is emphatic that "the goal of [biblical] hermeneutics is not the commentary but the sermon."[110] Nonetheless, the communicators of the word must first consider the "personal appropriation" (i.e., applying the message to themselves) before the sermon arrives at public application (i.e., transforming church listeners).[111] The goals of personal devotional study of Scripture involve not only *personal* fellowshiping with God, hearing his voice in Scripture, receiving guidance for daily decision in various situations, and sharing God's will in personal faith dialogue, but also grasping "the message of God for public preaching, as the pastor or Bible teacher confronts others with the biblical truths that have gripped his or her own life."[112] Osborne implies that personal devotion in reading Scripture and public preaching of Scripture should not be considered as two unrelated spiritual tasks. Rather, they are in a "spiral" relationship, progressing from personal application of the scriptural message to its public appropriation through preaching of the text, and returning to the initial step once again. Moreover, this dual aspect of application (i.e., personal-public appropriation) must necessarily involve the illuminating power of the Spirit (1 Cor 2:4–5), "who gives knowledge and wisdom to those who seek him. The Spirit anoints the utterances of the preacher."[113] Preachers are duly reminded to "strive for the Holy Spirit in exegeting as well as in proclaiming the Word of God."[114] It is the illuminating work of the Spirit that enables the preacher as well as the hearers to understand, discern, and apply the text.[115]

---

109. Vanhoozer, *First Theology*, 227.
110. Osborne, *Hermeneutical Spiral*, 434.
111. Osborne, *Hermeneutical Spiral*, 435, 437–38.
112. Osborne, *Hermeneutical Spiral*, 439.
113. Osborne, *Hermeneutical Spiral*, 435.
114. Osborne, *Hermeneutical Spiral*, 436.
115. Osborne, *Hermeneutical Spiral*, 436.

Some seminaries lean toward the traditional practice requiring seminarians to have separate times/occasions for devotional reading and "sermonic" reading (i.e., Scripture reading for sermon preparation that necessarily involves exegeting). It seems to be a spiritual taboo for seminarians (or preachers) to merge devotional reading and disciplined interpretation, as if the applications from personal reading are unrelated to the applications from preaching. Carson provides insightful advice that calls to strive for a healthy balance between devotional reading and interpretive study:

> It is not helpful to tell such students that, on the one hand, they simply need to get on with the discipline of study [for their homework assignments], and, on the other, they need to preserve time for devotional reading of the Bible. That bifurcation of tasks suggests there is no need to be devotional when using technical tools, and no need for rigor when reading the Bible devotionally. Far better to insist that even when they are wrestling with difficult verbal forms and challenging syntax, what they are working on is the Word of God—and it is always imperative to cherish that fact, and treat the biblical text with reverence. And similarly, if when reading the Bible for private edification and without reference to any assignment, one stumbles across a passage one really does not understand, one is not sinning against God if one pulls a commentary or two off the shelf and tries to obtain some technical help. In short, one should not be seduced by merely technical disciplines, nor should one eschew them. In every case, the Bible remains the authoritative Word of God regardless of the "tools" one deploys to understand it better, and it functions authoritatively in our lives when we manage a better integration of technical study and devotional reading.[116]

Although Carson does not directly write about seminarians' sermon preparation, the implication remains the same. If seminaries insist on maintaining the bifurcation of seminarians' devotional reading and technical reading, this guilt-driven tension will carry into their preaching or pastoral ministry—devotional reading versus "sermonic" reading. Ideally, devotional reading and diligent interpretation ought to be in a "spiral" relationship.

Second, the theological nature of sermons. As observed by Treier and Anizor, and approved by Vanhoozer, Western theologians and preachers are prone to work more comfortably and frequently with didactic literature (e.g., wisdom, epistles), rather than narrative literature (e.g., poems, stories, parables) in Scripture because the latter's literary forms are not as easily translatable

---

116. Carson, "Subtle Ways to Abandon," 10–11; partially cited by this writer elsewhere in 池峈鋒 (Tie, Peter), 〈為今日華人教會〉, 176.

into propositional concepts or theological statements.[117] Preaching narrative passages, on the other hand, is preferable for Asian and/or Chinese cultures that esteem stories.[118] Regardless of one's inclination towards the didactic or the narrative, every sermon is *theological*. While teaching-preaching could be in a topical, exegetical/textual, or expository form depending on occasions,[119] all sermons are, in fact, theological in nature.

For a topical sermon (e.g., on "the jealousy of God," "the return of Christ," "marriage," or "prayer"), a preacher-teacher must collect and study all relevant and appropriate texts that ultimately give rise to a key theological principle or affirmation on the topic, that is, "a *theological* affirmation must reflect the Bible's total teaching [on a subject], not only some select or isolated texts."[120] For an exegetical/textual sermon, a preacher may emphasize the diversity of the respective messages/texts by different biblical authors. Ultimately, one has to strive for *theological* unity of the messages, under the conviction that the Spirit, as the ultimate author of the entire canon, has a theologically unified message for his people.[121] In other words, anytime anyone preaches or teaches a text exegetically, the person must acknowledge the immediate literary as well as the larger canonical contexts to bear upon

---

117. Vanhoozer, "Love's Wisdom," 262; Treier and Anizor, "Theological Interpretation," 14.

118. Song claims, "In [stories] we find popular theology at its most unsophisticated and yet at its most profound, at its simplest and yet at its deepest, at its most unadorned and yet at its most moving. Jesus himself frequently resorted to stories to drive home to his listeners the message of God" (Song, *Tell Us Our Names*, ix). Song attempts to do "story theology," deriving theological implications through reflecting theologically on histories and stories of the ordinary people, including fairytales or folktales (3–4), as well as "the history of other peoples, other faiths, other cultures, and other ideologies" (57). Song also asserts, "Doing theology with folktales in Asia teaches an important lesson: stories of people, not preconceived theological ideas and criteria, lead us to deeper truths about humanity and God" (*Third-Eye Theology*, 11).

119. For a concise explanation of topical, exegetical/textual, and expository sermon structures, refer to Chapell, *Christ-Centered Preaching*, 127–29. Chapell states that the "*technical definition of an expository sermon* requires that it expound Scripture by deriving from a specific text main points and subpoints that disclose the thought of the author, cover the scope of the passage, and are applied to the lives of the listeners" (129; italics original).

120. Klein et al., *Introduction to Biblical Interpretation*, 585; emphasis added.

121. The "theologically unified message" does not mean there is "merely one meaning" in Scripture. This "unified message" of Scripture or the "truth of God is many-faceted," that is, Scripture consists of diverse genres; teaching about various doctrines and morals; speaking to the people in different ages and of various ages; and yet, all are displaying together "the incredible richness of our salvation in Jesus Christ" (Frame, "Spirit and the Scriptures," 219). Stanglin states, "Scripture is, in a word, 'multivalent'"; it teaches diverse doctrines (faith) and morals (practice), and yet all are unified in the person and work of Christ (*Letter and Spirit of Biblical Interpretation*, 215).

the fuller meaning of the particular text.¹²² Lastly, expository preaching is also theological in nature. While expository sermons may give prominence to the "application" element, one must still first identify the "cross-cultural principle" component from the text.¹²³ This principle must be further tested against the larger canonical context, especially against clearer teachings elsewhere within Scripture, in order to confirm its theological validity before it arrives at life application.¹²⁴

In summary, the work of establishing theological principles (or truths) that are clearly reflected in the individual texts, firmly testified in the whole canon, and universally applicable to the present real-life context, is an indispensable aspect in Scripture interpretation as well as public communication.¹²⁵ These theological principles are intimately connected to the "fuller meaning" (*sensus plenior*) intended by the Spirit, beyond that of the original human authors, and yet they are to remain faithful to the canonical boundary providentially guarded by the Spirit through the church, i.e., the community of the redeemed.¹²⁶ Put concisely, this *theological preaching of Scripture* (TPS, tentatively called) functions collaboratively with theological interpretation of Scripture (TIS).¹²⁷

---

122. Klein et al., *Introduction to Biblical Interpretation*, 584; see also Moo, "Problem of *Sensus Plenior*," 205.

123. Köstenberger and Patterson, *Invitation to Biblical Interpretation*, 792–93; Chapell, *Christ-Centered Preaching*, 140, 146.

124. Köstenberger and Patterson, *Invitation to Biblical Interpretation*, 793; Duvall and Hays, *Grasping God's Word*, 237–46. For practical guidelines of formulating theological principles for all of the NT's and OT's genres, see Duvall and Hays, *Grasping God's Word*, 259–63 (Epistles); 275–82 (Gospels); 299–306 (Acts); 325–28 (Revelation); 350–51 (Narrative); 364–66 (Law); 388–91 (Poetry); 407–11 (Prophets); and 428–41 (Wisdom).

125. Köstenberger and Patterson see "theology" as the goal of biblical interpretation, after the historical and literary aspects, and yet theology must eventually lead to personal application and public proclamation (Köstenberger and Patterson, *Invitation to Biblical Interpretation*, 689, 692–95, 727).

126. Moo's analysis suggests the validity of the delicate interaction between *sensus plenior* and the canonical approach for a proper theological interpretation of Scripture (Moo, "Problem of *Sensus Plenior*," 202–11).

127. For a concise assessment of TIS, please see Plummer, *40 Questions*, 315–19; for a critical assessment of TIS, see Porter, "Biblical Hermeneutics and *Theological* Responsibility," 39–46. Porter observes that TIS gives an "ambiguous role . . . of the Holy Spirit in the interpretive process" (40); however, he is rather convinced TIS is not a responsible biblical hermeneutic (46). Despite the difficulty of providing a concise definition of TIS as an interpretive discipline, this writer is convinced TIS must continue to discuss the themes of dual authorship, *sensus plenior*, and theological principalization in light of Spirit illumination in order to better support theological preaching to the churches.

Concluding Statements for Further Conversation

This chapter has discussed some significant theological and practical implications for holding to Scripture's dual authorship or concursive inspiration. The conviction of dual authorship responds directly to the delicate interplay between "Spirit illumination" and "saint interpretation." Achieving a healthy balance between the two have a direct impact on all believers in churches and seminaries. I have first surveyed a handful of basic biblical hermeneutics textbooks to demonstrate the disproportional emphasis on the anthropological factor over the pneumatological aspect. To remedy this problem, I have attempted to explore the illuminating work of the Spirit through three main, intertwined concepts—product-canonicity, process-community, and purpose-communication—in search for a more proper interpretation that is faithful to the "dual-authorship" conviction.

The illumination of the Spirit does not mean that the Spirit will normally "whisper in our ears" vocally while we practice our devotional reading of Scripture, nor does it mean that the Spirit works "predictably through the normal channels of [seminary] education so that those with advanced degrees automatically have the greatest spiritual perception."[128] The Spirit typically moves in free, mysterious, and sovereign ways, and yet Christians are responsible for the disciplined study of Scripture in intimate interrelation with the Spirit's perennial work of illumination.

This chapter does not claim to cover all crucial aspects of Spirit illumination in Christian interpretation. In fact, there is one more relevant concept that deserves further exploration, namely, the promise of the Spirit—consummation. The Spirit's illumination is not only indispensable in the whole production of canon, the interpretive process of community, and the ongoing purpose of communicating the messages in Scripture, but also vital in fulfilling the ultimate goal of consummating the saints in Christlike glory, resulting in the glorification of God (Eph 1:13-19; 3:16-21; 2 Cor 3:7-8, 17-18; Rom 8:5, 11, 16, 29-30). This means that Spirit illumination is vital from beginning to end, from Scripture's inspiration to its complete fulfillment. This awaits further exploration.

Bibliography

Allison, Gregg R. "Theological Interpretation of Scripture: An Introduction and Preliminary Evaluation." *Southern Baptist Journal of Theology* 14 (2010) 28–36.

---

128. Frame, "Spirit and the Scriptures," 234.

Anizor, Uche. *How to Read Theology: Engaging Doctrine Critically and Charitably.* Grand Rapids: Baker, 2018.

Aquino, Frederick D. "A Theology of Informed Judgment." *Restoration Quarterly* 45 (2003) 115–25.

Barker, Kit. "Speech Act Theory, Dual Authorship, and Canonical Hermeneutics: Making Sense of Sensus Plenior." *Journal of Theological Interpretation* 3 (2009) 227–39.

Brown, Raymond E. "The Problems of the *Sensus Plenior.*" *Ephemerides Theologicae Lovanienses* 43 (1967) 460–69.

Brueggemann, Walter. "Biblical Authority: A Personal Reflection." *Christian Century*, January 3–10 (2001) 14–16. http://fpcperu.org/wp-content/uploads/2013/01/Brueggemann-on-Biblical-Authority.pdf.

Carson, D. A. "Subtle Ways to Abandon the Authority of Scripture in Our Lives." *Themelios* 42 (2017) 1–12.

Chapell, Bryan. *Christ-Centered Preaching: Redeeming the Expository Sermon.* Grand Rapids: Baker, 1994.

Cole, Graham A. *He Who Gives Life: The Doctrine of the Holy Spirit.* Edited by John S. Feinberg. Foundations of Evangelical Theology. Wheaton, IL: Crossway, 2007.

Dockery, David S. *Christian Scripture: An Evangelical Perspective on Inspiration, Authority and Interpretation.* Nashville: Broadman & Holman, 1995.

———. "A People of the Book and the Crisis of Biblical Authority." In *Beyond the Impasse? Scripture, Interpretation, and Theology in Baptist Life*, edited by Robinson B. James and David S. Dockery, 17–39. Nashville: Broadman, 1992.

———. "Study and Interpretation of the Bible." In *Foundations for Biblical Interpretation*, edited by David S. Dockery et al., 36–54. Nashville: Broadman & Holman, 1999.

Duvall, Scott J., and J. Daniel Hays. *Grasping God's Word: A Hands-On Approach to Reading, Interpreting, and Applying the Bible.* 3rd ed. Grand Rapids: Zondervan, 2012.

Erickson, Millard J. *Christian Theology.* 3rd ed. Grand Rapids: Baker, 2013.

Fee, Gordon D. *God's Empowering Presence: The Holy Spirit in the Letters of Paul.* Grand Rapids: Baker, 2009.

Fee, Gordon D., and Douglas Stuart. *How to Read the Bible for All its Worth.* 4th ed. Grand Rapids: Zondervan, 2014.

Feinberg, John S. *Light in a Dark Place: The Doctrine of Scripture.* Foundations of Evangelical Theology. Wheaton, IL: Crossway, 2018.

Frame, John M. "The Spirit and the Scriptures." In *Hermeneutics, Authority, and Canon*, edited by D. A. Carson and John D. Woodbridge, 213–35. Grand Rapids: Baker, 1995.

Green, Joel B. "Spiritual Hermeneutics." In *Third Article Theology: A Pneumatological Dogmatics*, edited by Myk Habets, 153–72. Minneapolis: Fortress, 2016.

Hauerwas, Stanley. *Unleashing the Scripture: Freeing the Bible from Captivity to America.* Nashville: Abingdon, 1993.

Hobbs, Herschel H. *You are Chosen: The Priesthood of All Believers.* San Francisco: Harper & Row, 1990.

Holmes, Steve. "John Webster Dies at 60: Tribute to a Leading Theologian of His Day." *Christian Today*, May 26, 2016. https://www.christiantoday.com/article/john-webster-dies-at-60-tribute-to-a-leading-theologian-of-his-day/86908.htm.

James, Robinson B., and David S. Dockery, eds. *Beyond the Impasse? Scripture, Interpretation, and Theology in Baptist Life*. Nashville: Broadman, 1992.

Keener, Craig S. *Spirit Hermeneutics: Reading Scripture in Light of Pentecost*. Grand Rapids: Eerdmans, 2016.

Kelsey, David H. *To Understand God Truly: What's Theological about a Theological School?* Louisville: Westminster John Knox, 1992.

Klein, William W., et al. *Introduction to Biblical Interpretation*. 3rd ed. Grand Rapids: Zondervan, 2017.

Köstenberger, Andreas J., and Richard D. Patterson. *Invitation to Biblical Interpretation: Exploring the Hermeneutical Triad of History, Literature, and Theology*. Invitation to Theological Studies. Grand Rapids: Kregel, 2011.

LaSor, William S. "Prophecy, Inspiration, and *Sensus Plenior*." *Tyndale Bulletin* 29 (1978) 49–60.

Levering, Matthew. *Mary's Bodily Assumption*. Notre Dame: University of Notre Dame Press, 2014. Kindle Edition.

Lightfoot, J. B. *The Acts of the Apostles: A Newly Discovered Commentary*. Vol. 1 of the Lightfood Legacy Set. 3 vols. Edited by Ben Witherington III and Todd D. Still. Downers Grove, IL: IVP Academics, 2014.

Melick, Charles L., Jr. "Can We Understand the Bible?" In *In Defense of the Bible: A Comprehensive Apologetics for the Authority of Scripture*, edited by Steven B. Cowan and Terry L. Wilder, 89–116. Nashville: B&H, 2013.

Moo, Douglas J. "The Problem of *Sensus Plenior*." In *Hermeneutics, Authority, and Canon*, edited by D. A. Carson and John D. Woodbridge, 175–211. Grand Rapids: Baker, 1995.

Osborne, Grant R. *The Hermeneutical Spiral: A Comprehensive Introduction to Biblical Interpretation*. Rev. and expanded ed. Downers Grove, IL: InterVarsity, 2006.

Plummer, Robert L. *40 Questions about Interpreting the Bible*. Grand Rapids: Kregel, 2010.

Porter, Stanley E. "Biblical Hermeneutics and *Theological* Responsibility." In *The Future of Biblical Interpretation: Responsible Plurality in Biblical Hermeneutics*, edited by Stanley E. Porter and Matthew R. Malcolm, 29–50. Downers Grove, IL: IVP Academic, 2013.

Quarles, Charles L. "Higher Criticism: What Has it Shown?" In *In Defense of the Bible: A Comprehensive Apologetics for the Authority of Scripture*, edited by Steven B. Cowan and Terry L. Wilder, 63–88. Nashville: B&H, 2013.

Song, Choan-Seng. *Tell Us Our Names: Story Theology from an Asian Perspective*. Maryknoll, NY: Orbis, 1984.

———. *Third-Eye Theology: Theology in Formation in Asian Settings*. Maryknoll, NY: Orbis, 1979.

Stanglin, Keith D. *The Letter and Spirit of Biblical Interpretation: From the Early Church to Modern Practice*. Grand Rapids: Baker, 2018.

Theilicke, Helmut. *A Little Exercise for Young Theologians*. Translated by Charles L. Taylor. Grand Rapids: Eerdmans, 1962.

Tie, Peter L. *Restore Unity, Recover Identity, and Refine Orthopraxy: The Believers' Priesthood in the Ecclesiology of James Leo Garrett Jr.* Eugene, OR: Wipf & Stock, 2012.

Treier, Daniel, and Uche Anizor. "Theological Interpretation of Scripture and Evangelical Systematic Theology: Iron Sharpening Iron?" *Southern Baptist Journal of Theology* 14 (2010) 4–17.

Vallet, Ronald E. *Stewards of the Gospel: Reforming Theological Education.* Grand Rapids: Eerdmans, 2011.

Vanhoozer, Kevin J. *Biblical Authority after Babel: Retrieving the Solas in the Spirit of Mere Protestant Christianity.* Grand Rapids: Brazos, 2016.

———. *First Theology: God, Scripture & Hermeneutics.* Downers Grove, IL: InterVarsity, 2002.

———. *Is There a Meaning in This Text? The Bible, the Reader, and the Morality of Literary Knowledge.* Grand Rapids: Zondervan, 1998.

———. "Love's Wisdom: The Authority of Scripture's Form and Content for Faith's Understanding and Theological Judgment." *Journal of Reformed Theology* 5 (2011) 247–75.

Webster, John. "Illumination." *Journal of Reformed Theology* 5 (2011) 325–40.

Wright, William M., and Francis Martin. *Encountering the Living God in Scripture: Theological and Philosophical Principles for Interpretation.* Grand Rapids: Baker, 2019.

于中旻 (Yu, JAMES C. M.), 〈宋尚節〉. http://www.aboutbible.net/Ab/E.59.JohnSung.html.

池峈鋒 (Tie, Peter L. H.). 〈為今日華人教會重尋與實踐唯獨聖經〉.《義配恩源 蕩蕩流: 宗教改革五百周 年文集》, 167–84. 香港: 牧職神學院, 2017.

2

From "the Spirit of the Lord *Clothed* Gideon" to "*Put On* the New Man"

Kwang-Chi Liu

Introduction

DURING THE DAYS WHEN I was writing a commentary for the book of Judges, I came across several key points in the narratives with the phrase "the Spirit of the Lord" (רוּחַ יְהוָה). This aroused my curiosity about the work of the Holy Spirit (on humans) in the Old Testament. Obviously, the number of occurrences for the "Spirit of the Lord" (or "the Spirit of God": רוּחַ אֱלֹהִים) in the Old Testament is not as high as the "Holy Spirit" recorded in the New Testament; likewise, the scope of coverage is not as wide as in the New Testament. In this chapter, I attempt to begin my investigation on "the Spirit of the Lord" from Judges with further study into other relevant passages in the Old Testament, and expand into New Testament for discussion of the above-mentioned topics, and further study and compare/contrast the works of the Holy Spirit on humans in both the Old and New Testaments.

A Description of the Work of "the Spirit of the Lord" in Judges

The Hebrew word for "Spirit" in the Old Testament of the Bible is רוּחַ.[1] There are nine occurrences of רוּחַ in the book of Judges.[2] Besides its use, 9:23 describes the "evil spirit" (רוּחַ רָעָה) which was sent by God[3], and in 15:19 "his spirit" (רוּחוֹ) refers to Samson's "spirit"; the remaining seven are all used to refer to "the Spirit of the Lord." In the remaining seven verses, two of them connect the verb היה ("to be") with the preposition עַל ("on, upon") to say that the Spirit of the Lord came upon someone (Judg 3:10; 11:29).[4] Bruce K. Waltke argues that it is customary grammar to indicate that "an urgent, compulsive, overwhelming force empowers him to achieve a God-ordained objective."[5] The result of the action for Othniel in chapter 3 was to become the judge for the Israelites, to go out to war[6] and to overcome the suppression of Israel's gentile enemy "Cushan-rishathaim king of Mesopotamia."[7] For Jephthah in chapter 11, when "the Spirit of the Lord" came upon him, he walked through the land of the east of the Jordan to call on the people, and finally

---

1. Besides "spirit," the Hebrew term רוּחַ consists of many other meanings in different contexts, including "wind" (2 Sam 22:11; 1 Kgs 18:45; 2 Kgs 3:17), "breeze" (Gen 3:8), "air" (Jer 14:6), "breath" of humans or animals (Gen 7:15, 22–23; 1 Sam 1:15; Ezek 37:5; Ps 104:25, 29), God's "breath" (Job 4:9; 27:3), human "mind" (Ps 32:2), "courage" (Josh 2:11), etc. Payne, "רוּחַ," *TWOT*, 836–37; Holladay, *Concise Hebrew*, 377.

2. The term רוּחַ appears in Judg 3:10; 6:34; 9:23; 11:29; 13:25; 14:6, 19; 15:14, 19.

3. Since the "evil spirit" (רוּחַ רָעָה) was sent by God, and the traditional Chinese Union Version has translated it into "Devil" (惡魔), this has created confusion in readers: "Why did the holy and just God send the 'Devil' to do his work?" As a matter of fact, the so-called "evil spirit" refers to the "disaster-producing spirit." See 劉光啟,《士師記反思》, 188, 195n2.

4. Hamilton, "הָיָה," *TWOT*, 214.

5. Waltke and Yu, *Old Testament Theology*, 597.

6. This does not mean Othniel did not know how to do battle because Judg 1:13 clearly recorded that he was a skilled warrior. Therefore, rather than taking Judg 3:10 to mean "the Spirit of the Lord gives him the ability of war," it is better to say "the Spirit of the Lord bestows upon Othniel more power and courage to confront the enemy. Or it can be said that what was given here is increased "effectiveness" or "heightened capacity," not mere "power" (Thiselton, *Holy Spirit*, 11–12).

7. Since no external literature other than the Bible mentions "Cushan-rishathaim" (כּוּשַׁן רִשְׁעָתַיִם), there is no consensus among scholars about this person. His name means "Cushan-of-double-wickedness; it is probably a play on words by the author of Judges (Webb, *Book of Judges*, 159–60). Compared with other enemies who suppressed Israel in the Judges, "Cushan-rishathaim of Mesopotamia" recorded in Judg 3:8–10 is quite noteworthy because he is not like the king of Moab, king of Ammon, king of Hazor, or like regional rulers or forces of the Philistines, or like the nomads of the Midian, but far away in the north of the two rivers. It is likely he was the most powerful force among the many gentile rulers that appeared in the Judges.

led the Israelites to strike the Ammonites who oppressed them with a great blow (Judg 11:33). Daniel I. Block points out that the phrase "the Spirit of the Lord came upon . . ." not only expresses the call of the Lord to the people in the book of Judges, but also in other Old Testament Scriptures to specify the power of the Lord in some people (cf. 1 Sam 11:6; 16:13–14).[8]

In addition to the two above-mentioned sources, there are another three verses highlighting רוּחַ in the book of Judges (Judg 14:6, 19; 15:14). They all couple the verb צלח ("to rush") with the preposition עַל ("on, upon"), demonstrating that the Spirit of the Lord came upon the chosen one in an urgent manner and empowered the person to perform the assigned task (cf. 1 Sam 13:6; 16:13).[9] The three verses mentioned here are related to Samson, since the scripture says "the Spirit of the Lord rushed upon him." As a result, Samson "tore the lion in pieces (as one tears a young goat)," "struck down thirty (Ashkelon) men," and "the ropes that were on his arms became as flax that has caught fire, and his bonds melted off his hands." These showed the ability of Samson, though amazing, was not of himself but a special gift from God.[10] Another narrative about Samson in relation to the Spirit of the Lord appeared in 13:25: "And the Spirit of the Lord began to stir him in Mahaneh-dan, between Zorah and Eshtaol." The verb "stir" is פעם, and this is the only verse with the *qal* form. However, its passive/reflexive (*niphal*) form means "be disturbed" (Gen 41:8; Ps 77:5 [4]; but 2:3). Therefore, it should have a meaning of "incitement."[11] Many English translations, such as NASB, RSV, NRSV, NIV, or NLT, are translated here as "stir," which means "incitement, motivation."[12] This account of "the Spirit of the Lord stirs up Samson" becomes the beginning of a series of attacks of Samson on the Philistines.[13]

---

8. Block, *Judges, Ruth*, 154.

9. It is worth noting that the root meaning of the verb צלח is "be successful, be prosperous." Luc, "צלח," *NIDOTTE*, 3:804. However, some scholars think this person had a "sudden possession by the Spirit of God" (*BDB*, 852).

10. Several manifestations of Samson's power, however, were connected with his anger and his desires, which had little to do with the salvific work of the Lord. 畢維廉, "Spirit of God," 66–67.

11. Van Rooy, "פעם," *NIDOTTE*, 3:649; Clines, *Concise Dictionary*, 362.

12. A few standard Hebrew encyclopedias, such as *BDB*, *TWOT*, Holladay, etc., suggest the original meaning as "thrust," "impel," or "push (*BDB*, 821; Holladay, *Concise Hebrew*, 295; Hamilton, "פָּעַם," *TWOT*, 730). In addition, KJV and JPS *Tanakh* translate the verb into "move," and NET has understood it as "control." Lee R. Martin even translated the verb as "to trouble" because it was the spirit of the gods that "excited" Samson, which later made him the "trouble" of the Philistines (Martin, "Power to Save!?," 43).

13. If the chapter and verses are omitted as in the original Bible, the last verse of the thirteenth chapter is obviously causally related to the following 14:4–7 (Block, "Empowered by the Spirit of God," 45).

In addition to the above-mentioned verses, the narrative of Gideon in 6:34 is noteworthy: "But the Spirit of the Lord clothed Gideon, and he sounded the trumpet, and the Abiezrites were called out to follow him." (וְרוּחַ יְהוָה לָבְשָׁה אֶת־גִּדְעוֹן וַיִּתְקַע בַּשּׁוֹפָר וַיִּזָּעֵק אֲבִיעֶזֶר אַחֲרָיו). This "to clothe" description is a synonym to the verb היה coupled with preposition "עַל" in 3:10 and 11:29, and is translated as "came upon/on" in some bible versions, such as KJV, NASB, and NIV.[14] Literally, it seems that Gideon (outwardly) "wore or put on" a certain kind of divine spiritual robe or armor; but in essence, it was the Spirit of the Lord working in the heart (inwardly) of this undeserved mighty man of valor (Judg 6:12–16), turning this ordinary man into His vessel,[15] so that Gideon could rely on the power and encouragement of God to call everyone up for war.[16] Thus, RSV, NRSV and NET translate this verb as "took possession/control." In fact, if we compare this to the narrative in the earlier part of chapter 6 where the Israelites were frightened facing the allied army of the Midianites and the Amalekites (Judg 6:2, 6, 11), or the tribe of Gibeon, the Abiezrite, prepared to put Gideon to death due to his demolition of the altar of Ba'al; and now the immediate following of the Abiezrite (Judg 6:34b), and the active response and readiness for operation of the other tribes towards the calling of Gideon (Judg 6:35), manifesting the results of the work of the Spirit of the Lord on Gideon.

The above Scriptures from the book of Judges shows that the Spirit of the Lord took initiative "to come upon, to move, to inspire" certain specific people and empowered them with special abilities to call on the people to complete the mission entrusted by God. However, it is noteworthy that Gideon, Jephthah, and Samson[17] did not live an unequivocal qualitative

---

14. ESV, however, translated it as "clothed," according to its original meaning, and yet, JPS *Tanakh* translated it as "enveloped."

15. Compared to the description in Isa 51:9 ("wake up, wake up . . . *clothe* [לבש] yourself with strength"), the so-called "clothe" in Judg 6:34, in fact, should be understood as the Spirit of God came into Gideon's life, using him as a robe, allowing him to be a vessel for the work of the Lord (Coleson et al., *Joshua, Judges, Ruth*, 277; Richter, "What Do I Know of Holy?," 30n23).

16. Block, "Empowered by the Spirit of God," 45. Nahum M. Waldman pointed out that in the ancient Semitic language expressions in the Near East, the so-called "clothing, covering" by "divine spirit," "evil spirit," or some supernatural existence usually refers to "empowering." And these descriptions are often related to war (Waldman, "Imagery of Clothing," 61–70).

17. Of the four judges mentioned above in relation to the Spirit of the Lord, Othniel can be said to be one of the exceptions. In fact, in addition to 1:11–15, the passage in 3:7–11 did not give much comment on Othniel. But if you use the "negative list" method to compare him with the later judges, one may find that: Othniel has not secretly assassinated anyone (cf. 3:21–22); he did not nail anyone's head to the ground (cf. 4:21); he did not arbitrarily test God (cf. 6:39); he did not make any foolish oath (cf.

spiritual life with the dwelling of the Spirit of the Lord. Conversely, they made many mistakes despite the descent of the Spirit of the Lord.[18] Gideon tempted God in order to conquer in the war (Judg 6:36–40),[19] broke into anger resulting in a massacre of two east Jordan cities which were reluctant to provide supply (Judg 8:5–17), and took private revenge for "his mother's sons" under guise of public justice (Judg 8:18–21). Jephthah's foolish vow had ruined his only daughter (Judg 12:30–31,34–40), and his fiery personality had caused a heavy toll in the civil war within the tribe of Ephraim (Judg 12:1–6). Samson's errors were enormous even after "the Spirit of the Lord stirred him"—not only did he marry a daughter of the Philistines at Timnah (Judg 14:1–20), go in to a prostitute at Gaza (Judg 16:1–3), and hang out with the infamous Delilah (Judg 16:4–22), but he also repeatedly violated the vow of the Nazirites (Judg 14:6, 8–9, 10, 12; 15:15; 16:7, 17–19).[20] It is quite intriguing that Judg 16:20 records that when the most obvious sign of the Nazirites, "the seven locks of his head" which Samson had kept thus far, was finally shaved off by the Philistines, causing him to lose his power, "he did not know that the Lord had left him." Although the Scriptures do not mention it directly, the most reasonable explanation should be: at this time the Spirit of the Lord left him.[21]

11:30); and he did not have sexual relations with any prostitute (cf. 16:1) (Hamilton, *Handbook on the Historical Books*, 112; Block, *Judges, Ruth*, 149).

18. Lee R. Martin, comparing the "circular mode" presented by Judg 2:11–19 with the "Othniel's cycle" in Judg 3:8–11, suggests the mention of "the Spirit of the LORD came on him (Othniel)" in 3:10 is actually a sign as in 2:18a "(the LORD) is with the judge," indicating this particular person had been a chosen savior by God. Furthermore, 2:18a mentions: "The LORD is with the judge, he will save them from the hands of their enemies—in all the days of the judge" (original translation: וְהָיָה יְהוָה עִם־הַשֹּׁפֵט וְהוֹשִׁיעָם מִיַּד אֹיְבֵיהֶם כֹּל יְמֵי הַשּׁוֹפֵט), and the reason for special mention of "the LORD left Samson" (Judg 16:20) indicates "the Spirit of the Lord" had been with these judges continuously after his coming (Martin, "Power to Save!?," 26–27, 31). Lu, however, believes "the mission of the judges was mostly of an urgent nature, that is, fighting against the enemies of Israel. After the completion of the mission, the gift of the Holy Spirit would disappear." 呂紹昌, 〈撒母耳記中的聖靈〉, 79.

19. For a positive and negative evaluation of "Gideon used wool fleece to seek the Lord's confirmation," see 劉光啟, 《士師記反思》, 138–39, 142–43nn16–17.

20. Concerning how Samson repeatedly violated the vow of a Nazirite, and moved toward self-destruction, see 劉光啟, 〈士師參孫的眼見〉, 2–5.

21. Dragga, "In the Shadow," 42; Younger, *Judges and Ruth*, 320.

The Work of "the Spirit of the Lord/God" in OT Narrative Scriptures besides Judges

The above discussion in the book of Judges is related to Israel's leadership. The narration is about the leaders attaining power through the Spirit of the Lord to face the challenges and needs before them. Similar narrations and descriptions also appear in other Old Testament narrative Scriptures:

In Genesis, Pharaoh described his dream interpreter, Joseph as: "a man in whom the Spirit of God is" (אִישׁ אֲשֶׁר רוּחַ אֱלֹהִים בּוֹ, Gen 41:38). Although Pharaoh did not know the so-called "the Spirit of the Lord," he realized that the extraordinary power and wisdom of this man would come from God (cf. Dan 5:14);[22] in fact, Genesis repeatedly described one of the features of Joseph, that is, "the Lord was with Joseph" (Gen 39:2, 3, 21, 23).

In Exodus, besides instructing Moses about the details of the facilities of the tabernacle and the priestly dress, the Lord also told Moses that He had called by name Bezalel the son of Uri, son of Hur, of the tribe of Judah (and Oholiab, the son of Ahisamach, of the tribe of Dan) saying: "I have filled him with the Spirit of God (וָאֲמַלֵּא אֹתוֹ רוּחַ אֱלֹהִים), with ability and intelligence, with knowledge and all craftsmanship" (Exod 31:3, 6; cf. Exod 28:3; 35:31). In the past, the Creator Lord created all things with his own Spirit (cf. Gen 1:2), and now through His Spirit empowering the gift of craftsmanship and teaching with these two leaders, they would lead the involved people in the completion of the holy works of the tabernacle.[23]

In Numbers, the prolonged of the grumbling of the people led to Moses' burnout, the Lord had Moses gather the seventy chosen elders and promised Moses: "And I will take some of the Spirit that is on you and put it on them (וְאָצַלְתִּי מִן־הָרוּחַ אֲשֶׁר עָלֶיךָ וְשַׂמְתִּי עֲלֵיהֶם),[24] and they shall bear the burden of the people with you, so that you may not bear it yourself alone." (Num 11:17; cf. 24–30). "Portion" of the Spirit of the Lord was shared among these elders from Moses at this time, so that they could be involved in the responsibility of leadership and management. Obviously, the Spirit of the Lord had been with Moses (cf. Exod 3:12 the promise of the Lord to be with Moses) despite the fact that there is no direct record

---

22. Hamilton, *Book of Genesis*, 503.

23. Hildebrandt, *Old Testament Theology*, 106–7; Hess, "Bezalel and Oholiab," 161–72.

24. The statement "from the Spirit which is upon you" (מִן־הָרוּחַ אֲשֶׁר עָלֶיךָ) in Num 11:17 does not clearly explain the precise identity of the "spirit," but Moses affirmed later in verse 29, "that the LORD would put *His Spirit* upon them" (כִּי־יִתֵּן יְהוָה אֶת־רוּחוֹ עֲלֵיהֶם), clearly specifying that it is "the LORD's Spirit."

in the scripture.²⁵ Thus, in the forty years of Moses' service, many miracles and wonders performed by Moses were the manifestation of the power of the Spirit of the Lord. The Spirit of the Lord worked not only in these elders, but also with Joshua, Moses' assistant, and the Lord said to Moses, "Joshua, the son of Nun, a man in whom is the Spirit" (אֶת־יְהוֹשֻׁעַ בִּן־נוּן אִישׁ אֲשֶׁר־רוּחַ בּוֹ, Num 27:18a). The Spirit of God made him wise to replace Moses and govern the whole congregation (cf. Deut 34:9).

In Samuel, the Spirit of the Lord "rushed upon" (the verb צלח coupled with the preposition עַל) Saul, so that he not only prophesied, but also called and led the Israelites to strike Nahash the Ammonite King (1 Sam 10:10; 11:6). After Saul committed critical mistakes, the prophet Samuel was ordered to anoint David, and from that day onward the Spirit of the Lord "rushed upon" (צלח) this future king (1 Sam 16:13);²⁶ and immediately the book of Samuel records "Now the Spirit of the Lord departed from Saul (וְרוּחַ יְהוָה סָרָה מֵעִם שָׁאוּל),"²⁷ and instead "a harmful spirit from the Lord tormented him (וּבִעֲתַתּוּ רוּחַ־רָעָה מֵאֵת יְהוָה)" (1 Sam 16:14).²⁸ From then on Saul encounter similar tortures repeatedly (cf. 1 Sam 16:23; 18:10; 19:9). It is noteworthy that after this, the Spirit of the Lord "came upon" (the verb היה coupled with the preposition עַל) Saul so that he went to Naioth in Ramah to arrest David; but this time he was not himself, only able to prophesy (1 Sam 19:23–24).

The above examples are mostly related to the leadership and governance, or the ability to engage in certain work skills. The books of Kings and Chronicles also mention another level—the prophetic service.²⁹ Although

25. Kaiser, "Pentateuch," 8–10; Ashley, *Book of Numbers*, 211.

26. Ps 139:7—David's claim of "Where can I go from your Spirit? Where can I flee from your presence?" reflects David's heartfelt experience with "the presence of the Lord's Spirit."

27. This means the LORD's favor had been transferred from Saul, the king who disobeyed God, to the future king, David (Tsumura, *First Book of Samuel*, 426; Firth, *1 & 2 Samuel*, 187). Howard points out 1 Sam 16:13–14 presents a very complete fan-shaped structure, showing this is a transfer of power/authority, whether in spiritual or political terms (Howard, "Transfer of Power," 473–83). Robert P. Gordon comments that David's fear, as reflected in Ps 51:11, is exactly what Saul had experienced, that is, abandonment by God (Gordon, *I & II Samuel*, 152).

28. The statement in the Chinese Union Version "惡魔從耶和華那裡來" (1 Sam 16:14b) "the evil spirit from the LORD" (רוּחַ־רָעָה מֵאֵת יְהוָה), should be similar to Judg 9:23, "被神所差派、邪惡的靈" "being sent by God, the evil spirit" (Butler, *Judges*, 244; Howard, "Transfer of Power," 482).

29. In 1 Kgs 22:19–25 (=2 Chr 18:18–24), the prophet Micahia mentioned a vision: in the presence of the Lord, a "spirit" in the heavenly multitudes offered to the Lord, "I will be a lying spirit in the mouth of all his prophets" (וְהָיִיתִי רוּחַ שֶׁקֶר בְּפִי כָּל־נְבִיאָיו), so that the king of Israel, Ahab, would listen to the message of the false prophet and go to

the book of Kings did not directly mention how the Spirit of the Lord influenced the service of the prophet Elijah, Obadiah, the servant of Ahab, and the disciples of Elijah believed that the Spirit of the Lord could suddenly "lift or carry" (נשׂא) Elijah from the current position to another place (1 Kgs 18:12; 2 Kgs 2:16).[30] When Elijah was about to pass away, his disciple, Elisha, who followed him also asked: "Please let there be a double portion of your spirit on me" (וִיהִי־נָא פִּי־שְׁנַיִם בְּרוּחֲךָ אֵלָי, 2 Kgs 2:9b).[31] Later, the other disciples also observed that "the spirit of Elijah rests on Elisha" (נָחָה רוּחַ אֵלִיָּהוּ עַל־אֱלִישָׁע, 2 Kgs 2:15a).[32] In fact, none of these verses mention "the Spirit of the Lord." The spirit of Elijah seen by the disciples on Elisha should not be understood as "the spirit of Elijah attached to Elisha,"[33] and it is not merely saying, "The spirit of Elijah is with him." The indication is more towards to the source of the authority, wisdom, revelation, and power of Elijah, which is the Spirit of the Lord.[34] Obviously, many signs and wonders of Elijah and Elisha were the result of the works of the Spirit of the Lord.

In addition to Elijah and Elisha, 2 Chr 15:1 contains the verb היה coupled with the preposition עַל, mentioning "The Spirit of God came upon

---

the battlefield to be killed. Clearly, the רוּחַ in this passage refers to the spirit that serves the Lord, which is different from the "Spirit of the LORD" as discussed in this chapter; but it is worth noting that 1 Kgs 22:24 states, "Zedekiah son of Kenaanah went up and slapped Micaiah in the face. 'Which way did the spirit from the Lord go when he went from me to speak to you?' he asked." Apparently, the people there thought: the message of the prophet must be from the revelation of "the Spirit of the LORD" (Japhet, *I & II Chronicles*, 764).

30. Since the Hebrew word רוּחַ can also be understood as "wind" or "breath" of God in certain contexts, some scholars believe "the Spirit of the LORD" (רוּחַ יְהוָה) in 1 Kgs 18:12 and 2 Kgs 2:16 may also refer to "the wind caused by the LORD" or "the breath from the LORD." For relevant discussion, see Chisholm, "'Spirit of the LORD,'" 306–17.

31. The so-called "doubling" (פִּי־שְׁנַיִם) of Elisha does not mean it has to be doubled that of Elijah; a similar phrase has the meaning of "two-thirds" in the ancient Near East. The phrase also appears in Deut 21:17, referring to the "double portion" of the inheritance for the eldest son. In other words, what Elisha expected was to be like a disciple who inherited the mantle of his master Elisha, continued his ministry, and experienced his unique relationship with God (Watson, "Note on the 'Double Portion,'" 70–75; House, *1, 2 Kings*, 25).

32. The verb נוה is used here, often referring to the fact that certain people stop moving around, "to rest, settle down" (Holladay, *Concise Hebrew*, 231; BDB, 628).

33. If the disciples had really thought "the spirit of Elijah attached to Elisha," they would not ask Elisha, "we your servants have fifty able men. Let them go and look for your master. Perhaps the Spirit of the Lord has picked him up and set him down on some mountain or in some valley" (2 Kgs 2:16).

34. Fretheim, *First and Second Kings*, 137–38; Block, "Empowered by the Spirit of God," 46; Fritz, *1 & 2 Kings*, 235.

Azariah the son of Oded" (וַעֲזַרְיָהוּ בֶּן־עוֹדֵד הָיְתָה עָלָיו רוּחַ אֱלֹהִים).³⁵ With the Spirit of the Lord, the prophet Azariah reminded Asa the King of Judah: "The Lord is with you while you are with him. If you seek him, he will be found by you, but if you forsake him, he will forsake you" (2 Chr 15:2). This message also prompted the King of Judah to begin a series of religious reforms (2 Chr 15:8–19). The Spirit of the Lord *came upon* him (הָיְתָה עָלָיו רוּחַ יְהוָה), "Jahaziel the son of Zechariah, son of Benaiah, son of Jeiel, son of Mattaniah, a Levite of the sons of Asaph" (2 Chr 20:14), or the Spirit of God *clothed* (וְרוּחַ אֱלֹהִים לָבְשָׁה) Zechariah the son of Jehoiada the priest (2 Chr 24:20a),³⁶ so that they could preach the message from God to the kings and the people of the kingdom of Judah during that period of time (2 Chr 20:15–17; 24:20b). On one hand, Jehoshaphat was willing to obey the message of Jahaziel, and led the people to experience the victory given by the Lord (2 Chr 20:18–28); but on the other hand, Joash turned a deaf ear to the warning of Zechariah and persuaded the people to kill the prophet with stones in the house of the Lord (2 Chr 24:21–22).

From the comprehensive survey above, it can be concluded that when the Spirit of the Lord is mentioned in the Old Testament narrative, the most striking and explicit is the wonderful power that He has given to man. The few chosen leaders, such as Moses, Joshua, the elders, the judges, and the kings, were the receivers of the power of the Lord.³⁷ The Spirit of the Lord makes them wise and talented to lead and manage the people, or to plan and have courage to face all kinds of war. Apart from this, the Spirit of the Lord also came upon some people with special missions, such as Joseph who being sold to Egypt, served Potiphar the prison warden and later Pharaoh (also Daniel who served in the palace of Babylon), Bezalel and Oholiab who were involved in the construction of the tabernacle, and the prophets who received

---

35. Sara Japhet thinks this has the same meaning with the use of the verb היה with the preposition עַל ("the Spirit of God" came upon) in 2 Chr 20:14, and the appearance of לבש "to clothe" in 1 Chr 12:19 (verse 18 in the Chinese Union Version) (Japhet, *I & II Chronicles*, 717).

36. In addition to Judg 6:34 and 2 Chr 24:20, 1 Chr 12:19 (verse 18 in the Chinese Union Version) also uses the verb לבש (to clothe): "Then the Spirit 'came on' Amasai, chief of the Thirty, and he said: 'We are yours, David! We are with you, son of Jesse! Success, success to you, and success to those who help you, for your God will help you.'" These people were later received by David and became warriors who fought side by side with him.

37. Quite intriguingly, apart from Saul and David, the books of Kings and the Chronicles do not directly mention the "the Spirit of the LORD" with any kings—but there are several references that "The LORD is with (a certain king)." These include Solomon (2 Chr 1:1), Asa (2 Chr 15:9), and Hezekiah (2 Kgs 18:7).

revelation and proclaimed the message of the Lord.[38] When the Spirit of the Lord is working, the surrounding people would be aware of the intervention of the divine power, and when they are willing to respond to God with obedience, they would be involved in the plan of God; but when they refuse, they would later experience the consequences of disobedience. Most of these verses describe the functions of "the Spirit of the Lord" to indicate the channel and results of the work of God. As for the more "inner" portion, did the Spirit of the Lord only dwell temporarily for the use of these "God's chosen vessels" or was he with them for a long period of time? The texts do not provide a clear answer. In the Old Testament, these "people who were used by the Spirit of the Lord," besides ability empowerment, gifts execution and mission fulfillment, how were their personalities influenced by the Spirit of the Lord? The memoirs of the Scriptures are not obvious.

"The Spirit/Holy Spirit of the Lord" and the Inner Character of Man

Nevertheless, there are two noteworthy characters in the Scriptures that are related to the Spirit of the Lord: when Samson repeatedly defiled himself, "the Lord had left him" (Judg 16:20); and when Saul has repeatedly sinned, "The Spirit of the Lord departed from Saul" (1 Sam 16:14)—these two characters were the tragic heroes of the Old Testament.[39] However, there are comparative characters to these two in the Old Testament Scriptures.

For Samson, though with the Spirit of the Lord, he repeatedly indulged in lusts, walked in his own way according to the sight of his eyes (see Judg 14:3, 7; 16:1, 4), neglected the divine vow of a Nazarite, and abused the great power of God. Compared to Samson, when facing the temptation of lust, Joseph said in tremble, "How then can I do this great wickedness and sin against God?" (Gen 39:9b). With a great opportunity for vengeance to

---

38. Interestingly, in most of the prophetic books before or after, the prophets did not use "the Spirit of the LORD came to (someone)" as their opening proclamation; instead, they used "the word of the LORD came to (someone)" (וַיְהִי דְבַר־יְהוָה אֶל־) (e.g., 1 Sam 15:10; 2 Sam 7:4; 24:11; 1 Kgs 13:20; 16:1, 7; Isa 38:4; Jer 1:2; 7:1; Ezek 3:16; Hos 1:1; Joel 1:1; Nah 1:1; Zeph 1:1; Hag 1:3; Zech 1:1, etc.). This "formula of proclamation" had also been used many times by the prophets Elijah and Elisha, as discussed in this chapter (see 1 Kgs 17:2; 18:1; 21:17, 28).

39. Simcha S. Brooks pointed out that there are many similarities between Samson's and Saul's records, including style of descriptions, their experiences, personality traits, and their failures. In fact, the turning point of Saul's life is in 1 Sam 16:14: "The Spirit of the LORD left Saul." Although he was still the king of Israel at that time, he was actually heading toward a path of self-destruction (Brooks, "Saul and the Samson Narrative," 19–25).

his "enemies," he replied, "Do not fear, for am I in the place of God? As for you, you meant evil against me, but God meant it for good, to bring it about that many people should be kept alive, as they are today" (Gen 50:19–20). Although "the Lord was with him, and whatever he did, the Lord made it succeed," Joseph actually went through tremendous hardships to obey the Lord to maintain such "togetherness."

Despite the presence of the Lord, Saul intended to expand his own territory, to consolidate his power, and to pursue his ambitions; he gradually stepped away from the call of God, deviated from the law of God, and finally journeyed to the path of self-destruction.[40] Compared to Saul, with the same presence of the Lord, David was willing to seek the will of God. However, this does not mean that he had no personal desire for power (see 2 Sam 24:1–25).[41] Conversely, he even committed a heinous crime (see 2 Sam 11:1–27). In his psalms writing, he also realized the evilness of sin and pleaded with the Lord, "take not your Holy Spirit from me" (וְרוּחַ קָדְשְׁךָ אַל־תִּקַּח מִמֶּנִּי Ps 51:11b).[42] But unlike Saul, after David sinned, he was willing to humble himself before God to admit his sins, to repent, and to rebuild the relationship with God.

---

40. Saul has been called the "ambitious person" by Gordon MacDonald. The "ambitious people" have the following characteristics: achievements alone can satisfy the "ambitious people"; the sign of achievement has already occupied the "ambitious people"; there is no ending to the pursuit of expansion on the part of "ambitious people"; "ambitious people" give honesty a wide scale; "ambitious people" usually have limited, immature interpersonal skills; "ambitious people" tend to compete with people; "ambitious people" always feel angry; "ambitious people" are always too busy. 麥哥登,《心意更新》, 31–41.

41. Robert Alter mentions: in the narratives related to David and Saul's daughter Michal, the layouts or depictions of the Scriptures show some of David's tactics and plans (see 1 Sam 18:17–29; 19:8–17; 25:43–44; 2 Sam 3:12–16; 6:16–23) (Alter, *Art of Biblical Narrative*, 114–30). Furthermore, in David's command to Solomon in his later years (1 Kgs 2:1–9), one may also find out how he planned to destroy some of his enemies (Halpern, *David's Secret Demons*, 52–53).

42. The Hebrew Bible only uses the phrase "Holy Spirit" in Isa 63:10 and 11, and Ps 51:11 (verse 13 in the Chinese Union Version) to depict the Spirit of the LORD; all in absolute noun with pronominal suffix קֹדֶשׁ ("holiness"), preceded by the construct noun רוּחַ. Such expressions (Isaiah's רוּחַ קָדְשׁוֹ or in Psalms' רוּחַ קָדְשְׁךָ) seem to be a little different from the NT's usage on the Third Person of the Trinity, "the Holy Spirit" (πνεῦμα ἅγιον). The possible emphasis was the psalmist's inner desire for God's holiness, so as to help realize the only way to reach such a holy standard and to approach God is to rely on the Spirit of the LORD (Estes, "Spirit and the Psalmist in Psalm 51," 131–32). In addition, Dan 4:8–9, 18; 5:11–14 (the Aramaic parts) also mentions "the spirit of holy gods" (רוּחַ־אֱלָהִין קַדִּישִׁין), but those parts belong to the respect and description of him by those people who were around Daniel; and the word "holy" (קַדִּישׁ) is more a description of God (אֱלָהּ).

Quite intriguingly, the prophet Isaiah reminded the people of God who accepted His salvation and blessing: "But they rebelled and grieved his Holy Spirit (וְהֵמָּה מָרוּ וְעִצְּבוּ אֶת־רוּחַ קָדְשׁוֹ), therefore he turned to be their enemy, and himself fought against them" (Isa 63:10). The word "grieved" is the verb עצב in *piel* form. Its root word sometimes depicting the pain of the body, sometimes referring to the pain of the heart or affectional pain.[43] The use of "holiness" (קֹדֶשׁ) to describe the Spirit of the Lord should not be taken as a kind of honor, but a deliberate expression: It is a great offense for the people of God sin, rebel, and refuse to continue to trust in Him, which bring great pain to God, and will provoke His wrath.[44] Regardless of the experience of Samson and Saul, or the Old Testament Scriptures which concern of the "Holy Spirit," it is obvious that: if the Spirit of the Lord departs from certain people because of their disobedience, then the 'Holy Spirit' (רוּחַ קָדְשׁוֹ) of the Lord must have concern about the personalities of those who He dwells upon. As mentioned before, although most of the Old Testament Scriptures refer to the Spirit of the Lord as "explicit ability and work," there are still a few verses that refer to "changes in the inner life," especially in Jeremiah 33 and Ezekiel 36. It is noteworthy that these two passages have the same tendency that points to the future on the New Testament.

"New Heart," "New Spirit," and "New Covenant"

Ezekiel 36 is about the promise of the return of Israel from the captivity (cf. vv. 8–15), and the Lord declares, "I will take you from the nations and gather you from all the countries and bring you into your own land" (v. 24). However, God does not only bring the people back to their homeland, but He will do great things: "I will sprinkle clean water (מַיִם טְהוֹרִים) on you, and you shall be clean (וּטְהַרְתֶּם) from all your uncleannesses, and from all your idols I will cleanse (אֲטַהֵר) you" (v. 25). The metaphorical image here is the root word "טהר," which means that God is to bring in the wholesome, not the only (literally) ritual of cleansing, but to let them depart from the past corrupt evilness (cf. vv. 17–21, 29a).[45] The key is that "And I will give you a new heart, and a new spirit I will put within you. And I will remove the heart of stone from your flesh and give you a heart of flesh" (v. 26; cf. 11:19; 18:31). The repeated word "heart" (לֵב) refers to the inner thought, will, and emotion of man.[46] The so-called "heart of stone" is cold, hard, numb and

---

43. Allen, "עצב," *TWOT*, 688; *BDB*, 780.
44. Oswalt, *Book of Isaiah*, 607; Smith, *Isaiah 40–66*, 672.
45. Block, *Book of Ezekiel*, 354–55; Wright, *Message of Ezekiel*, 293–94.
46. Bowling, "לֵב," *TWOT*, 466; Clines, *Concise Dictionary*, 189–90.

senseless, which was the rebellious spirituality towards God of the past Israelites (cf. 2:4; 3:7). Here the Lord emphasizes that He gives (נתן) a "new heart" which is "a heart of flesh" (לֵב בָּשָׂר).[47] In Ezekiel 11:19, the parallel scripture shows that it is "one heart" (לֵב אֶחָד).[48] In other words, this "transplant" of the "spiritual surgery" is a heart which is living, warm and soft, sensible to the will of God, and committed to God.[49] In addition, the Lord further declares, "And I will put my Spirit within you" (וְאֶת־רוּחִי אֶתֵּן בְּקִרְבְּכֶם, v. 27a).[50] The result of this action is to "cause you to walk in my statutes and be careful to obey my rules" (v. 27b). It is worth noting that the Lord went on saying, "you shall be my people, and I will be your God" (וִהְיִיתֶם לִי לְעָם, וְאָנֹכִי אֶהְיֶה לָכֶם לֵאלֹהִים, v.28b; cf. Ezek 11:20; 14:11; 37:27). Such declarations are not uncommon in the Old Testament (cf. Deut 26:17–18; 29:13; 2 Sam 7:23–24; 1 Chr 17:22; Jer 7:23; 24:7; 32:38; Zech 8:8; 13:9), which expresses a unique "covenant relationship" between the Lord and His people.[51] However, this relationship had been destroyed in the past due to the rebellion and idolatry of the Israelites, yet the Lord took the initiative to repair and renew the relationship. Although this passage has not appeared in the "New Testament," but this concept is vividly portrayed.

In fact, the above-mentioned message regarding the "new heart" and "new spirit" in Ezekiel 36, echo with the message of the "new covenant" in Jeremiah: like Ezekiel's "new heart" message, Jeremiah's "new covenant" message is placed after the message of "the return of the exile" (cf. Jer 31:1–14, 15–22, 23–30). Firstly, the Lord proclaims, "Behold, the days are coming" (הִנֵּה יָמִים בָּאִים, v. 31a); that day is concerning "the new covenant" (בְּרִית חֲדָשָׁה) that the Lord will make with the house of Israel and the house of Judah. Just as Ezekiel's "new heart" is in comparison to the "heart of stone," the "new" covenant in Jeremiah naturally reflects there is the so-called

---

47. Nancy R. Bowen points out that this "heart of flesh" (לֵב בָּשָׂר) is a unique expression of Ezekiel (Bowen, *Ezekiel*, 223).

48. The so-called "united heart" (לֵב אֶחָד) in Ezek 11:19 has a direct meaning of "one heart"; this "one" (אֶחָד) should mean undividedness or singleness. Thus, the NIV translated it as "undivided heart," and the NLT "singleness of heart" (Tuell, *Ezekiel*, 59; Longman and Garland, *Jeremiah-Ezekiel*, 702).

49. Block, *Book of Ezekiel*, 355. Wright, *Message of Ezekiel*, 296. Although there are different meanings for "heart" (לֵב), Paul Joyce asserts that it mainly means "moral will" in Ezek 26:26 (Joyce, *Divine Initiative and Human Response in Ezekiel*, 108–9).

50. Daniel I. Block points out: at first glance, the "heart" (לֵב) and "spirit" (רוּחַ) in 36:26 seem to be "synonyms" in the parallel structure of poetry, but the parallelism of Hebrew poetry is rarely "completely synonymous"; in fact, verse 27a clearly states the so-called "new spirit" refers to the Spirit of the Lord (Block, "Prophet of the Spirit," 38–39).

51. Joyce, *Divine Initiative and Human Response in Ezekiel*, 120.

"old" covenant.[52] Then the Lord continues saying, "not like the covenant that I made with their fathers on the day when I took them by the hand to bring them out of the land of Egypt" (v. 32a). This points to the covenant of Mount Sinai in Exodus, whence the Israelites accepted the Lord as their lord, and were willing to do according to His statutes and decrees (cf. Exod 19:1—24:11).[53] Similar to the coldness of the "heart of stone" resulted in disobedience, the results of the "old covenant" was "my covenant that they broke though I was their husband (וְאָנֹכִי בָּעַלְתִּי)" (Jer 31:32b).[54] Therefore, the Lord declares, "For this is the covenant that I will make with the house of Israel after those days: 'I will put my law within them, and I will write it on their hearts. And I will be their God, and they shall be my people'" (v. 33). For the old covenant, the law is written by God on stone; but in the picture of Jeremiah's message, the "heart of man" is like the tablet given to Moses in Mount Sinai, with "the law of God written" on it (cf. Exod 32:15-16; 34:1-3, 28). In fact, "the words of God to be out into the heart of man" is not a new concept in the Old Testament, because Moses had repeatedly pleaded with earnest exhortations to people in Deuteronomy: "And these words that I command you today shall be on your heart" (Deut 6:6; 11:18; 32:46). However, it was in vain,[55] but now it is "God's initiative to put it in the heart

---

52. Scholars differ as to whether the "new" here should be understood as "new"/discontinuity, or "renew"/continuity. The former views that the work of the Holy Spirit is not continuous in the NT and OT; the latter believes the two stages have certain connections. Many scholars do not think it is a completely new and noncontinuous "covenant/stage." For an introduction to the "spectrum of opinion" of various scholars, see Hamilton, *God's Indwelling Presence*, 7-24.

53. In addition to the covenant ceremony at Mount Sinai, YHWH and the Israelites have repeatedly reaffirmed such covenant relations at different times, including Deut (plains of Moab), Josh 8:30-35; 24:1-28 (Mount Ebal/Shechem), etc. (Longman, *Jeremiah, Lamentations*, 211).

54. The Hebrew verb בעל, having been translated into "was a husband" by many translations, is derived from the noun בַּעַל. The term has many meanings in different contexts, including "lord," "owner," "husband," "citizen," or even a proper noun—the Canaanite deity, "Baal" (Koopmans, "בעל," *NIDOTTE*, 1:682-83). Although Jer 31:32b can be understood here as "a husband," it is probably not about the husband's love for his wife, but rather the "covenant relationship" between them (like a marriage contract) or the "sovereignty" of the Lord over Israel (McKane, *Critical and Exegetical Commentary*, 819).

55. Wright, *Message of Jeremiah*, 327. Quite intriguingly, in the message of Jer 17:1, 9, Jeremiah said: "Judah's sin is engraved with an iron tool, inscribed with a flint point, on the tablets of their hearts and on the horns of their altars . . . The heart is deceitful above all things and beyond cure. Who can understand it?" Therefore, "the heart of man" is deeply wicked, incompatible with the holy law of God (Lalleman-de Winkel, *Jeremiah and Lamentations*, 234).

of man"—in the mind and will of man. This is another "spiritual surgery," which is the law of the Lord marked into the heart of man.[56]

There are two ramifications for the relationship of this "new covenant." On one hand, "And no longer shall each one teach his neighbor and each his brother, saying, 'Know the Lord,' for they shall all know me, from the least of them to the greatest" (Jer 31:34a). As long as the Spirit of the Lord lives within, regardless of the level of identity, they will know this God. The word "know" (ידע), is not only the knowledge of the objective information, that is to know the attributes of the greatness, holiness, and righteousness of God, but also includes the building of life relationship,[57] understanding and experiencing this loving and faithful God, and honoring Him in fear.[58] This action and relationship of "knowing" God is an alternative expression as in the book of Ezekiel, "cause you to walk in my statutes and be careful to obey my rules" (Ezek 36:27b). On the other hand, "For I will forgive their iniquity, and I will remember their sin no more" (v. 34b). The word "remember" (זכר) is not only remember something, but also expresses taking action because of the remembrance (cf. Jer 2:2).[59] In fact, the "remembrance" of the Lord was the judgment toward Israel with a series of severe punishment (Jer 5:1, 7, 29) which was resulted from the many sins of Israel provoking the wrath of God.[60] But now the Lord initiated the offer of sins forgiving. This gift is reflected and also emphasized as "clean" in the book of Ezekiel for the purpose of "breaking away from all uncleannesses" (Ezek 36:25).

If we compare Jeremiah 31:33 with Ezekiel 36:27–28, we will find two very similar statements about the covenant at the end of the passages: "you shall be my people, and I will be your God." and "I will be their God, and they shall be my people." At the beginning of the two passages, the Lord proclaimed to the Israelites through Ezekiel, "I will put[61] my Spirit within

---

56. Only through this "branding" in the heart will a person be able to truly live out the commandment in Deut 6:5, "Love the Lord your God with all your heart and with all your soul and with all your strength" (Carvalho, *Reading Jeremiah*, 103).

57. On the one hand, here refers to "each other," indicating it does indeed contain personal understanding and relationship with God. On the other hand, it also says "from the least of them to the greatest," that is to say, the building of the relationship with God also occurs in the faith community. Wright, *Message of Jeremiah*, 329.

58. Gilchrist, "ידע," *TWOT*, 366–67. Fretheim, "ידע," *NIDOTTE*, 2:411–14.

59. Holladay, *Jeremiah 2*, 199.

60. Wright, *Message of Jeremiah*, 330–31.

61. In the Chinese Union Version, the phrase "我要放" ("I put" נָתַתִּי) of Jer 31:33a is a completed action, usually translated into the past tense, but except for the Leningrad Codex, which is based on the current prevalent Hebrew Bible *Biblia Hebraica Stuttgartensia* (*BHS*), many Hebrew Bible manuscripts have a so-called "continuous vav" in front of the verb (*vav*-consecutive), making it an unfinished ונתתי; therefore,

you" (וְאֶת-רוּחִי אֶתֵּן בְּקִרְבְּכֶם), and through Jeremiah the Lord said, "I will put my law within them" (נָתַתִּי אֶת-תּוֹרָתִי בְּקִרְבָּם). Both statements use the same verb (נתן, "to give, put") and similar sentence structure, "my spirit" (רוּחִי) and "my law" (תּוֹרָתִי).[62] This becomes a very special analogy. For the "old covenant," the "law" was written by the Lord in Mount Sinai and stored in the "ark" (cf. Exod 25:21; Deut 10:1–2). Later, Moses copied the "book of the law" (סֵפֶר הַתּוֹרָה הַזֶּה) and placed it beside the "ark" (Deut 31:26). And the "ark" is placed in the tabernacle /temple representing the presence of the Lord. Then, in the relationship of the "new covenant," God not only places "His law" into "the heart of man," but also by His presence through "His Spirit," "the heart of man" becomes the dwelling place of God.[63] It is also because of the guidance of "His Spirit" in the heart of man, one could truly know God and obey His "law." Nevertheless, Ezekiel was careful with his ink about the so-called "new covenant" while Jeremiah had no further explanation on how God would "forgive the sins of man." These are unanswered questions in the "old covenant."

The "Work of the Holy Spirit" through the "New Covenant" by Jesus Christ

The above-mentioned unresolved questions in the Old Testament are believed not to be an inexplicable mystery for many Christians, because when Jesus took the cup on the night he was betrayed, saying "This cup is the new covenant in my blood. Do this, as often as you drink it, in remembrance of me" (1 Cor 11:25), there is no doubt that when Jesus mentioned "new covenant," it will be reminiscent of the promise in Jeremiah 31.[64] In fact, The Epistle of Hebrews pens more contrast about the "new covenant" and "old covenant." Hebrews 7 states that Jesus is priest forever, "after the order of

---

the English translations often translate its futuristic sense, "I *will* put" (Holladay, *Jeremiah 2*, 154).

62. Block, "Prophet of the Spirit," 39.

63. Hamilton, *God's Indwelling Presence*, 43.

64. Gordon D. Fee compares the words spoken by Jesus at the last supper in Mark 14:24 and 1 Cor 11:25. Mark recorded, "This is my blood of the covenant, which is poured out for many." The "blood of the covenant" mentioned here is reminiscent of what Moses said to the people at Mount Sinai: "This is the blood of the covenant that the Lord has made with you in accordance with all these words." In other words, it is directly connected to the OT. Although 1 Cor 11:25 does not mention the covenant of Sinai, the mention of the "new covenant" links the words of Jesus to the promise of Jeremiah (Fee, *First Epistle*, 554–55).

Melchizedek" and He offered his body as "sacrifice once for all." [65] In chapter 8, it directly quotes Jeremiah 31:31–34 (Heb 8:8–12), and sandwiched with: "For if that first covenant had been faultless, there would have been no occasion to look for a second" (Heb 8:7) and "In speaking of a new covenant, he makes the first one obsolete. And what is becoming obsolete and growing old is ready to vanish away" (Heb 8:13). Hebrews 9–10 clarify that the high priest of the descendants of Aaron must enter the sanctuary every year to make atonement for himself and the people; Jesus as the high priest also entered the most holy place—He did not enter the tabernacle or the temple on earth, but into the most holy place in heaven. The sacrificial system of the Old Testament could not really solve the problem of sin, because in those sacrifices there is a reminder of sins year after year; but Jesus enter the sanctuary with his blood only once to accomplished the eternal atonement. The author of the Hebrews here quotes Jeremiah: "For by a single offering he has perfected for all time those who are being sanctified. And the Holy Spirit also bears witness to us; for after saying, 'This is the covenant that I will make with them after those days, declares the Lord: I will put my laws on their hearts, and write them on their minds', then he adds, 'I will remember their sins and their lawless deeds no more.' Where there is forgiveness of these, there is no longer any offering for sin" (Heb 10:14–18).[66]

The Epistle of Hebrews shows that the sin of man is forgiven (cf. Jer 31:34) due to the eternal sin offering by the high priest Jesus in light of the "new covenant."[67] Through the sin offering of Jesus on the cross, man is able to accept the "new spirit" to truly know God and act according to the law of God (cf. Ezek 36:27; Jer 31:34). As Jesus mentioned to the disciples before he proceeded to the cross: "the Spirit of truth" (τὸ πνεῦμα τῆς ἀληθείας) will come,[68] and He will "dwell with you and will be in you" (John 14:17); He is the "helper/advocate" (παράκλητος)[69] "to teach you all

---

65. From 7:27 onward, the book of Hebrews uses the adverb ἐφάπαξ (once for all) to describe Jesus' self-offering as unique and only once. It was a complete sin offering, ending the problem of sin (cf. Heb 9:12; 10:10) (Bruce, *Epistle to the Hebrews*, 175n82; Ellingworth, *Epistle to the Hebrews*, 394–96).

66. On the connection between Heb 8–10 and Jer 31, and other detailed discussion, see Beale, *New Testament Biblical Theology*, 731–40.

67. Alan K. Hodson points out that Heb 9–10 closely links the death of Jesus with the work of the Holy Spirit, including the revelation of the Holy Spirit, the promise of the new covenant, and the salvation of Jesus (Hodson, "Hebrews," 231–32).

68. More emphasis is placed on the power of the Holy Spirit than the Old Testament or Synoptic Gospels. The Gospel of John mentions even more about the person of the Holy Spirit (Third Person of the Trinity) and his work in the life of the believers (Marshall, *New Testament Theology*, 522).

69. The so-called "保惠師" (Chinese Union Version) of John's Gospel (*paraclētos*, παράκλητος) originally meant "one who is called to someone's aid." In different

things, and to remind you of all that I have spoken to you" (John 14:26). He wants to glorify Jesus (John 16:14), to testify for Jesus (John 15:26), and He will "will teach you all things and bring to your remembrance all that I have said to you" (John 16:13). In addition, He "will convict the world concerning sin and righteousness and judgment" (John 16:8).[70] However, the essential work of the Holy Spirit is to cause a person to be "born again" (γεννηθῇ ἄνωθεν; John 3:3),[71] that is "born of water and the Spirit" (γεννηθῇ ἐξ ὕδατος καὶ πνεύματος, John 3:5). This is the requisite condition for a person to enter the kingdom of God and receive "eternal life" (John 3:3, 5, 15–17). Although scholars have different opinions about "of water and the Spirit,"[72] the phrase clearly points to the new life given by the Holy Spirit (cf. John 7:37–39).[73] Rather intriguing, in Ezekiel 36, on one hand, the Lord promised, "I will sprinkle 'clean water' on you, and you shall be clean" (v. 25); and on the other hand, God said, "I will put 'my Spirit' within you, and cause you to walk in my statutes and be careful to obey my rules" (v. 27). The description of the prophet and the statement of Jesus though different, it leads to the same results.[74]

---

contexts, it can be understood as "helper," "succorer," "mediator," "advocate," "intercessor," "comforter," etc. BDAG, 766; Verbrugge, *New International Dictionary*, 436–37.

70. On the other hand, Paul also stated in 1 Cor 12:3, "Therefore I want you to know that no one who is speaking by the Spirit of God says, 'Jesus be cursed,' and no one can say, 'Jesus is Lord,' except by the Holy Spirit."

71. Concerning γεννηθῇ ἄνωθεν," translated in the Chinese Union Version as "重生" (literally, "rebirth"), the adverb ἄνωθεν, used to describe the verb "to beget" (γεννάω), can be understood as "again" in terms of time, and also as "from above" in terms of position. It is known from John 3:4 that Nicodemus's understanding is the former, but Jesus pointed to the heavenly origin—"born of the Holy Spirit" (John 3:5, 6, 8). It is also very likely that Jesus played a word game; just like he constantly mentioned πνεῦμα in this paragraph, sometimes referring to "wind," but sometimes to "Spirit" (Klink, *John*, 196–97).

72. Some suggest "born of water" refers to "natural/first birth," which is distinct from "of the Spirit/second birth"; some think it means "water baptism" and "baptism by the Holy Spirit"; others claim "born of water" actually describes "of water which is Spirit" (Carson, *Gospel According to John*, 191–95; Köstenberger, *John*, 123–24).

73. In John 7:37–38, Jesus said, "Let anyone who is thirsty come to me and drink. Whoever believes in me, as Scripture has said, rivers of living water will flow from within them." John continued to explain, "By this he meant the Spirit, whom those who believed in him were later to receive. Up to that time the Spirit had not been given, since Jesus had not yet been glorified" (v. 39). Here, John connected "the Spirit . . . given" (work on the disciples, see John 20:22) with "Jesus . . . glorified." Jesus mentioned in 3:14–15 and 12:32 that he would be "lifted up." As such, "lifted up" was a unique way of being "glorified." This action referred to the cross and resurrection of Jesus (John 12:16, 23–33) (Schnelle, *Theology of the New Testament*, 699–700).

74. Harris, "Theology of John's Writings," 197–98; Hamilton, *God's Indwelling Presence*, 127–31. Regarding the metaphor of "water," Jesus also mentioned to the Samaritan

The redemptive work of Jesus established the realization of the "new covenant" and it also resulted in "the filling of the Holy Spirit" during the day of Pentecost (Acts 2:1–4). In his message during Pentecost, Peter pointed out that this was the fulfillment of the prophecy of God through the prophet Joel of the Old Testament: "And in the last days it shall be, God declares, that I will pour out my Spirit on all flesh, and your sons and your daughters shall prophesy, and your young men shall see visions, and your old men shall dream dreams; even on my male servants and female servants in those days I will pour out my Spirit, and they shall prophesy. And I will show wonders in the heavens above and signs on the earth below, blood, and fire, and vapor of smoke; the sun shall be turned to darkness and the moon to blood, before the day of the Lord comes, the great and magnificent day. And it shall come to pass that everyone who calls upon the name of the Lord shall be saved" (Acts 2:17–21; Joel 2:28–32 [3:1–5]). These series of events were proclaimed by John the Baptist, the pioneer of Jesus (Luke 3:15–18; cf. Luke 24:45–49).[75] Compared to the "old covenant" era where the Spirit of the Lord worked only in a few leaders or those who have special mission, in the "new covenant" era, pointed out by Joel's prophecy, the Holy Spirit "pour[ed] out on all flesh" towards different ages, sex, status, and even races, for God wants to establish a different relationship from the past with them.[76] In fact, Acts recorded the work of the Holy Spirit, the spread of the Gospel—from the Jews (chapter 2), the Samaritan (chapter 8), the gentiles (chapter 10), to the "disciples of John" (chapter 19)—for all to witness the universality of the work of the Holy Spirit.[77]

---

woman by the well in Sychar, "whoever drinks the water I give them will never thirst. Indeed, the water I give them will become in them a spring of water welling up to eternal life (John 4:14). This is not only related to the salvation of a person, but also to true worship, that is, as Jesus taught, one "must worship in spirit and truth" (ἐν πνεύματι καὶ ἀληθείᾳ δεῖ προσκυνεῖν, John 4:24) (Burge, "Gospel of John," 112–13).

75. Bock, "Theology of Luke-Acts," 97.

76. Hildebrandt, *Old Testament Theology*, 97–98; Williams, *Acts*, 49–50. Some scholars believe "all the flesh" (כָּל־בָּשָׂר) in Joel 2:28–32 (Hebrew Bible 3:1–5) refers only to the people of Israel/Judah. Martin Clay, however, argues that according to the usage of the phrase in this verse and its context, it actually has a "universal" sense (Clay, "Book of the Twelve," 80–82).

77. Such a development corresponds to what Jesus promised at the beginning of Acts: "But you will receive power when the Holy Spirit comes on you; and you will be my witnesses in Jerusalem, and in all Judea and Samaria, and to the ends of the earth" (Acts 1:8). Matthias Wenk also pointed out that the beginning of this series of work of the Holy Spirit, i.e., the "Pentecostal event," is the reversal of the "Babel incident" (Gen 11:1–9); the latter used the confusion of language to scatter the people, but the former used "tongues/dialects" to form a new community of God by breaking down the language/ethnic boundaries (Wenk, "Acts," 119).

After the day of Pentecost in Acts, the records of Holy Spirit are enormous in the New Testament (after the books of Gospel),[78] and this chapter naturally could not discuss all in detail. Nevertheless, according to the inductive work of Keith Warrington on these New Testament texts, he concluded the following: (1) The Holy Spirit and evangelical work: The Holy Spirit encourages believers to testify Jesus with faith and to give them the ability and timely words to preach the gospel to different targets (Acts 1:8; 13:4-12) – even in difficult situations (Acts 4:1-3). Although the proclamation with the power of Holy Spirit may not convince all (Acts 6:8—7:60), the power of God, through miracles and wonders, was manifested during the process of evangelical work by the believers in the Holy Spirit (Acts 3:1-26; 14:8-19). (2) The Holy Spirit guides the believer: Whether it be an individual (Acts 5:3-9; 8:29-40) or in a group (Acts 13:1-3), the Holy Spirit guides the people of God in a variety of ways (Acts 16:6-10). The believers must be willing to seek and follow the guidance of the Holy Spirit, which the Holy Spirit expects the believer to continue to seek—because this is crucial (Acts 8:29-40; 11:12-15; 13:2-4). (3) The Holy Spirit resists flesh and affirms the believer: Although the believer is "free," the Holy Spirit expects the believer to put to death of the flesh in the Holy Spirit (Rom 8:1-13); the Holy Spirit affirms the believers in their heart as the children of God (Rom 8:14-23); the Holy Spirit has empathy with the weak believer (Rom 8:26-27). (4) The Holy Spirit provides different gifts: The spiritual gift is the gift from God through the Holy Spirit, for the benefit of others and church (1 Cor 12:4-7). They are diverse and abundant (1 Cor 12:8-10, 28-30; Rom 12:6-8; Eph 4:11), which is the manifestation of the work of the Holy Spirit (1 Cor 12:11). There the spiritual gifts are to be used (Rom 12:6-8). (5) The Holy Spirit and the change of life: When the believer is born again (Gal 4:1-7), he follows the Holy Spirit (Gal 5:16) which transcends the law (Gal 5:18). The Holy Spirit guides the believer for life-changing fruit-bearing (Gal 5:22-6:2). (6) The Holy Spirit becomes the seal and assurance of the salvation of the believer (Eph 1:13-14). (7) The Holy Spirit provides the channel to God: The believer could access to God through the Holy Spirit (Eph 2:18). The Holy Spirit makes the believer /church into a holy temple in the Lord, where God lives through the Holy

---

78. The "Holy spirit" in the NT or the "spirit" in the "Spirit of God" use Greek πνεῦμα, which is also the Greek translation (the Septuagint, LXX), of the Hebrew Bible, רוּחַ. Like in the OT, although not all πνεῦμα refers to the "Holy Spirit," but it is the most important usage. In the NT, πνεῦμα appeared at least 354 times in all 260 chapters (approximately 1.36 times in every chapter). Compared with the OT that has 378 occurrences in 929 chapters (about 0.4 per chapter), the frequency of the "Holy Spirit" in the NT is significantly higher than that of the OT. In addition, if one removes the 90 times of πνεῦμα in the four Gospels, the frequency of πνεῦμα is increased to about 1.54 times per chapter, based on the remaining 171 chapters in the NT.

Spirit (Eph 2:21–22). (8) The Holy Spirit and Unity: The Holy Spirit has given unity (Eph 4:1–3), and through love makes unity in the people in the process of church building (Eph 4:11–16). Therefore, the believers grieve the Holy Spirit when they deviate from the will of God (Eph 4:25–32). (9) Filled with the Holy Spirit: The life of the believers should be filled with the Holy Spirit and be in charge by the Lord (Eph 5:18), and this will be manifested in all aspects of life of the believers (Eph 5:19—6:18). In addition, the sword of the Holy Spirit /the word of God and prayers are the powerful weapons of the believers facing war.[79]

The Comparison of "the Work of the Holy Spirit" in the Old and New Testaments

Comparing the texts regarding the work of the Holy Spirit in the New Testament and the relevant texts in the Old Testament, it is found that the continuity between the two is much greater than the discontinuity. The New Testament not only has more texts of which similar to the Old Testament, but also presents a deeper and wider work of the Holy Spirit:[80]

In the Old Testament, the Spirit of the Lord came upon the God chosen leaders, those who had special missions, or prophets who proclaimed the message of the Lord. On the other hand, the New Testament shows that the Holy Spirit continues to come upon people not limited to few specific targets, but "pour out on all flesh," even to the Gentiles.

In the Old Testament, the most striking aspect of "the Spirit of the Lord" is the supernatural, miraculous wonders upon His accompaniment. The power of God is manifested from the ten plagues in Egypt before the Israelites left the country, to the miracles of Elijah and Elisha. In the New Testament, through the Holy Spirit, the apostles healed the sick, cast out demons, and even resurrected the dead, testifying to their preaching.[81] In the Old Testament era, "the Spirit of the Lord" gave the Judges the power of leadership, gave wisdom to the leaders of Israel, empowered Bezalel and Oholiab with the gift of craftsmanship, and revealed the words of God to many prophets. In the New Testament era, the Holy Spirit not only revealed

79. Warrington, *Message of the Holy Spirit*, 121–30, 142–49, 153–244.

80. Van Pelt et al., "רוּחַ," *NIDOTTE*, 3:1077.

81. In the NT, Luke's writings (Luke and Acts) has the most records of signs and wonders. As Luke's "work of the Holy Spirit" revolves around the "power in ministry," 劉彼得 points out three pertinent dimensions: "empowerment" (by preaching and miracles), "renewal" (through salvation given by Jesus), and "sanctification" (by the baptism of fire, driving away the forces of darkness, cleansing human hearts, and overcoming trials). 劉彼得,〈靈風屢颳〉, 31–69.

the mystery of God through the apostles and the prophets (Eph 3:5), but also provided many different types of gifts to the church. These gifts, include healing, casting out demons, teaching and preaching the word of God, administering the church, caring for others with compassion, which are distributed among the believers, not concentrated to certain minorities, so that the body of Christ will grow under the collaboration of the gifts. These gifts in the New Testament seem to focus on the construction of the church when compared with the description of the Old Testament. In fact, the "gift" of "the Spirit of the Lord" in the Old Testament era was more or less to restore the relationship between man and God with an ultimate goal for humans to be obedient to God.

In addition to the above description of "functionality," the major focus of the work of the Holy Spirit appears to be more on inner work in human beings.[82] In the Old Testament, unlike Samson and Saul who sinned and failed after the Spirit of the Lord came upon them, Joseph was willing to obey, and David was repenting in humility. In spite of this, they are, after all, a handful of those minority who had experienced the work of the Holy Spirit, but not a solution to the fundamental problem of sin. Chapter 11 of the Epistle to the Hebrews ranks them as the "Faithful Heroes" (Heb 11:21–22, 32), but the author of Hebrews reminds this at the end of the passage: "And all these though commended through their faith did not receive what was promised, since God had provided something better for us, that apart from us they should not be made perfect" (Heb 11:39–40). In other words, these past great faithful heroes lived in accordance to the expectation of God, but they have not seen the fulfillment of the promise of God and the eternal kingdom in the years of their life, for there is a better covenant in the future.[83]

The "new covenant" established by Jesus (cf. Jer 31:31) does bring epoch-making changes: through the eternal sin offering of Jesus, the sins of man are forgiven and the hearts of man are cleansed (Jer 31:34b; Ezek 26:25). The "Holy Spirit" is a precious gift of God that lives in the heart of man and becomes the seal of believers belonging to God (Ezek 36:26). In addition, the Holy Spirit engraves the law of God in the heart of man (Jer 31:33), in order to obey the law and truth of God, and establish a close relationship with God

---

82. If one refers to the nine functions Keith Warrington summed up in the previous paragraph of this chapter, six of them clearly belong to "the Holy Spirit's inner work in human beings," including: (3) "The Holy Spirit resists the flesh and gives the believers assurance," (5) "The Holy Spirit and change of life," (6) "The Holy Spirit becomes the believers' seal and assurance of salvation," (7) "The Holy Spirit provides the channel to God," (8) "The Holy Spirit and unity," and (9) "The filling of the Holy Spirit."

83. Hagner, *Hebrews*, 207–8; Bruce, *Epistle to the Hebrews*, 330.

(Jer 31:34a; Ezek 36:27). In fact, many New Testament verses point out that human "heart" (καρδία)[84] is critical throughout the process:

Jesus had reminded the disciples that "Either make the tree good and its fruit good, or make the tree bad and its fruit bad for the tree is known by its fruit" (Matt 12:33; cf. Matt 7:15–20; Luke 6:43–44). The outward fruit seen by people is in fact reflecting "good treasure brings forth good" or "evil treasure brings forth evil" (Matt 12:34–35; Luke 6:45). In John 15:1–16, Jesus mentioned His relationship with the disciples is a metaphor associated with the fruit: Jesus is the vine, the disciples are the branches, and the Father is the vinedresser—"Abide in me, and I in you. As the branch cannot bear fruit by itself, unless it abides in the vine, neither can you, unless you abide in me" (John 15:4). The key for the disciples to bear fruit is that the disciples are "in Christ," and Christ is "in the disciples"; in some way, the Holy Spirit is "in the disciples."[85] Regarding bearing fruit, Paul in Gal 5:22–23 says: "the fruit of the Spirit is love, joy, peace, patience, kindness, goodness, faithfulness, gentleness, self-control; against such things there is no law." The list of many quality personalities is from the work of the Holy Spirit to contend with our flesh. Gordon D. Fee points out that the usage of "fruit" instead of "work" by Paul in Galatians 5:22 is to emphasize the gift of the Holy Spirit, but not the own work of man.[86] Such results and expression of life, just as Peter has described, not only "having [us] escaped from the corruption that is in the world because of sinful desire," but also "become partakers of the divine nature" (2 Pet 1:4; cf vv. 5–8).[87]

The quality of the "new life" described above is according to "the new man" (τὸν καινὸν ἄνθρωπον) description by Paul in chapter 4 of the Epistle to the Ephesians. Paul reminds followers of Christ: "But that is not the way you learned Christ! —assuming that you have heard about him and were

---

84. The Greek καρδία ("heart") in the NT is very similar to the meaning of the OT לֵב. Except for the occasional meaning of "heart" as the human body, it mostly refers to a person's inner life, that is, the center of emotion, will, cognition, conscience, and spirituality (Verbrugge, *New International Dictionary*, 288–89; Gingrich, *Shorter Lexicon*, 100).

85. Mary L. Coloe believes the metaphor of the "branches and the vines" is another symbol of the "temple of the Holy Spirit"; both show the connection of "Make your home in Me, as I make Mine in you" (Coloe, *God Dwells with Us*, vii, 159–60, 208–9). Joseph C. Dillow also uses 1 John 3:24 and 4:13 to point out that what John calls "in Christ" is the fellowship of believers with Christ through the Holy Spirit (Dillow, "Abiding is Remaining in Fellowship," 50).

86. Fee, *God's Empowering Presence*, 443–44.

87. I. Howard Marshall observes that the series of characters listed in 2 Pet 1:4–8, "faith, goodness, knowledge, self-control, perseverance, godliness, and love," is intimately connected to Gal 5:22–23 (Marshall, *New Testament Theology*, 676–77).

taught in him, as the truth is in Jesus, to put off your old self, which belongs to your former manner of life and is corrupt through deceitful desires, and to be renewed in the spirit of your minds, and to put on the new self, created after the likeness of God in true righteousness and holiness" (Eph 4:20–24). It is noteworthy that, although the fruit is the product of the power of the Holy Spirit and the result of the "spiritual surgery" by God, which no man could do by himself, the person to receive the "change of heart" has the responsibility "to put off (ἀποθέσθαι) your old self,[88] which belongs to your former manner of life." The old self is the influence of the corrupted customs in the world and the indulgence of own desires of words and deeds, which should be treated as dirty clothing to be put off. The person also has the responsibility "to put on (ἐνδύσασθαι) the new self," just like putting on new clothing, that would obey God and not grieve the Holy Spirit (cf. 4:25—5:2).[89] The key to this process is "to be renewed in the spirit[90] of your mind (ἀνανεοῦσθαι δὲ τῷ πνεύματι τοῦ νοὸς ὑμῶν)"—just as the exhortations from Romans 12:2, "Do not be conformed to this world but be transformed by the renewal of your mind." This is a process of continuation of renewal by the Holy Spirit, gradual life transformation, and reflection of the glory image of the Lord (cf. Col 3:10; 2 Cor 3:18; 4:16).[91] Although such changes are originated from the power of the Holy Spirit, the believer needs to "walk according to the Spirit and set the mind on the Spirit" (cf. Rom 8:3–6), and co-work with the Holy Spirit in one's mind, decision and action.

Comparing "put on the new man" in the New Testament and "the Spirit of the Lord clothed someone" in the Old Testament, although both of them are the work of the Holy Spirit and the receivers of the Holy Spirit face

---

88. Eph 4:22–24 use three consecutive "infinitives": "put off" (ἀποθέσθαι), "made new" (ἀνανεοῦσθαι), and "put on" (ἐνδύσασθαι) There are four possible explanations: (1) treating them all as imperatives; (2) continuing the description of verse 21, indicating the previous learning purpose of the recipients; (3) referring to the results obtained by the recipients after being taught; or (4) an explanation to the teaching in verse 21. From the context of the passage (especially the subsequent series of reminders in 4:25—5:2), however, the "infinitives" are more like the command and exhortation to the recipient (Lincoln, *Ephesians*, 283–84; Best, *Ephesians*, 430–31).

89. The "old" and the "new" here may refer to the inner life of an "individual"—"old self" and "new self"; but they may also refer to the "way of life" influenced by the external world—"after the flesh" and "after God's heart." In any case, they obviously refer to two mutually opposing inclinations (Gombis, *Drama of Ephesians*, 165–67).

90. Concerning the definite article (τῷ πνεύματι) that comes with the word in Eph 4:23, biblical scholars disagree on if it refers to the "human will" (in the spirit) or the "renewal" (in the Spirit). Nevertheless, all generally agree this is the work of the "Holy Spirit" in "human hearts" (Fee, *God's Empowering Presence*, 710–12; Lincoln, *Ephesians*, 286–87).

91. Hoehner, *Ephesians*, 599–600, 607. Bruce, *Epistles to the Colossians*, 358.

different difficult challenges and temptations, the establishment of "new covenant" by Jesus changes one inside out where the sin of man is forgiven and separation between man and God is demolished through the atonement of Jesus. Man is given a "new heart" because he is born again in the Holy Spirit making one possible to obey the law of God. The relationship of God and man is changed because of the guidance of the Holy Spirit enabling one to call the most holy God "Abba! Father!" The human heart could be reminded, helped, guided, encouraged, and comforted because of the presence of the Counselor, Holy Spirit. Man could continue to live in holiness and not corrupted by the customs of the world because of the constant renewal of human heart by the Holy Spirit. A new life with the Holy Spirit could not only bear fruit, but also fulfill the mission entrusted by God according to the will of God, by the spiritual gifts, and through the power of the Holy Spirit. The ultimate goal of the mission is to "lead people to the Lord, build the church, and reconcile man to God." These series of work of the Holy Spirit could not be experienced by the saints in the Old Testament era. If the "clothe" of the former covenant shows great ability of external gift, then the "put on" of the latter covenant emphasizes the inner life—because once the "heart" is changed, many external things change along the way. This external manifestation is outflow from the inner life.

Conclusion: The Inside-Out Work of the Holy Spirit

"Behold, the Lord's hand is not shortened, that it cannot save, or his ear dull, that it cannot hear" (Isa 59:1). From this research, we could see that from the Old Testament to the New Testament, the Spirit of God has been enthusiastic on wonderful events—whether from the journey of exodus to the land of Canaan, from the ministries of Elijah to Elisha, from the preaching of Jesus to the establishing of the churches by the apostles—the Holy Spirit has been manifesting the great power of God. On the other hand, the signs and wonders that intervene into the natural law are not happening whenever and wherever, because it is due to the sovereignty of God. It is done out of the will of God and His arm is not shortened.

The supernatural signs and wonders are not visible every day, but the supernatural work of God by the Holy Spirit in the heart of the people—to give people a "new heart," to make a "new relationship" with God, to be "new person," to live out a "new life," and to receive "new ability"—these miracles are happening every day. Therefore, the responsibility of the believer is to keep his heart in Christ, to obey the word of God and the guidance of the Holy Spirit, to build an intimate relationship with the Lord as the branch to the vine and willing to be trimmed to bear much fruit, and to glorify the Father in heaven.

Bibliography

Allen, Ronald B. "בצע." In *TWOT*, 688.
Alter, Robert. *The Art of Biblical Narrative*. New York: Basic, 1981.
Archer, Gleason L., et al., eds. *Theological Wordbook of the Old Testament*. Chicago: Moody, 1980.
Ashley, Timothy R. *The Book of Numbers*. New International Commentary on the Old Testament. Grand Rapids: Eerdmans, 1993.
Beale, G. K. *A New Testament Biblical Theology: The Unfolding of the Old Testament in the New*. Grand Rapids: Baker, 2011.
Best, Ernest. *Ephesians*. International Critical Commentary on the Holy Scriptures of the Old and New Testaments. Edinburgh: T. & T. Clark, 1998.
Block, Daniel I. *The Book of Ezekiel*. Vol. 2, *Chapters 25–48*. 2 vols. New International Commentary on the Old Testament. Grand Rapids: Eerdmans, 1998.
———. "Empowered by the Spirit of God: The Holy Spirit in the Historiographic Writings of the Old Testament." *The Southern Baptist Journal of Theology* 1 (1997) 42–61.
———. *Judges, Ruth*. New American Commentary 6. Nashville: Broadman & Holman, 1999.
———. "The Prophet of the Spirit: The Use of RWḤ in the Book of Ezekiel." *Journal of the Evangelical Theological Society* 32 (1989) 27–49.
Bock, Darrell L. "A Theology of Luke-Acts." In *A Biblical Theology of the New Testament*, edited by Roy B. Zuck, 87–166. Chicago: Moody, 1994.
Bowen, Nancy R. *Ezekiel*. Abingdon Old Testament Commentaries. Nashville: Abingdon, 2010.
Bowling, Andrew. "לֵב." In *TWOT*, 466.
Brooks, Simcha Shalom. "Saul and the Samson Narrative." *Journal for the Study of the Old Testament* 21 (1996) 19–25.
Brown, Francis, et al., eds. *A Hebrew and English Lexicon of the Old Testament*. Oxford: Clarendon, 1952.
Bruce, F. F. *The Epistles to the Colossians, to Philemon, and to the Ephesians*. New International Commentary on the New Testament. Grand Rapids: Eerdmans, 1984.
———. *The Epistle to the Hebrews*. Rev. ed. New International Commentary on the New Testament. Grand Rapids: Eerdmans, 1990.
Burge, Gary M. "The Gospel of John." In *A Biblical Theology of the Holy Spirit*, edited by Trevor J. Burke and Keith Warrington, 104–15. Eugene, OR: Cascade, 2014.
Butler, Trent C. *Judges*. Word Biblical Commentary 8. Nashville: Thomas Nelson, 2009.
Carson, D. A. *The Gospel According to John*. The Pillar New Testament Commentary. Grand Rapids: Eerdmans, 1991.
Carvalho, Corrine L. *Reading Jeremiah: A Literary and Theological Commentary*. Reading the Old Testament. Macon, GA: Smyth & Helwys, 2016.

Chisholm, Robert B. "The 'Spirit of the LORD' in 2 Kings 2:16." In *Presence, Power, and Promise: The Role of the Spirit of God in the Old Testament*, edited by David G. Firth and Paul D. Wegner, 306–17. Downers Grove, IL: IVP Academic, 2011.

Clay, Martin. "The Book of the Twelve." In *A Biblical Theology of the Holy Spirit*, edited by Trevor J. Burke and Keith Warrington, 71–83. Eugene, OR: Cascade, 2014.

Clines, David J. A., ed. *The Concise Dictionary of Classical Hebrew*. Sheffield: Sheffield Phoenix, 2009.

Coleson, Joseph E., et al. *Joshua, Judges, Ruth*. Cornerstone Biblical Commentary 3. Carol Stream, IL: Tyndale House, 2012.

Coloe, Mary L. *God Dwells with Us: Temple Symbolism in the Fourth Gospel*. Collegeville, MN: Liturgical, 2001.

Danker, Frederick W., ed. *A Greek-English Lexicon of the New Testament and Other Early Christian Literature*. 3rd ed. Chicago: University of Chicago Press, 2000.

Dillow, Joseph C. "Abiding is Remaining in Fellowship: Another Look at John 15:1–6." *Bibliotheca Sacra* 147 (1990) 44–53.

Dragga, Sam. "In the Shadow of the Judges: The Failure of Saul." *Journal for the Study of the Old Testament* 12 (1987) 39–46.

Ellingworth, Paul. *The Epistle to the Hebrews: A Commentary on the Greek Text*. New International Greek Testament Commentary. Grand Rapids: Eerdmans, 1993.

Estes, Daniel J. "Spirit and the Psalmist in Psalm 51." In *Presence, Power, and Promise: The Role of the Spirit of God in the Old Testament*, edited by David G. Firth and Paul D. Wegner, 122–34. Downers Grove, IL: IVP Academic, 2011.

Fee, Gordon D. *The First Epistle to the Corinthians*. New International Commentary on the New Testament. Grand Rapids: Eerdmans, 1987.

———. *God's Empowering Presence: The Holy Spirit in the Letters of Paul*. Peabody, MA: Hendrickson, 1994.

Firth, David G. *1 & 2 Samuel*. Apollos Old Testament Commentary 8. Nottingham, UK: Apollos, 2009.

Fretheim, Terence E. *First and Second Kings*. Westminster Bible Companion. Louisville: Westminster John Knox, 1999.

———. "ידע." In *NIDOTTE*, 2:411–14.

Fritz, Volkmar. *1 & 2 Kings: A Continental Commentary*. Translated by Anselm C. Hagedorn. Continental Commentaries. Minneapolis: Fortress, 2003.

Gilchrist, Paul R. "ידע." In *TWOT*, 366–67.

Gingrich, F. Wilbur, ed. *Shorter Lexicon of the Greek New Testament*. 2nd ed. Chicago: University of Chicago Press, 1979.

Gombis, Timothy G. *The Drama of Ephesians: Participating in the Triumph of God*. Downers Grove, IL: InterVarsity, 2010.

Gordon, Robert P. *I & II Samuel: A Commentary*. Library of Biblical Interpretation. Grand Rapids: Zondervan, 1986.

Hagner, Donald A. *Hebrews*. New American Commentary 14. Peabody, MA: Hendrickson, 1990.

Halpern, Baruch. *David's Secret Demons: Messiah, Murderer, Traitor, King*. The Bible in its World. Grand Rapids: Eerdmans, 2001.

Hamilton, James M. *God's Indwelling Presence: The Holy Spirit in the Old & New Testaments*. NAC Studies in Bible & Theology. Nashville: B&H, 2006.

Hamilton, Victor P. *The Book of Genesis*. Vol. 2, *Chapters 18–50*. 2 vols. New International Commentary on the New Testament. Grand Rapids: Eerdmans, 1995.

———. *Handbook on the Historical Books: Joshua, Judges, Ruth, Samuel, Kings, Chronicles, Ezra-Nehemiah, Esther*. Grand Rapids: Baker, 2001.

———. "הָיָה." In *TWOT*, 214.

———. "פָּעַם." In *TWOT*, 730.

Harris, W. Hall. "A Theology of John's Writings." In *A Biblical Theology of the New Testament*, edited by Roy B. Zuck, 167–242. Chicago: Moody, 1994.

Hess, Richard S. "Bezalel and Oholiab: Spirit of Creativity." In *Presence, Power, and Promise: The Role of the Spirit of God in the Old Testament*, edited by David G. Firth and Paul D. Wegner, 161–72. Downers Grove, IL: IVP Academic, 2011.

Hildebrandt, Wilf. *Old Testament Theology of the Spirit of God*. Peabody, MA: Hendrickson, 1995.

Hodson, Alan K. "Hebrews." In *A Biblical Theology of the Holy Spirit*, edited by Trevor J. Burke and Keith Warrington, 226–37. Eugene, OR: Cascade, 2014.

Hoehner, Harold W. *Ephesians: An Exegetical Commentary*. Grand Rapids: Baker, 2002.

Holladay, William L., ed. *A Concise Hebrew and Aramaic Lexicon of the Old Testament*. Grand Rapids: Eerdmans, 1971.

———. *Jeremiah 2*. Hermeneia. Minneapolis: Fortress, 1989.

House, Paul R. *1, 2 Kings*. New American Commentary 8. Nashville: Broadman & Holman, 1995.

Howard, David M., Jr. "The Transfer of Power from Saul to David in 1 Samuel 16:13–14." *Journal of the Evangelical Theological Society* 32 (1989) 473–83.

Japhet, Sara. *I & II Chronicles: A Commentary*. Old Testament Library. Louisville: Westminster John Knox, 1993.

Joyce, Paul. *Divine Initiative and Human Response in Ezekiel*. JSOT Supplement Series 51. Sheffield: Sheffield Academic, 1989.

Kaiser, Walter C., Jr. "The Pentateuch." In *A Biblical Theology of the Holy Spirit*, edited by Trevor J. Burke and Keith Warrington, 1–11. Eugene, OR: Cascade, 2014.

Klink, Edward W. *John*. Zondervan Exegetical Commentary on the New Testament. Grand Rapids: Zondervan, 2016.

Koopmans, William T. "בעל." In *NIDOTTE*, 1:649.

Köstenberger, Andreas J. *John*. Baker Exegetical Commentary on the New Testament. Grand Rapids: Baker, 2004.

Lalleman-de Winkel, Hetty. *Jeremiah and Lamentations*. Tyndale Old Testament Commentaries 21. Downers Grove, IL: InterVarsity, 2013.

Lincoln, Andrew T. *Ephesians*. Word Biblical Commentary 42. Dallas: Word, 1990.

Longman, Tremper. *Jeremiah, Lamentations*. New International Biblical Commentary 14. Peabody, MA: Hendrickson, 2008.

Longman, Tremper, and David E. Garland, eds. *Jeremiah-Ezekiel*. Rev. ed. Expositor's Bible Commentary 7. Grand Rapids: Zondervan, 2010.

Luc, Alex. "צלח." In *NIDOTTE*, 3:804.

Marshall, I. Howard. *New Testament Theology: Many Witnesses, One Gospel*. Downers Grove, IL: InterVarsity, 2014.

Martin, Lee Roy. "Power to Save!? The Role of the Spirit of the Lord in the Book of Judges." *Journal of Pentecostal Theology* 16 (2008) 21–50.

McKane, William. *A Critical and Exegetical Commentary on Jeremiah*. International Critical Commentary on the Holy Scriptures of the Old and New Testaments. Edinburgh: T. & T. Clark, 1996.

Oswalt, John N. *The Book of Isaiah*. Vol. 2, *Chapters 40–66*. 2 vols. New International Commentary on the Old Testament. Grand Rapids: Eerdmans, 1998.

Payne, J. Barton. "רוּחַ." In *TWOT*, 836–37.

Richter, Sandra. "What Do I Know of Holy? On the Person and Work of the Holy Spirit in Scripture." In *Spirit of God: Christian Renewal in the Community of Faith*, edited by Jeffrey W. Barbeau and Beth Felker Jones, 23–38. Downers Grove, IL: InterVarsity, 2015.

Schnelle, Udo. *Theology of the New Testament*. Translated by M. Eugene Boring. Grand Rapids: Baker, 2009.

Smith, Gary V. *Isaiah 40–66*. New American Commentary 15B. Nashville: B&H, 2009.

Thiselton, Anthony C. *The Holy Spirit—In Biblical Teaching, through the Centuries, and Today*. Grand Rapids: Eerdmans, 2013.

Tsumura, David Toshio. *The First Book of Samuel*. New International Commentary on the Old Testament. Grand Rapids: Eerdmans, 2007.

Tuell, Steven. *Ezekiel*. Understanding the Bible Commentary. Grand Rapids: Baker, 2012.

Van Pelt, Miles V., et al. "רוּחַ." In *NIDOTTE*, 3:1073–78.

Van Rooy, Harry F. "פעם." In *NIDOTTE*, 3:649–50.

Verbrugge, Verlyn D. *New International Dictionary of New Testament Theology*. Abridged ed. Grand Rapids: Zondervan, 2000.

Waldman, Nahum M. "The Imagery of Clothing, Covering, and Overpowering." *Journal of Ancient Near Eastern Society* 19 (1989) 161–70.

Waltke, Bruce K., and Charles Yu. *An Old Testament Theology: An Exegetical, Canonical, and Thematic Approach*. Grand Rapids: Zondervan, 2007.

Warrington, Keith. *The Message of the Holy Spirit: The Spirit of Encounter*. Bible Speaks Today. Downers Grove, IL: InterVarsity, 2009.

Watson, Paul. "A Note on the 'Double Portion' of Deuteronomy 21:17 and II Kings 2:9." *Restoration Quarterly* 8 (1965) 70–75.

Webb, Barry G. *The Book of Judges*. The New International Commentary on the Old Testament. Grand Rapids: Eerdmans, 2012.

Wenk, Matthias. "Acts." In *A Biblical Theology of the Holy Spirit*, edited by Trevor J. Burke and Keith Warrington, 116–28. Eugene, OR: Cascade, 2014.

Williams, David J. *Acts*. New International Biblical Commentary 5. Peabody, MA: Hendrickson, 1990.

Wright, Christopher J. H. *The Message of Ezekiel: A New Heart and a New Spirit*. Bible Speaks Today. Downers Grove, IL: InterVarsity, 2001.

———. *The Message of Jeremiah: Against Wind and Tide*. Bible Speaks Today. Downers Grove, IL: InterVarsity, 2014.

Younger, K. Lawson. *Judges and Ruth*. NIV Application Commentary. Grand Rapids: Zondervan, 2002.

呂紹昌.〈撒母耳記中的聖靈〉.《聖靈古今論：從聖經, 歷史, 神學看神的同在：戴紹曾牧師七十壽慶論文集》, 許宏度編, 71–99. 台北市: 中華福音神學院, 1999.

畢維廉. "Spirit of God in the Book of Judges." In《聖靈古今論：從聖經, 歷史, 神學看神的同在：戴紹曾牧師七十壽慶論文集》, 許宏度編, 131–54. 台北市: 中華福音神學院, 1999.

麥哥登.《心意更新: 如何調整內心生活》. 吳李金麗譯. 香港: 福音證主協會, 1988.

劉光啟.〈士師參孫的眼見〉.《浸神院訊》179 (2009) 2–5.

———.《士師記反思: 沉淪與拯救》. The Way. 香港: 浸信會出版社, 2013.

劉彼得.〈靈風屢颳—路加聖靈三工: 添力、更新、成聖〉.《聖靈工作的神學課題》, 陳若愚編, 31–69. 華人教會路向叢書. 香港: 中國神學研究院, 1996.

3

You Have Made All Things Beautiful in Their Time

Reflections on the Spirit of Beauty

JUSTIN T. T. TAN

Introduction

IN HIS DARK NOVEL about lost love and final redemption of sorts, John Hart speaks about the meaning of inspiration through the protagonist's mother. It merits a full quotation:

> In the Dark Ages, no one understood the things that made some people special, things like imagination or creativity or vision. People lived and died in the small village. They had no idea why the sun rose or set or why winter came. They grubbed in dirt and died young in disease. Every soul in that dark, difficult time faced the same limitations, every soul except a precious few who came rarely to the world and saw things differently, the poets and inventors, the artists and stonemasons. Regular folks didn't understand how a person could wake up one day and see the world differently. They thought it was a gift of God. Thus the word *inspiration*. It means "breathed upon."[1]

---

1. Hart, *Redemption Road*, 44–45 (italics original).

And the story goes to show how Elizabeth Black, the protagonist, whom her mother perceives has the gift of the poet, would swim through the waves of intrigue and darkness of the human souls, to finally reach the wellnigh impossible shore of redemption.

There seems to be some pathways through perceptions of beauty and imagination that lead to the elevation of the mundane. And we can almost say that in every culture, perception and creation of beauty and imagination are seen as a gift from the Beyond, especially in its representation of religious belief.

The recent interest in Western theology on the role of aesthetics as expressions of faith has spark the explorations into not just theological aesthetic, but on the very nature of God as Beauty.[2] The "breathed upon" is gradually being associated with the role of the Holy Spirit in the world, opening up the very possibility of the concept in dialogue with cultures and worldviews.

The following is an attempt to look at this possibility from the Chinese perspective, bringing with it the fruits of theological thoughts to bear on how the "Eastern" eyes can gaze at the Beauty of the Infinite, and at the same time appreciate the integration of Christian Theology into Chinese thoughts. And how this is related to the role of the Holy Spirit is at the core of our investigation. I emphasize the word "reflections" in the title as this is hardly a mature theological treatise but an exploration of the possibility and potential of contribution of Chinese theology in its global reflections.

Aesthetics and the Role of the Holy Spirit

Aesthetics has met with contention and polarized discussion in recent Western thinking.[3] Patrick Sherry succinctly portrays the theme of beauty as a "subterranean stream" in Christian theology, which erupts from time to time as a corrective to theology's intellectualization.[4] In terms of the language of theology, some scholars bemoan the paucity of "Spirit language" comparative to "God language" and "Christ language."[5] The role of the Holy Spirit is also subsumed into the activities of God the Father and God the

---

2. Preeminent by far is Hans Urs von Balthasar, see especially *Seeing the Form*, and theology of beauty in Jonathan Edwards. See for example Strachan and Sweeney, *Jonathan Edwards on Beauty*; Louie, *Beauty of the Triune God*. See also Milbank et al., *Theological Perspectives on God*; Viladesau, *Theological Aesthetics*; Hart, *Beauty of the Infinite*.

3. Dreyer and Burrows, "Spirituality and Aesthetics," 299.

4. Sherry, *Spirit and Beauty*.

5. Taylor, "Spirit and Beauty," 45.

Son. The theme of beauty is often concentrated on the Father or the Son's glory.[6] Thus there is a sense that the role of the Holy Spirit is being denigrated, and being considered as a supportive role. W. D. O. Taylor observes that "it is easy to see how the Spirit over time becomes merely the harmony of the Trinity rather than the harmonizing One, a divine person bereft of active agency."[7] But more and more theologians, sensing the movements of the Spirit in the world, are moving to eradicate this.

However, the link between aesthetics and the spiritual has existed in cultures all over the world. It seems that many Western theologies have not taken it to mind, and what the Eastern Christians from the past are taught is to concentrate on the redemptive side of the theological equation. In fact, it is very difficult to find any substantial work on this in Chinese theological thinking.[8] Thus there is a need to reflect on this and perhaps to bring a new dimension to Chinese Theology as a whole.

Balthasar surely points us in the right direction when he says that ". . . a doctrine of God and the Trinity really speaks to us only when and as long as the *theologia* does not become detached from the *oikonomia*, but rather lets its every formulation and stage of reflection be accompanied and supported by the latter's vivid discernibility."[9] It seems that the manifestation of the beauty of the Trinity outweighs the speculation of its nature.[10]

Some theologians regard holiness as a kind of beauty: "worship God in the beauty of Holiness." Indeed, Jonathan Edwards described God's holiness as "the infinite beauty and excellence of his nature,"[11] and when God communicates virtue and holiness to his creation, they share in His "moral excellency, which is properly the beauty of the divine nature." And Sherry adds that, "The power and the wonder it evokes explain why beauty is often listed together with truth and goodness as subject of utmost importance, rather than associating it with, say, humour—though that also is an area of human creativity."[12]

From the Chinese point of view, philosophy and religious beliefs have always been depicted through the medium of the Arts, i.e., paintings, calligraphy, and poetry. There is a sense that artistic creations lead to the deepest

6. Certainly Jonathan Edwards's appreciation of beauty is within this theme.

7. Taylor, "Spirit and Beauty," 45.

8. Samuel S. H. Ho is a lonely voice in this, but his work is deemed to be theoretical, even though it goes a long way to address the paucity of works on aesthetics and the spiritual: 何崇謙, 《超然的啓視》 *(From Vision of the Sublime to Visio Dei)*.

9. Balthasar, *Glory of the Lord*, 125.

10. Sherry, *Spirit and Beauty*, 71–72.

11. Edwards, *Unpublished Essay*, 97

12. Sherry, *Spirit and Beauty*, 3.

meaning of one's belief and lifestyle. And not just that, the artists are viewed as people who are entrusted by the Divine to create harmony and beauty in this Earthly world in which they lived. If Sherry's formulations above are to apply to Chinese theological thought, it seems that there is much to commend in that, inherent in Chinese religious thoughts, aesthetic and the spiritual can be related to the role of the Holy Spirit more readily than other Western style formulations.

Sherry summarizes the attempt to put Theological Aesthetic onto close to the center of theology in this way:

> The full development of this idea involves the claims that the Spirit of God communicates God's beauty to the world, both through Creation, in the case of natural beauty, and through inspiration, in the case of artistic beauty; that earthly beauty is thus a reflection of divine glory, and a sign of the way in which the Spirit is perfecting creation; and that beauty has an eschatological significance, in that it is an anticipation of the restored and transfigured world which will be the fullness of God's kingdom.[13]

Using Sherry's premises in reflecting on the Spirit and Beauty, we can see a fourfold understanding of how the Spirit engages with the Created world: manifesting beauty; inspiring beauty; communicating beauty; and perfecting beauty.

Manifesting Beauty: Beauty as a Way to God

Humans are never meant to anchor themselves on this world alone, the fact that they are always portrayed also as spiritual beings, that indeed points toward a desire for transcendence. This is what John O'Donohue means by the pursuit of beauty:

> At the centre of the mind's mirror there is a splinter of horizon that never allows us to see anything without some trace of desire in it. The beyond is constantly beckoning us in dream, thought and feeling; it protrudes into the present and into presence. That is what makes us urgent, passionate and open. This ardent kinship with beyond is at the heart of our love of beauty.[14]

And from the point of view of Christian theology, the Divine Spirit is right in the midst of this. O'Donohue puts it this way: "Beauty addresses us

13. Sherry, *Spirit and Beauty*, 2.
14. O'Donohue, *Divine Beauty*, 228.

from a place beyond; it captures our complete attention because it resonates with the sense of the beyond in us . . . it settles at once into the 'elsewhere' within us. It is as if we are in exile and home comes to visit us for a while. This is some of the completion and satisfaction we feel in the presence of the Beautiful."[15] The realization of exile in this ugly world and the glimpse of home is juxtaposed when the Divine Spirit of Beauty begin to take residence in the deepest access of the wondering heart.

From the perspective of the theology of beauty, that the Spirit is calling to mind (remember) all truth (John 16:12), has a particular importance. We can begin the "re-calling" via Graham Ward's description of the process. He starts his contemplation of beauty with desire as "one of the constitutive principles governing the manifestation of God's beauty . . . Desire reaches forward toward that which it already, inchoately possesses. It apprehends that which it cannot see and then attains an understanding of that apprehension in the delivery of what it desired,"[16] and memory comes into play, "the beautiful becomes, then, a mode of re-cognition in an operation of desire."[17]

Richard Viladesau[18] provides a pathway to view this aesthetically: "God [provides] the 'condition of possibility' not only of thought and love but also apprehension of beauty."[19] The sense of beauty as the contact point in encountering transcendence is well-known in Eastern thought, even with people without overt contact with religion. It somehow resonates, strengthen, and validates the existence of a presence above and beyond the mundane experience of being human.[20] Viladesau put it succinctly, "There seems to be no doubt that experiences of beauty can lead the spirit to God and confirm people in devotion, and that therefore the aesthetic dimension is one that must have a place in communication of religious truth."[21]

The thought of Pseudo-Dionysius would find its natural home in the Chinese mind on beauty. There is the sense that beauty is never lost in the person who is captivated by its brilliance and glory. It stirs up the spirit,

---

15. O'Donohue, *Divine Beauty*, 228.

16. Ward, "Beauty of God," 39. Although Ward speaks in terms of the theology of icons, it does serve our purpose well in recognizing the Holy Spirit at work in the human in comprehending the beauty of God.

17. Ward, "Beauty of God," 39.

18. Viladesau, *Theological Aesthetics*, 103–40.

19. Viladesau, *Theological Aesthetics*, 103. He uses the premises of theology much like that of theologian Rahner and Lonergan.

20. See, e.g., Jiang Xun, an art critic, who expresses the Eastern thought throughout his book 蔣勳:《新編美的曙光》.

21. Viladesau, *Theological Aesthetics*, 104.

knocks on the door of the world beyond, and lifts the spirit to a higher, ethereal level.[22] Not only this, manifestation of beauty brings tears to the eyes, not only because it causes the spirit to be lifted up, but more than this, it is the heart touching the deepest of feelings, because it is in this that expectations of life and hope are enacted at the moment of appreciation, that there is always hope beyond the mundane: it is as if the inner life of the self is given the opportunity to dialogue with the Universe, "like the feeling of being 'filled,' and this has never happen before. By 'being filled,' I mean, in reality our sense perception is like a container; when it is empty, it is very lonely and isolated, but when filled, brings about contentment, and overflowing joy."[23] And this contentment and joy inevitably lead one towards the transcendent thought and imagination.

However, with the advancement of age and knowledge, the young soul is forcefully taught to restraint from the so-called excesses of feelings. Confucian philosophy would teach that, "The middle way is to keep joy, anger, sorrow and happiness at bay."[24] As a result, there seems to be a loss of wonder in the philosophical speculations, instead, suppression of emotion and imagination becomes more prominent. Confucianism values human emotion in as far as human beings are not overly dependent on it, the norm is self-control. But at the same time, poets and artists rebelled against such wanton monopoly of nonaffective philosophy, and they created works of art that play to the emotions and mood, in one aspect to counteract this, and in a more positive aspect, to bring back the very basic and instinctive facade of being human. Their efforts were not in vain. Poets and artists were regarded highly in the centuries of Tang, Sung, Yuan and Ming period. And all through the modern period, i.e., Qing and Modern China, one can almost say that they are the ones carrying on the Chinese ethos.

But we are not looking to this wonder of the beautiful as if it could instinctively evoke the thought of a transcendent being. Graham Ward helpfully makes this distinction.[25] He agrees that, "A work of art may trigger experiences of wonder . . . associated with the religious, the spiritual—experiences that transport us or expand our consciousness of the world and ourselves,"[26] but this has to be distinguished "between the warm (or foreboding) feelings that are described as religious or spiritual and the

22. Jiang (蔣勳), 《新編美的曙光》, 239.
23. Jiang (蔣勳), 《新編美的曙光》, 240.
24. "喜怒哀樂之未發謂之中", see, Jiang (蔣勳), 《新編美的曙光》, 241.
25. Ward, "Beauty of God," 61.
26. Ward, "Beauty of God," 61.

theological apprehension of the beauty of God."²⁷ Here we would suggest that the beauty that is the Holy Spirit, would bring about "the mode of apprehension, participation, and the analogical practice that has taught the recipient how to receive (that is, discern)."²⁸ Christians would believe that the Beautiful God would yearn for His creatures to appreciate the harmony and enjoyment to be had in the world around them, so the initiation of the Spirit, who is co-creator and beautifier of the creator world, would surely create a restless yearning for the perfect beauty that can only be discerned in the Creator, thus creating the journey back to Himself.

Inspiring Beauty

Religions in China have always relied on the Arts to convey their ethos.²⁹ What the ancient Greek termed the inspiration of artists that come from the Muses, the Chinese look to as inspiration by the Great and Universal Qi. And this, may we suggest, is the meeting point of the Spirit of Beauty with Eastern Universal Qi. What is termed Qi has been subject of many investigations in conjunction with The Theology of the Holy Spirit.³⁰ Among other things that are said about Qi, one that is relevant here is to find the origin of inspirations in Qi, a creative spirit, that is inherent in the human spirit in response to the world around them. Art is a visible response to the prompting of Qi. This has particular relevance to the indigenization of Christian theology, as humans are looked at in our analysis below, as co-creative partners of the creative Spirit.

However, James Martin Jr.³¹ has helpfully delineated what he views as "holiness and beauty in Eastern thought" in the categories of philosophy, religion and aesthetics. In what he terms as "Eastern Thought," he takes "beauty" as a surrogate for "aesthetic excellence" and "holiness" as "surrogate for what may be felicitously called 'ultimateness' in a sense that has an affinity with

---

27. Ward, "Beauty of God," 61. However, Ward's argument adheres to his idea of the analogical connectivity to the divine beauty, and the incarnational aspect of the image of God, a very christological reflection, what Ward concludes as "A Christian aesthetics is founded upon the implication of the incarnation" (61).

28. The quotation comes from Ward, which is applied to Christ (Ward, "Beauty of God," 61), but this would fit more appropriately to the Holy Spirit, as the Spirit speaks to the spirit of the receiver.

29. Aesthetic philosopher Jiang Shu Zhuo has tabled this in his book on Art in Religion in Chinese culture and philosophy (蔣述卓),《宗教藝術論》(*On Art in Religion*).

30. See for example, Yun, *Holy Spirit and Ch'I (Qi)*.

31. Martin, *Beauty and Holiness*.

the analyses by Tillich and others."[32] And yet he recognizes the need to place theories under the broad heading of "experience,"[33] recognizing with Indian art philosopher Ananda Coomaraswamy, that "Modern [western] aesthetic theory errs in placing the ground and goal of aesthetic experience in the life of feeling, true art is ultimately ideational and cognitive."[34] And here lies the intimate relationship between holiness and beauty, in the sense that it brings the worshipper into the realm of the Holy: "Prizing aesthetic as an end in itself is a modern form of idolatry or dehumanization. Ultimate human apprehension of the real also transcends even the experience of the beauty of the good; it is completed in contemplation, which should both guide and perfect human life."[35] Thus, aesthetics is a Christian term that should point to the very inspiration of the Spirit in creativity.

The Bible narratives witness to that. There are extensive exploration of the creation/garden of Eden motif in the construction of the Wilderness tabernacle and the Solomonic Temple.[36] Hess puts it succinctly, "The Bible identifies God as the Creator of the 'temple of the cosmos.' However, in accordance with the decision to give to humanity the ongoing work of creation and dominion over the earth (Gen 1:26–28), the divine decision was made to appoint human agents to build the tabernacle and the temple in Jerusalem."[37] To him there is a quasi-direct relationship between the creativity of God and the creativity of humanity in terms of the divine command. Hess utilizes the figures of Bezalel and Oholiab[38] as biblical examples for a wider significance. And Hess points out that, "They create the tabernacle with skill that comes from God's direct endowment."[39] The construction of the tabernacle bring with it the affirmation of this direct endowment via God's own Spirit (Exod 28:3; 35:21). Thus the ongoing blessing of the Creative God, through his Spirit, has given humanity the God-given creativity to redeem beauty from the curse of ugliness. If beauty pertains to the Holy Spirit, then ugliness such as violence, oppression, economic enslavement and social irrationality have

---

32. Martin, *Beauty and Holiness*, 137.

33. Martin, *Beauty and Holiness*, 139, what he calls "the grounding of theory in personal practice . . . [because] in the East, comments on beauty and holiness have been judged in terms of both the character and the practice of the persons offering the comments" (132).

34. Martin, *Beauty and Holiness*, 141.

35. Martin, *Beauty and Holiness*, 141.

36. See, e.g., Wenham, "Sanctuary Symbolism," 399–404.

37. Hess, "Bezalel and Oholiab," 162.

38. They appear in the narrative of the building of the tabernacle, i.e., Exod 31:2; 35:30; 36:1, 2; 37:1; 38:22; 1 Chr 2:20; 2 Chr 1:5.

39. Hess, "Bezalel and Oholiab," 163.

no place in the economy of God, of which George Steiner terms a "systematic turn-about towards bestialization."[40]

Communicating Beauty: The Holy Spirt, Creation and Co-creativity

The role of the Holy Spirit in the Old Testament is questioned from the perspective of its (lack) of mention in the texts themselves. G. von Rad adamantly stated that "the Old Testament nowhere knows of such a cosmological significance for the concept of the spirit of God."[41] Thus what the Old Testament mention as the spirit of God is another way of saying the activity or the action of God.[42] But this is to fall into the trap of the systematic theologians which they set for themselves. The Old Testament sometimes defies systemization, and Robert Hubbard's careful analysis of Genesis 1:2 celebrates the nuances that bring out the "magic" of the text.[43] We only state some of his conclusions here in as far as they help to solidify our thoughts on beauty and the Spirit here. The description of the *ruah Elohim* is that of her "incredible influence on people and nature,"[44] at creation, "the spirit is invisible, but the spirit is there to act, not to watch"[45] and,

> Just as divine 'breath' breathes life into lifeless humans (Gen 2:7; Job 12:10), so the *ruah* breathes a specifically *life-giving* breath into the scene. Its mention signals that God is about to breathe life into the lifeless wasteland—to cause the barren, empty earth to flower and flourish and become inhabitable by all God's creatures. Made alive, the world will provide a beautiful, bountiful home for the 'living soul' that God will create and place there.[46]

---

40. Steiner, cited in Moore, "Hope of Beauty," 155–72.

41. Rad, *Genesis*, 49–50. R. P. C. Hanson has the same assertion: "When I say that there is no doctrine of the Holy Spirit in the Old Testament, I do not mean that there is no mention of a holy spirit or the spirit of God in the Old Testament. There are of course plenty of such references. But they do not, all put together, amount to anything remotely approaching or even anticipating the Christian doctrine of *the* Holy Spirit . . . [they] cannot seriously be described as foreshadowings of the Christian concept of God the Holy Spirit, not even as much as the Messianic texts are foreshadowings of the Christian concept of God the Son" (*Attractiveness of God*, 116).

42. Hanson, *Attractiveness of God*, 116–17.

43. Hubbard, "Spirit and Creation," 71–94.

44. Hubbard, "Spirit and Creation," 82.

45. Hubbard, "Spirit and Creation," 89.

46. Hubbard, "Spirit and Creation," 89.

With that as our inroad into the activity of the Holy Spirit in creation, Hubbard links this with the very intriguing hypothesis proposed by Amos Yong:[47] the co-creativity between God and the creation: "rather than act or command action, God calls the earth on its own to produce seed-bearing plants and trees . . . God asks the earth to act as, in essence, co-creator without surrendering his absolute sovereignty as Creator."[48] This has huge potential in reflecting the nature and activity of the Holy Spirit, what Amos Yong termed "the dynamic, particularizing, relational, and life-giving presence and activity of the Spirit of God."[49] The on-going role of the Holy Spirit in sustaining and beautifying Creation is brought to stark relief. What God himself deemed as "It was good" has the hallmark of the Spirit over it; only the disobedient act of his Creation marred the prospect of it remaining life-sustaining and harmonious and beautiful: "Cursed is the ground because of you; in toil you shall eat it all the days of your life. Both thorns and thistles it shall grow for you; and you shall eat the plants of the field; by sweat of your face, you shall eat bread, till you return to the ground" (Gen 3:17–19, NASB). But it is by the sheer grace of God that the task and enjoyment of being co-creating agency have not been entirely taken away.

Thus, the task of beautifying is communicated by the Holy Spirit to again fulfill the mission of creation that was in the beginning entrusted to it.

Perfecting Beauty: Beauty as Eschatological Fulfillment

Admittedly there is little evidence of the relationship of the divine spirit and the realm of creation in Chinese metaphysics, therefore the doctrine of the Spirit in creation in Christian theology can serve as corrective and illuminative to the otherwise depleting concept. In a Western secularized culture, the idea of beauty has become muddled, what Graham Ward terms "opacity of creation," it is akin to "a denial [that] alters the very possibility not only for the concept of the beautiful, but the representation or re-presentation of Beauty."[50] But the recent and very positive assertion of theological aesthetic in theological agenda has indeed opened up fresh formulation of the whole economy of God. W. D. O. Taylor puts this succinctly, "The Spirit secures the logic of each created thing and thereby its

---

47. Yong, "Ruah," 183–204.
48. Hubbard, "Spirit and Creation," 90.
49. Yong, "Ruah," 198.
50. Ward, "Beauty of God," 36.

own way of being beautiful, while also drawing it into the life of God in Christ, in whom all things holds together."[51]

James Martin Jr. endeavours to place religious thought in cultural contexts that embrace many other human activities.[52] He maintains that beauty and holiness in the Western context can be equivalent to the "Eastern" concept of aesthetic excellence and ultimateness: "In the East, comments on beauty and holiness have been judged in terms of both the character and the practice of the persons offering the comments."[53] The spirituality of the persons becomes the witness of their beliefs and outlook in life: "Political, economic, aesthetic, and religious factors have been more subtly intertwined in the east than in the West." What tend to be defined as holy and beautiful are ethical and moral behaviours, but the acts are always related back to the sense of the Holy, and in some circle, a sense of the Divine, that the moral person is deemed to be infused with.

Chinese theological reflection can gain much in contemplating this role of the Spirit of beauty in the whole redemptive economy of God. What Alan Jones in his essay calls "falling in love is the work of the Spirit"[54] is precisely this recalling of desire for the beauty of God in the worshipper. Out of the three transcendentals, Truth and Goodness invokes awe, appreciation and gratefulness, but beauty invokes love. It is this that becomes an apparent contradiction in the Chinese faithfuls, whilst the puritan thoughts that were passed on to the Chinese, Truth and Goodness becomes paramount, capitalizing on the Confucian way of thinking, and yet the sense of beauty that many Chinese Christians recalled when they first encountered Christianity is somehow suppressed, to be taken over by the so called "right living and right behaviour." The sense of wonder is gradually lost in the busyness of keeping the "Truth" and doing "Good."

However, what has been said about beauty and the Holy Spirit cannot ignore or bypass the redemptive economy of God. Ultimately, the work of the Holy Spirit involves conversion, not just accommodation. There will be no beauty without the benevolence of the God, no beauty if the ultimate source of all beauty is not fully acknowledged. The doctrine of the Spirit of Beauty can only be fully appreciated in the redemptive work of the Cross. W.D.O. Taylor puts it well: "The argument is that all things in creation, whether 'natural' or human-made, are able to be beautiful, and that it is the Holy Spirit who takes responsibility for deepening the particular reality of

---

51. Taylor, "Spirit and Beauty," 48.
52. Martin, *Beauty and Holiness*, 137.
53. Martin, *Beauty and Holiness*, 139.
54. Jones, "Falling in Love," 376.

each thing's beauty as well as perfecting each thing by bringing it, through Christ, into reconciled relationship with the Father."[55]

Thus, when we talk of the work of the Holy Spirit, the emphasis should be turned to the eschatological fulfillment of God's purpose for the World, not just anthropological alone, as is often emphasized in Protestant theology (conviction, justification, spiritual guidance, sanctification and even glorification), although this is crucial to Pauline theology, the New Testament also bears witness to God's involvement in the world by the Holy Spirit. This involvement is focused in Jesus Christ and those who are in him, and yet it holds out hope for the whole creation, as the Spirit bears witness (Rom 8:1–27). So human redemption may be looked at as part of the plan of the manifestation of the glory of God, in terms of the consummation of the eschaton and the beautifying of the final creative process of God's ultimate design. Thus the Spirit's role is the crucial one in bringing the whole creation to final *akouluthia*, perfecting beauty.

Bibliography

Balthasar, Hans Urs von. *The Glory of the Lord: A Theological Aesthetics*. Vol. 1, *Seeing the Form*. 3 vols. Edinburgh: T. & T. Clark, 1982.

Dreyer, Elizabeth A., and Mark S. Burrows. "Spirituality and Aesthetics." In *Minding the Spirit: The Study of Christian Spirituality*, edited by Elizabeth A. Dreyer and Mark S. Burrows, 299–302. Baltimore: Johns Hopkins University Press, 2005.

Edwards, Jonathan. *An Unpublished Essay of (Jonathan) Edwards on the Trinity*. Edited by George Park Fisher. New York: Scribner, 1903.

Hanson, Richard Patrick Crosland. *The Attractiveness of God: Essays in Christian Doctrine*. London: SPCK, 1973.

Hart, David Bentley. *The Beauty of the Infinite: The Aesthetics of Christian Truth*. Grand Rapids: Eerdmans, 2003.

Hart, John. *Redemption Road*. Waterville, ME: Thorndike, 2016.

Hess, Richard S. "Bezalel and Oholiab: Spirit and Creativity." In *Presence, Power and Promise: The Role of the Spirit of God in the Old Testament*, edited by David G. Firth and Paul D. Wegner, 161–74. Nottingham, UK: Apollos, 2011.

Hubbard, Robert L., Jr. "The Spirit and Creation." In *Presence, Power and Promise: The Role of the Spirit of God in the Old Testament*, edited by David G. Firth and Paul D. Wegner, 71–94. Nottingham, UK: Apollos, 2011.

Jones, Alan. "Falling in Love: The Work of the Holy Spirit." *Anglican Theological Review* 83 (2001) 375–86.

Louie, Kin Yip. *The Beauty of the Triune God: The Theological Aesthetics of Jonathan Edwards*. Eugene, OR: Pickwick, 2013.

Martin, James Alfred, Jr. *Beauty and Holiness: The Dialogue between Aesthetics and Religion*. Princeton: Princeton University Press, 1990.

---

55. Jones, "Falling in Love," 376.

Milbank, John, et al. *Theological Perspectives on God and Beauty*. Rockwell Lecture Series. Harrisburg, PA: Trinity Press International, 2003.

Moore, T. M. "The Hope of Beauty in an Age of Ugliness and Death." *Theology Today* 61 (2004) 155–72.

O'Donohue, John. *Divine Beauty: The Invisible Embrace*. London: Bantam, 2004.

Rad, Gerhard von. *Genesis: A Commentary*. Old Testament Library. Philadelphia: Westminster, 1972.

Sherry, Patrick. *Spirit and Beauty: An Introduction to Theological Aesthetics*. Oxford: Clarendon, 1992.

Steiner, George. *Grammars of Creation: Originating in the Gifford Lectures for 1990*. New Haven: Yale University Press, 2001.

Strachan, Owen, and Douglas A. Sweeney, eds. *Jonathan Edwards on Beauty*. Chicago: Moody, 2010.

Taylor, W. David O. "Spirit and Beauty: A Reappraisal." *Christian Scholar's Review* 40 (2014) 45–59.

Viladesau, Richard. *Theological Aesthetics: God in Imagination, Beauty, and Art*. New York: Oxford University Press, 1999.

Ward, Graham. "The Beauty of God." In *Theological Perspectives on God and Beauty*, edited by John Milbank et al., 35–65. Rockwell Lecture Series. Harrisburg, PA: Trinity Press International, 2003.

Wenham, Gordon J. "Sanctuary Symbolism in the Garden of Eden Story." In *"I Studied Inscriptions from Before the Flood": Ancient Near Eastern, Literary, and Linguistic Approaches to Genesis 1–11*, edited by Richard S. Hess and David Toshio Tsumura, 399–404. Sources for Biblical and Theological Study 4. Winona Lake, IN: Eisenbrauns, 1994.

Yong, Amos. "Ruah, the Primordial Chaos, and the Breath of Life: Emergence Theory and the Creation Narratives in Pneumatological Perspective." In *The Work of the Spirit: Pneumatology and Pentecostalism*, edited by Michael Welker, 183–204. Grand Rapids: Eerdmans, 2006.

Yun, Koo Dong. *The Holy Spirit and Ch'i (Qi): A Chiological Approach to Pneumatology*. Princeton Theological Monograph Series 180. Eugene, OR: Pickwick, 2012.

何崇謙.《超然的啟視：從藝術到靈性》 *(From Vision of the Sublime to Visio Dei)*. Hong Kong: Tao Fong Shan Christian Centre, 2006.

蔣述卓.《宗教藝術論》 *(On Art in Religion)*. 廣州：暨南大學出版社, 1998.

蔣勳.《新編美的曙光》. 看世界的方法 33. 台北市：有鹿文化, 2012.

Historical-Theological Perspective

4

Charismata in the Early Church

Samuel H. H. Chiow

Introduction

He who invokes the past is always secure. The dead will not rise to witness against him.

—Czesław Miłosz[1]

THE EMERGENCE OF THE Pentecostal-Charismatic movement as a global phenomenon breathes new life into the biblical *charismata* and their significance into the contemporary church. Such focus on the *charismata* has also brought about changes of understanding and attitude concerning *charismata* and its place in the life of the Chinese church. A historical investigation and evaluation of the gifts of the Spirit in the history of Christianity betrays the theological biases of the one doing the investigation. History often retrieves information from its dusty bin to prove or defend novel or old ideas. For many scholars, it has proved to be an effective ally in the battle for the truth. For the Pentecostal-Charismatics, history offers many instructive precedents, and it has been given maximum exposure (publicity, attention) to bolster what is viewed as the cornerstone of their theology. They have argued impassionedly that history is on their side in amply demonstrating that the Pentecostal-Charismatic movement is as old as the church itself and even that such movements are a semi-permanent part of the church.

---

1. Miłosz, *New and Collected Poems*, 86.

Particularly, on the question of the gifts of the Spirit, it has been part and parcel of the church and its manifestation today is as equally valid now as in the days of the apostles.

On the contrary, the Non-Pentecostal-Charismatics, especially conservatively oriented evangelicals, have met the movement with the skepticism of Thomas. They have stressed the insignificance and spotty occurrences of some of the gifts of the Spirit during the history of the church, and even exaggerated the negative features which have accompanied it. Some stout opponents of the Pentecostal-Charismatic movement have even gone to the extreme, contending that gifts such as tongues-speaking is the work of demons rather than of God.[2]

The conservative non-Pentecostal-Charismatics have relied on a tradition of the cessation of the gifts of the Spirit. Perhaps, the most influential case was set forth by Benjamin B. Warfield of Princeton Theological Seminary in the early part of the twentieth century. In his book *Counterfeit Miracles*, published in 1918, in the chapter entitled "The Cessation of the Charismata," Warfield maintained that spiritual gifts are uniquely associated with the apostles, and occurred for the purpose of authenticating them. It was an evidential sign for the apostolic age and such a sign was needed to establish the truth of Christianity. When the apostolic period ended and the church was established, the need for these gifts also ceased. Warfield elaborated:

> These gifts were not the possession of the primitive Christian as such; nor for that matter of the Apostolic Church or the Apostolic age for themselves; they were distinctively the authentication of the Apostles. They were part of the credentials of the Apostles as the authoritative agents of God in founding the church. Their function thus confined them to distinctively the Apostolic Church, and they necessarily passed away with it.[3]

The view of Warfield has been widely adopted and even frequently used to defend and give credibility for an anti-Pentecostal-Charismatic position.[4] Warfield's cessation theory has shown to be not only influential but deeply entrenched among the non-Pentecostal-Charismatics. Even today

---

2. Ward, "Anti–Pentecostal Argument," 101–22.
3. Warfield, *Counterfeit Miracles*, 6.
4. Williams, *Renewal Theology*, 162–67. Please note Williams's careful refutation of Warfield. Also check Deere, *Surprised by the Power*, 229–41. Deere represents another recent response to the cessation theory (MacArthur, *Charismatic Chaos*, 118, 200; Budgen, *Charismatics and the Word of God*, 113–14; Mallone, "Tidy Doctrine," 14–17).

Warfield's cessation theory echoes in the writings of his theological descendants. Peter Masters formulates his argument this way:

> Every example of healing [by the instrumentality of a person] in the Book of Acts is performed by an apostle, or an apostle's deputy, and if we go strictly by the biblical record, the only three "deputies" who had any involvement in healing were Stephen, Philip and possibly Barnabas if Acts 14:3 includes him [We shall comment in a moment on the hypothetical possibility that there were others also]. Outside this select group there are no "gifted" healing activities actually recorded in Acts or the epistles.... In these days of charismatic confusion, we need constantly to draw attention to the texts which prove that signs and wonders were peculiar to the apostolic band, and were not bestowed generally [author's emphasis].[5]

Despite the popularity of Warfield's argument, it is untenable because of its inherent contradiction in its concept of miracle and biblical hermeneutics. The basis of his cessationism is on post-Reformation and Enlightenment understanding of miracles as evidence. Warfield's cessationism relies too much on dogma instead of Scripture, which fail to see the biblical portrayal of the eschatological outpouring of the Spirit of prophecy as expressed in the *charismata*. Till the end of this age, the *charismata* are given by the exalted Christ as the manifestation of the advancing Kingdom of God.[6]

The cessation theory is extended in that, if spiritual gifts were strictly apostolic then logically such phenomena would not continue in the postapostolic history. The miracles and the gifts of the Spirit manifested during the apostolic age were irrefutable and authentic. The other side of this argument is that if spiritual gifts were not strictly limited to the apostolic age and ceased after that, then the expectation is that there would be "an unbroken line of occurrences from apostolic time to the present" as the Pentecostal-Charismatic would like to claim.[7] The historical evidence, thus, will be overwhelming, because the gifts are a permanent fixture of the church. However, the non-Pentecostal-Charismatic argues that the "very paucity and sporadic nature of alleged occurrences is evidence against this claim."[8] So it is impossible to establish a historical link between the New Testament gifts and the "charismatic" gifts of today.

5. Masters, *Healing Epidemic*, 69–70.
6. Ruthven, "On the Cessation," 15, 16–31.
7. Edgar, "Cessation of the Sign Gifts," 372–73.
8. Edgar, "Cessation of the Sign Gifts," 373.

Moreover, the non-Pentecostal-Charismatic maintains that if these spiritual gifts are genuinely of God, then, why are such gifts conspicuously absent throughout the history of the church? Here, on the heels of the historical-gap argument, the theological argument is added. The assumption behind such an argument is simple in that what is good and divine should continue. God would not withdraw from the church what is obviously beneficial for her existence. Thus, historical evidence contradicts the claims of the Pentecostal-Charismatic.[9]

The historical-gap argument is in part conceded by the Pentecostal-Charismatic. Declining charismatic activities seems evident in the postapostolic era. Often, John Wesley is quoted to explain leanness of evidence:

> The grand reason why the miraculous gifts were so soon withdrawn was not only that faith and holiness were well-nigh lost, but that dry, formal, orthodox men began then to ridicule whatever gifts they had not themselves and to cry them all as evil madness or imposture.[10]

George Malone has posited at least three basic reasons for the spotty evidence: the rise of clericalism within the church, the rise of scientism, and the loss of heart for the Lord.[11] Besides the above reasons, formalism, secularism, modernism, and acculturation were cited for the great diminution of the gifts after the apostolic age.[12]

Another way some Pentecostal-Charismatic had used to explain the diminution of the spiritual gifts after the apostolic age is that some of these gifts ceased, but have been restored in these "latter days." The end of the church age is imminent and, according to Joel 2:23, in the "latter days," the Spirit will be poured out on all humanity. So, the upsurge of "signs and wonders" is tied to Premillennial eschatology, and that in His sovereignty He will restore the New Testament experience. Such logic helps the Pentecostal-Charismatic to solve the problem of its discontinuity with apostolic form of Christianity. The restoration perspective turned out to be a legitimation for the long drought of charismatic activity from postapostolic time to the present.[13]

---

9. Edgar, "Cessation of the Sign Gifts," 373.
10. Wesley, cited in Mallone, "Tidy Doctrine," 24.
11. Mallone, "Tidy Doctrine," 24–26.
12. Hinson, "Significance of Glossolalia," 189.
13. Blumhofer, *Assemblies of God*, 18–21. See also Dayton, *Theological Roots of Pentecostalism*, 26–28; Edgar, "Cessation of the Sign Gifts," 374–375; Judisch, *Evaluation of Claims*, 80; Hoekema, *What about Tongue Speaking?*, 23.

Thus, the cessation of the *charismata* argument is important for both the Pentecostal-Charismatic and the Non-Pentecostal-Charismatic. The tendency for the Pentecostal-Charismatic, obviously, is to affirm and maximize all they can on the historical evidence. The non-Pentecostal-Charismatic, on the other hand, tends to deny and minimize the historical data. Also to be noted,

> Relatively little work has been done on the history of spiritual gift teaching as such. Prior to the advent of the Pentecostal/charismatic movement at the turn of the 20th century, there was relatively little to be explored. I do not mean that the church had no notion of the *charismata* before 1900. From the earliest centuries, Christian authors have preached and commented on 1 Cor 12, Rom 12, and Eph 4, and discussed prophecy, tongues, and miracles . . . But the attempt to distill a specific theology of spiritual gifts—one that defines a particular category or class of unique capacities for ministry granted to Christians, that names those capacities, explains their distinguishing qualities, tells believers how to identify which they have, and advises on their application to church ministry structures—that sort of literature is all but impossible to find before the most recent chapters in church history.[14]

The present chapter seeks neither to muffle or amplify the voice of church history for a specific theological end; it simply lays out the historical documents that are relevant to our discussion. It will sample several key church fathers of the early church, and note the role of the Spirit in the experience of Christian believers and especially their view of spiritual gifts.

Didache or *The Teaching of the Lord Through the Twelve Apostles to the Nations*, a manual of church order and discipline likely originated in Syria/Palestine and dated from the latter part of the first century. The date is of particular significance in that this document recorded the life of the church while the New Testament was still being written. Moreover, the church was still dealing with the gift of prophecy as if it were a general affair within the church. The document was highly valued in the early church. Eusebius placed it among the writings that were orthodox but rejected from the canon.[15] In this work, the author instructs the local congregation concerning travelling prophets. In *Didache* 10:7:

14. Radant, quoted in Berding, "'Gifts' and Ministries," 135.

15. Eusebius, *History of the Church*, 3.25.4. Eusebius has this to say about writings accepted as sacred and those not accepted: "Among spurious books must be placed the 'Acts' of Paul, the 'Shepherd' and the 'Revelation of Peter'; also, the alleged 'Epistle of Barnabas', and the 'Teaching of the Apostles', together with the Revelation of John, if

"In the case of prophets, however, you should let them give thanks in their own way."[16] Here, the prophets are spoken of favorably and are allowed the freedom to speak and to give thanks, implying that their message would be propitious to the church. Later in *Didache* 11:7 says:

"While a prophet is making ecstatic utterances (speaking in the Spirit), you must not test or examine him. For 'every sin will be forgiven,' but this sin 'will not be forgiven.'"[17]

For the author, the prophet is not only allowed to speak freely in the church but his message should also be respected. He further teaches that the prophetic message should be left alone without scrutiny. However, such positive acceptance of the prophets needs to be balanced with certain critical suspicions. Two tests are presented. The first is that the content of their teaching must be consistent with the early teaching in the *Didache*.

> Now, you should welcome anyone who comes your way and teaches you all we have been saying. But if the teacher proves himself a renegade and by teaching otherwise contradicts all this, pay no attention to him. But if his teaching furthers the Lord's righteousness and knowledge, welcome him as the Lord.[18]

This test applies also to other traveling teachers. The second test is moral in nature:

> However, not everybody making ecstatic utterances is a prophet, but only if he behaves like the Lord. It is by their conduct that false prophet and the [true] prophet can be distinguished.[19]

A moral test must be applied in discerning the true prophets from the false prophets. Their teaching and their lives must be in harmony. Thus, the ministry of the prophets must be tested and approved. After it is approved, it must be welcomed, in accordance to apostle Paul, who taught that the prophet's faithfulness to the confession of Christ (1 Cor 12:3) must be tested. So, false prophecies and heretical prophets continued to be an issue in the early church. From these passages in the *Didache*, it is clear that the office of charismatic prophet was important to the church, and that the

---

this seems the right place for it: as I said before, some reject it, others include it among the Recognized Books."

16. Richardson, *Early Christian Fathers*, 176.
17. Richardson, *Early Christian Fathers*, 176; Kydd, *Charismatic Gifts*, 7.
18. Richardson, *Early Christian Fathers*, 176 (11.1–2).
19. Richardson, *Early Christian Fathers*, 176–77.

controversy over "false prophets" was a lively one. Thus, the church does welcome prophets, and the prophetic gifts are still in evidence.[20]

The apostolic fathers volunteer little information on the charismatic gifts and their use. However, the continuance of prophetic gifts is confirmed by the writings of Ignatius of Antioch (c.35–c.107), who was born about the time of Jesus' resurrection. According to Eusebius, he was the third bishop of Antioch following St. Peter's successor, Euodius.[21] Little is known of his life, except the seven letters which he wrote between AD 98 and 117, on his way to martyrdom from Antioch to Rome.[22]

In the letter of Ignatius to Polycarp, who was bishop of Smyrna, the elder Ignatius instructs the younger bishop:

> But ask that you may have revelations of what is unseen. In that way, you will lack nothing and have an abundance of every gift.[23]

Here, we note that Ignatius encourages Polycarp to pray for revelation and the reason for such advice is that Polycarp may have an abundance of spiritual gifts. Such exhortation demonstrates that Ignatius has great respect for spiritual gifts and their exercise in the church.

In another letter to the Smyrneans, in reference to 1 Corinthians 1:7, Ignatius sanctions the spiritual gifts when speaking to the church at Smyrna: "By God's mercy you have received every gift; you abound in faith and love and are lacking in no gift. You are a wonderful credit to God and real saints."[24]

Moreover, in his letter to the Philadelphians, Ignatius establishes himself as the prophet, and claims to have been the vehicle of a prophetic utterance. He says:

> When I was with you I cried out, raising my voice—it was God's voice—"Pay heed to the bishop, the presbytery, and the deacons." Some, it is true, suspected that I spoke thus because I had been told in advance that some of you were schismatic. But I swear by Him for whose cause I am a prisoner, that from no

---

20. Kydd, *Charismatic Gifts*, 88; Kelsey, *Tongue Speaking*, 36; Campbell, "Charismata," 10. Interestingly, Budgen, after examining the same series of quotations, concludes negatively in that the reference to traveling prophets in the *Didache* illustrates the opposite. It shows more the decline and nonexistence of the gifts of prophecy (Budgen, *Charismatics and the Word of God*, 114).

21. Cross, *Oxford Dictionary*, 688.

22. Cross, *Oxford Dictionary*, 688. See also Burns and Fagin, *Holy Spirit*, 22; Maier, *Social Setting of the Ministry*, 147; Quasten, *Patrology*, 63.1.

23. Richardson, *Early Christian Fathers*, 118.

24. Richardson, *Early Christian Fathers*, 112.

human channels did I learn this. It was the Spirit that kept on preaching in these words: "Do nothing apart from the bishop; keep your bodies as if they were God's temple; value unity; flee schism; imitate Jesus Christ as he imitated his Father."[25]

Ignatius strongly emphasized the authority of the threefold, ordained ministry of deacon, presbyter, and bishop as being essential to the Body of Christ. The essential threefold level of leadership is "confirmed and established by his Holy Spirit."[26] However, at the same time, Ignatius recalled how he, under the guidance of the Holy Spirit, had exercised the gift of prophecy to settle a dispute in the congregation. For Ignatius, there seemed to be no conflict between the charismatic and episcopal interest.[27] He could have appealed to his authority as bishop, but instead he cited the authority of the prophetic word. When Ignatius said that He "cried out, raising my voice—it was God's voice" was similar to other accounts in early Christian and Hellenistic literature which describe prophetic or inspired pronouncements.[28] So, in the days of Ignatius when someone speaks in a loud voice, one is speaking as a prophet. From these passages in Ignatius's letters, spiritual gifts are positively affirmed and the prophetic ministry is operational.

In comparing with the apostolic fathers, the Apologists offer a bit more information concerning the use of spiritual gifts. Justin Martyr (c.100–c.165), the most outstanding of the "Apologists" born in Flavia Neapolis (ancient Shechem, modern Nablus), came to Rome and there composed two apologies, one to the Emperor and one to the Roman Senate. He also published a version of a dialogue in which he had earlier engaged with a Jew named Trypho, in which he spelled out the position of Israel in the history of salvation. Justin based the Christian claims to truth and universality on the divinity of Christ, the Logos of God.[29] He made certain observations in his writings that demonstrate the existence of spiritual gifts in the church around the middle of the second century. In his theological conversation with Trypho, Justin testified to the existence of spiritual gifts in the church around the middle of the second century:

> . . . He imparts to those who believe in Him, according as He deems each man worthy thereof. I have already said, and do again say, that this would be done by Him after His ascension

25. Richardson, *Early Christian Fathers*, 109–10.
26. Marshall, "Holy Spirit," 260–61, 268.
27. Campbell, "Charismata," 11.
28. Maier, *Social Setting of the Ministry*, 160. See Williams and Waldvogel, "History of Speaking in Tongues," 106.
29. Cross, *Oxford Dictionary*, 770.

to heaven. It is accordingly said, "He ascended on high, He led captivity captive, He gave gifts unto the sons of men." And again, in another prophecy it is said: "And it shall come to pass after this, I will pour out My Spirit on all flesh, and on My servants, and on My handmaids, and they shall prophesy."[30]

In this passage, Justin cited Psalm 68:16 and Joel 2:28 to speak of the outpouring of the Holy Spirit. This event for Justin was not simply a past event in history but a contemporary reality. Thus, Charismatic activity was still prevalent in his day. For Justin witnessed,

"Now it is possible to see among us women and men who possess gifts of the Spirit of God."[31]

Here, Justin noted that the Holy Spirit is continually present and observed that "among us," that is, in his own day, both men and women have been granted gifts (*charismata*) by the Spirit of God. Justin's dialogue, which was a decade or so before the emergence of Montanism, is a remarkable evidence for the continuance of the gift of the Spirit in both men and women.[32]

In his *Second Apology*, Justin reported the healing of demon-possessed persons in Rome and attributed such healings as *charismata*:

> For numberless demoniac throughout the whole world, and in your city, many of our Christian men exorcising them in the name of Jesus Christ, who was crucified under Pontius Pilate, have healed and do heal, rendering helpless and driving the possessing devils out of the men, though they could not be cured by all the other exorcists, and those who used incantations and drugs.[33]

Spiritual gifts during the days of Justin Martyr were widespread and he gave ample evidence to the fact, which serves to refute the claim that Charismatic gifts no longer appeared in the church, or had dropped away.

Irenaeus (c. 130–200), bishop of Lyon, took us to the western reaches of the Roman empire at the beginning of the third century. As a pastor and

30. *Dialogue of Justin* 87 (ANF 1:243).

31. *Dialogue of Justin* 88 (ANF 1:243). See Kelsey, *Tongue Speaking*, 37; Budgen, *Charismatics and the Word of God*, 115. Oddly, Budgen maintains that Justin's comments strictly "refers to events in New Testament times." Quite to our great chagrin, Budgen never explains himself on his interpretation of Justin's comments as limited to apostolic times rather than to postapostolic times. Also, Gromacki, *Modern Tongues Movement*, 12. He argues the spiritual gifts during the time of Justin were not to be identified with the spiritual gifts of 1 Cor because the gifts were once possessed by the Israelites and belonged to the Old Testament.

32. Stanton, "Spirit in the Writings of Justin Martyr," 331–34.

33. *Second Apology of Justin* 6 (ANF 1:190).

a theologian, Irenaeus spent most of his life in the defense of the Christian faith. He battled Gnosticism and left behind a careful and critical refutation of various strands of this early opponent that threatened the survival of the church. Irenaeus was pre-eminently a theologian of the Holy Spirit.[34] His work *Against Heresies*, written around 180–185, contained a large amount of material on the Holy Spirit, and afforded a great deal of information about glossolalia, prophecy, and healing. Irenaeus also dealt at some length with the role of the Holy Spirit in creation and revelation, in the teaching of the church, and in the salvation of the individual Christian.[35]

In Book Two of *Against Heresies*, Irenaeus speaks extensively about the *charismata* and gives us a list of gifts, which he knew existed in the church:

> Wherefore, also, those are in truth His disciples, receiving grace from Him, do in His name perform [miracles], so as to promote the welfare of other men, according to the gift which each one has received from Him. For some do certainly and truly drive out devils, so that those who have thus been cleansed from evil spirits frequently both believe [in Christ], and join themselves to the Church. Others have foreknowledge of things to come: they see visions, and utter prophetic expressions. Others still, heal the sick by laying their hands upon them, and they are made whole. Yea, moreover, as I have said, the dead even have been raised up, and remained among us for many years. And what shall I more say? It is not possible to name the number of the gifts which the Church, [scattered] throughout the whole world, has received from God, in the name of Jesus Christ, who was crucified under Pontius Pilate, and which she exerts day by day for the benefit of the Gentiles, neither practicing deception upon any, nor taking any reward from them [on account of such miraculous interpositions]. For as she has received freely from God, freely also does she minister.[36]

Here, Irenaeus spoke of how Christ, through the church, ministered to mankind. The list of spiritual gifts shown here was remarkable in that it included such gifts as the ability to cast out demons, knowledge about the future, visions, and prophetic speech. In a significant passage on the

---

34. Rusch, "Doctrine of the Holy Spirit," 71.

35. See Heron, *Holy Spirit*, 64–67.

36. Irenaeus, *Against Heresies* 11:32.4 (*ANF* 1:408); Warfield, *Counterfeit Miracles*, 14–16. Warfield, when considering this passage, argues that Irenaeus's reports on raising the dead refers only to people who had been raised from the dead in apostolic times. For Irenaeus, it was only hearsay. See also Kydd, *Charismatic Gifts*, 45.

charismatic gifts, Irenaeus referred not only to the contemporary exercise of general gifts but also specifically to tongue-speaking:

> . . . the apostle declares, "We speak wisdom among them that are perfect," terming those persons "perfect" who have received the Spirit of God, and who through the Spirit of God do speak in all languages (*universis linguis/pantodapais . . . glōssais*) through, as he used Himself also to speak. In like manner, we do also hear many brethren in the Church, who possess prophetic gifts, and who through the Spirit speak all kinds of languages, and bring to light for the general benefit the hidden things of men, and declare the mysteries of God whom also the apostle terms "spiritual."[37]

Moreover,

> For some (of Christ's true disciples) do certainly and truly drive out demons, so that those who are thus cleansed from the evil spirits often believe and join the church. Others have foreknowledge of future things, they see visions and utter prophetic words. Again others heal the sick by laying their hands upon them and let them rise up healthy. Moreover, as we have said, the dead even have been raised up and lived with us for many years. What shall I say further? It is impossible to name the number of all *charismata*, which the church, dispersed throughout the whole world, has received from God, in the name of Jesus Christ, who was crucified under Pontius Pilate, and which she exerts day by day for the benefit of the gentiles, without misleading anyone or accepting money . . .[38]

This passage has often been quoted by both the non-Charismatic-Pentecostal and Charismatic-Pentecostal. Questions have been raised concerning whether Irenaeus was actually an eyewitness of the phenomena. The phenomena of the passage are dismissed by maintaining that the phenomena described by Irenaeus did not occur in his day, but simply what had happened in the apostolic times. But such arguments are tenuous and require another set of exegeses.[39]

---

37. Irenaeus, *Against Heresies* 5:6 (*ANF* 1:531).
38. Irenaeus, *Against Heresies*, book II, chapter 32, 4.
39. See Hoekema, *What about Tongue Speaking?*, 12–15; Hunter, "Tongues–Speech," 130; Budgen, *Charismatics and the Word of God*, 116. Budgen simply repeats Hoekema that Irenaeus simply describes events in New Testament times and not those of his days. Also consult Robeck, "Irenaeus and 'Prophetic Gifts,'" 104–14.

Irenaeus clearly spoke from the standpoint of the wider church, and the church he described as charismatic. He offers us an eyewitness account of how various spiritual gifts were manifested in the church. So, the church that Irenaeus described was sensitive to the working of the Spirit and the gifts benefited the church greatly. It is of great interest and significance to note that he was dismayed at those of his own church who failed to accept the *charismata*. In the concluding section of his *Demonstration of the Apostolic Preaching* writes:

> Others do not accept the gifts of the Holy Spirit and cast the prophetic charisma far from their sight, through which man, when he is sprinkled with it, bears the life of God as fruit. These are the people of whom Isaiah said: 'Because (these), he says, will be like a terebinth tree that has lost all its leaves and like a garden without water' (cf. Isa. 1:30). And people like that have no use for God, because they bear no fruit.[40]

For Irenaeus, prophecy and other spiritual gifts should be an integral part of the life of the church. The gifts should serve the whole church. Thus, *charismata* for Irenaeus is the mark of a true church.

With Tertullian, a theologian from North Africa, *charismata* entered Latin theological literature as a transliterated loan-word with the general meaning of "gifts" and with the special meaning of the extraordinary spiritual gifts described in 1 Corinthians 12–14. As with Irenaeus, Tertullian believed that the presence of *charismata* was the mark of a true church. He spoke of the Holy Spirit in a variety of contexts. The Spirit strengthened the martyrs, whose power extended the peace of the church to those who had denied the faith. The Spirit is called Vicar of Christ because of his office of preserving the church in the teaching of Christ and apostles. The same Spirit comes down on the water of baptism and bestows its sanctifying power.[41]

The *Passion of Perpetua and Felicitas*, edited by Tertullian, even some of the chapters was authored by him. At the beginning of it we find:

> And thus we—who both acknowledge and reverence, even as we do the prophecies, modern visions as equally promised to us and consider the other powers of the Holy Spirit as an agency of the Church for which also He was sent, administering all gifts in all, even as the Lord distributed to everyone . . .[42]

---

40. Irenaeus, *Proof of the Apostolic Preaching* Vol 16; *Writings* (ANF 1:531).
41. Menzies, "Holy Spirit," 69. Heron, *Holy Spirit*, 67–69.
42. *Passion of the Holy Martyrs* Preface (ANF 3:699)

One note from the above passage is that Tertullian equated prophecies with the modern visions. Prophecies most likely referred to Old Testament prophecies, and the modern visions probably referred to those coming from the Montanists, which he joined in his later years. Also, significantly, both the Holy Spirit and the Lord were mentioned as dispenser of gifts to the church. Here, Tertullian showed great feelings for spiritual gifts which the Holy Spirit so generously distributed in the church.

At the end of the work *On Baptism*, Tertullian stated:

> Therefore, blessed ones, whom the grace of God awaits, when you ascend from that most sacred font of your new birth, and spread your hands for the first time in the house of your mother, together with your brethren, ask from the Father, ask from the Lord, that His own specialties of grace and distributions of gifts may be supplied you.[43]

In this passage, it is particularly important to note the phrase "distributions of gifts." Tertullian not just recommended but encouraged the newly baptized to seek the Lord for spiritual gifts. For him, there is a close connection between baptism, the receiving of the Spirit, and the *charismata*. Thus, for Tertullian, asking and receiving of spiritual gifts was a common Christian experience. In his famous treatise *Against Marcion*, Tertullian cited the evidences of spiritual gifts as proof of God's oneness and as a refutation of Marcion's doctrine of two God—the God of Wrath in the Old Testament and the God of Love revealed in Jesus of Nazareth:

> Let Marcion then exhibit, as gifts of his God, some prophets such as have not spoken by human sense, but with the Spirit of God, such as have both predicted things to come, and have made manifest the secrets of the heart; let him produce a psalm, a vision, a prayer—only let it be by the interpretation of tongues which has occurred to him; let him show to me also that any woman of boastful tongue in his community has ever prophesied from amongst those especially holy sisters of his. Now all these signs (of spiritual gifts) are forthcoming from my side without any difficulty, and they agree, too, with the rules, and the dispensations, and the instructions of the Creator; therefore, without doubt the Christ, and the Spirit, and the apostle, belong severally to my God.[44]

---

43. *On Baptism* 20 (ANF 3:679).
44. *Against Marcion* 5:8 (ANF 3:446–47).

This passage is often placed after Tertullian's conversion to Montanism. Thus, the spiritual gifts mentioned by Tertullian were often interpreted as naturally expected in light of the sectarian movement.[45] However, if one compares his pre-Montanist writings with his post-Montanist writings, his view on spiritual gifts remains the same. There are no major shifts in his theological thinking.[46]

As we reach the fourth century, Eusebius of Caesarea (c. 260–340) the "father of church history" in his monumental work *Historia Ecclesiastica* (Ecclesiastical History), records:

> It was at that very time, in Phrygia, that Montanus, Alcibiades, Theodotus, and their followers began to acquire a widespread reputation for prophecy; for numerous other manifestations of the miraculous gift of God, still occurring in various churches, led many to believe that these men too were prophets.[47]

Interestingly, in this passage, Eusebius tried to explain the rapid growth of Montanism, which occurred in early AD 170s. The reason he offered was that spiritual gifts were common in the church during this time. The expectation of the Christian matched the reality demonstrated by Montanus and his friend, thus acceptance of them was without difficulty.

Moreover, in his *Commentary on the Psalms*, Eusebius spoke of spiritual gifts as conferring glory to the body of Christ.

> The flashes of God's lightning appeared in all the world. What else are His lightnings but the radiances of the *charismata* of the Holy Spirit which flash throughout the whole inhabited world. There is a diversity of *charismata*, but the same Spirit. To some is given a word of wisdom by the Spirit and to another word of knowledge and another faith and so on, which, being excellent *charismata* of God, flash and bring radiance to His Church.[48]

Vividly, Eusebius spoke of the spiritual gifts as "flashes of God's lightning." He also confirmed that such reality was universal and listed various gifts granted by the Holy Spirit. He compares the divine powers and operations of the seraphim with the "holy men of God among men who shared in the most excellent *charismata*, as prophesying future events,

---

45. Gromacki, *Modern Tongues Movement*, 14; Hoekema, *What about Tongue Speaking?*, 15; Budgen, *Charismatics and the Word of God*, 118–19; Hunter, "Tongues-Speech," 130–31.

46. Kydd, *Charismatic Gifts*, 70.

47. Eusebius, *History of the Church*, Book 5, 3:4.

48. Eusebius, *Commentary on the Psalms* 76, 16–17.

healing diseases, raising the dead, and speaking in tongues, and sharing in wisdom and knowledge."[49]

Crossing into the fifth century, we have the testimony of Augustine (354–430). Augustine's testimony was particularly significant in that he represented much of Western theology and its view of the Holy Spirit's person and work. The Holy Spirit is the gift of the Father and the Son. Augustine strove to synthesize tendencies which had been developing in prior centuries. He elaborated a view of the Holy Spirit which integrated the mission to the church with the sanctification of the individual.[50]

Early in his career, Augustine in an exposition of 1 John 3:23 declared that the signs were adapted to the times:

> In the earliest times, "the Holy Ghost fell upon them that believed: and they spake with tongues," which they had not learned, "as the Spirit gave them utterance." These were signs adapted to the time. For there behooved to be that betokening of the Holy Spirit in all tongues, to shew that the Gospel of God was to run through all tongues over the whole earth. That thing was done for a betokening, and it passed away. In the laying on of hands now, that persons may receive the Holy Ghost, do we look that they should speak with tongues? Or when we laid the hand on these infants, did each one of you look to see whether they would speak with tongues, and, when he saw that they did not speak with tongues, was any of you so wrong-minded as to say. These have not received the Holy Ghost: for, had they received, they would speak with tongues as was the case in those times? If then the witness of the presence of the Holy Ghost be not now given through these miracles, but what is it given, by what does one get to know that he has received the Holy Ghost? Let him question his own heart.[51]

Here, Augustine offered a new interpretation of the significance of tongues. He contended that speaking in tongues of the day of Pentecost had been a sign "adapted to the time" which had vanished. Thus, the initial appearance of tongues at Pentecost was to "show that the Gospel of God was to run through all tongues over the earth." Tongues at Pentecost was historical and it simply demonstrated the universal nature of the gospel. Now the church, not individuals, spoke in tongues, for Christian communities existed throughout

---

49. Eusebius, *Commentary on Isaiah*, 6.2.
50. Heron, *Holy Spirit*, 87–98. See Augustine, *Trinity* (*NPNF* 1/2:490).
51. Augustine, *Tractates on the First Epistle of John* 6.10 (*NPNF* 1/7:497).

the known world, and the church spoke in the tongues of its diverse members. Also, when attacking the Donatists, Augustine stated:

> For the Holy Spirit is not only given by the laying on of hands amid the testimony of temporal sensible miracles, as He was given in former days to be the credentials of a rudimentary faith, and for the extension of the first beginnings of the Church. For who expects in these days that those on whom hands are laid that they might receive the Holy Spirit should forthwith begin to speak with tongues.[52]

According to this passage, miracles in the days of the apostles were simply "the credentials of a rudimentary faith." The miraculous was necessary in that it served to confirm the faith of the young church and to advance the gospel she preached. Especially for those who argued against the continuation of *charismata* after the times of the apostles, this passage serves to prove that, by the time of Augustine, there was no evidence of the gift of tongue-speaking in the Western church.[53]

> The testimony of Augustine . . . on this matter is extremely significant. For although rightly considered doctors of the church, they were no ivory-tower seminary professors. They were, on the contrary, active bishops and popular preachers on the front lines of the Lord's armies, in close contact with the current thought and practice of clergy and laity. So here we may rely on the authority of . . . Augustine with respect to the Western church.[54]

Despite such a negative view of the charismatic gifts and its manifestations, Augustine seemed to show greater acceptance when he wrote *The City of God* (413–426). In it, he detailed the miracles which were occurring in his day. There was a strong personal element implicit in these reports, since they happened in his church in Hippo. "For even now miracles are wrought in the name of Christ, whether by His sacraments or by the prayers or relics of His saints."[55]

Then in the same chapter, Augustine listed one miracle after another, from the healing of the blind, the exorcism of demons to the raising of the dead, as common events in his day. Moreover, he recognized the sovereign

---

52. Augustine, *Baptism; Against the Donatists* 3.16.21 (*NPNF* 1/4:443).

53. Hoekema, *What about Tongue Speaking?*, 17; Gromacki, *Modern Tongues Movement*, 17; Kelsey, *Tongue Speaking*, 40–41.

54. Judisch, *Evaluation of Claims*, 78–79.

55. Augustine, *Basic Writings*, 2:432. *City of God*, Book 22, chapter 8.

pleasure of God in these miracles. "Even now, therefore, many miracles are wrought, the same God who wrought those we read of still performing them, by whom He will and as He will."[56]

Also, Augustine declares,

> For we cannot listen to those who maintain that the invisible God works no visible miracles . . . God who made the visible heaven and earth, does not disdain to work visible miracles in heaven or earth, that He may thereby awaken the soul which is immersed in things visible to worship Himself, the Invisible.[57]

Augustine's negative assessment of the gift of tongues might be a reaction to its misuse in his day, however, it should be tempered with his later writings and his positive report of the miraculous in his church. Moreover, the larger question of the decline of the use of the *charismata* as shown in the writings of third and fourth century Fathers should be considered in light of an important shift in the religious intentionality of early Christianity.[58]

Conclusion

After sampling some of the early church fathers' writings on the *charismata*, there is little room to doubt that it is the general consensus of the church fathers that God intends to build up His church by means of the *charismata* of the Holy Spirit. Some of the Fathers were honest enough to acknowledge that the spiritual gifts were no longer manifested universally in the Church. However, none condemned them as being of demonic in origin or that the *charismata* belonged only to the apostolic church and were thereafter withdrawn. It is unquestionable that these Fathers were faithful and obedient to the word of God. The theology of these early church fathers was distinctly Spirit-centered, Charismatic, and Pentecostal.

If presuppositionless theology has been proven to be impossible, the same must be true of historical investigation. Thus, the point is that one's inquiry must be made independently of this influence. It is praise worthy that both Pentecostal-Charismatic and Non-Pentecostal-Charismatic take seriously the ramification of the historical data presented. For the non-Pentecostal-Charismatic argues that the historical date is insignificant:

---

56. Augustine, *City of God* 22.8 (*NPNF* 1/2:490).
57. Augustine, *City of God* 10.12 (*NPNF* 1/2:188–89).
58. Campbell, "Charismata," 17–19. Kydd, *Charismatic Gifts*, 87.

The history of the church, then reinforces the deduction we have drawn from Scripture, that the gifts of prophecy speaking in tongues, and performing miracles passed away with the apostles.[59]

Therefore, based on the above citations, any postapostolic continuation of spiritual gifts is of dubious credibility. On the other hand, the Pentecostal-Charismatic may read too much into the historical record to support their doctrine of Spirit-baptism. Indeed, one's theological commitments often prove to hamper objective analysis and color the reading of church history. Whatever one's theological commitment may be, one has to contend with the cumulative effect of the foregoing material which demonstrates that spiritual gifts did continue in the postapostolic church.

Bibliography

Augustine. *Basic Writings of Saint Augustine*. Edited by Whitney J. Oates. 2 vols. Grand Rapids: Baker, 1948.

Berding, Kenneth. "'Gifts' and Ministries in the Apostolic Fathers." *The Westminster Theological Journal* 78 (2016) 135–58.

Blumhofer, Edith L. *Assemblies of God: A Chapter in the Story of American Pentecostalism*. 2 vols. Springfield, MO: Gospel, 1989.

Budgen, Victor. *The Charismatics and the Word of God*. 2nd ed. Durham, UK: Evangelical, 1989.

Burns, J. Patout, and Gerald M. Fagin. *The Holy Spirit*. Wilmington, DE: Michael Glazier, 1984.

Campbell, Ted A. "Charismata in the Christian Communities of the Second Century." *Wesleyan Theological Journal* 17 (1982) 7–25.

Cross, Frank L., ed. *The Oxford Dictionary of the Christian Church*. Oxford: Oxford University Press, 1983.

Dayton, Donald W. *Theological Roots of Pentecostalism*. Grand Rapids: Baker Academic, 1987.

Deere, Jack. *Surprised by the Power of the Spirit*. Grand Rapids: Zondervan, 1993.

Edgar, Thomas R. "The Cessation of the Sign Gifts." *Bibliotheca Sacra* 145 (1988) 371–86.

Eusebius. *The History of the Church from Christ to Constantine*. Translated by Geoffrey Arthur Williamson. Minneapolis: Augsburg, 1965.

Gromacki, Robert Glenn. *The Modern Tongues Movement*. Grand Rapids: Baker, 1974.

Heron, Alasdair. *The Holy Spirit*. Philadelphia: Westminster, 1983.

Hinson, E. Glenn. "The Significance of Glossolalia in the History of Christianity." In *Speaking in Tongues: A Guide to Research on Glossolalia*, edited by Watson E. Mills, 181–204. Grand Rapids: Eerdmans, 1986.

Hoekema, Anthony. *What about Tongue Speaking?* Grand Rapids: Eerdmans, 1966.

---

59. Judisch, *Evaluation of Claims*, 81. Hoekema, *What about Tongue Speaking?*, 23. See also Gromacki, *Modern Tongues Movement*, 17–18.

Hunter, Harold D. "Tongues-Speech: A Patristic Analysis." *Journal of the Evangelical Theological Society* 23 (1980) 125–37.

Judisch, Douglas. *An Evaluation of Claims to the Charismatic Gifts*. Grand Rapids: Baker, 1978.

Kelsey, Morton T. *Tongue Speaking: An Experiment in Spiritual Experience*. Garden City, NY: Doubleday, 1968.

Kydd, Ronald. *Charismatic Gifts in the Early Church*. Peabody, MA: Hendrickson, 1984.

MacArthur, John. *Charismatic Chaos*. Grand Rapids: Zondervan, 1992.

Maier, Harry O. *The Social Setting of the Ministry as Reflected in the Writings of Hermas, Clement and Ignatius*. Waterloo, ON: Wilfrid Laurier University, 1991.

Mallone, George. "Tidy Doctrine and Truncated Experience." In *Those Controversial Gifts: Prophecy, Dreams, Visions, Tongues, Interpretation, Healing*, edited by George Mallone, 13–29. Downers Grove, IL: InterVarsity, 1988.

Marshall, I. Howard. "The Holy Spirit in the Pastoral Epistles and the Apostolic Fathers." In *The Holy Spirit and Christian Origins: Essays in Honor of James D. G. Dunn*, edited by Stephen C. Barton et al., 257–69. Grand Rapids: Eerdmans, 2004.

Masters, Peter. *The Healing Epidemic*. London: Wakeman Trust, 1988.

Menzies, William W. "The Holy Spirit in Christian Theology." In *Perspectives on Evangelical Theology*, edited by Kenneth S. Kantzer and Stanley N. Gundry, 67–79. Grand Rapids: Baker, 1979.

Miłosz, Czesław. *New and Collected Poems 1931–2001*. New York: HarperCollins, 2003.

Minns, Denis. *Irenaeus: An Introduction*. London: T. & T. Clark, 2010.

Quasten, Johannes. *Patrology*. Vol. 1, *The Beginnings of Patristic Literature*. 4 vols. Westminster, MD: Newman, 1983.

Radant, Kenneth G. "Are Our 'Lifekeys' the Right 'SHAPE' for Our 'Network'? Recent Trends in Spiritual Gift Teaching." Paper read at the annual meeting of the Evangelical Theological Society, Washington, DC, 2006.

Richardson, Cyril C., ed. and trans. *Early Christian Fathers*. Library of Christian Classics 1. Philadelphia: Westminster, 1953.

Robeck, Cecil M. "Irenaeus and 'Prophetic Gifts.'" In *Essays on Apostolic Themes: Studies in Honor of Howard M. Ervin*, edited by Paul Elbert, 104–14. Peabody, MA: Hendrickson, 1985.

Rusch, William G. "The Doctrine of the Holy Spirit in the Patristic and Medieval Church." In *The Holy Spirit in the Life of the Church*, edited by Paul D. Opsahl, 66–98. Minneapolis: Augsburg, 1978.

Ruthven, Jon. "On the Cessation of the Charismata: The Protestant Polemic of Benjamin B. Warfield." *Pneuma* 12 (1990) 14–31.

A Select Library of Nicene and Post-Nicene Fathers of the Christian Church. Edited by Philip Schaff and Henry Wace. 28 vols. in 2 series. 1886–89. Reprint, Peabody, MA: Hendrickson, 1994.

Stanton, Graham. "The Spirit in the Writings of Justin Martyr." In *The Holy Spirit and Christian Origins: Essays in Honor of James D. G. Dunn*, edited by Graham Stanton et al., 321–34. Grand Rapids: Eerdmans, 2004.

Ward, Horace S. "The Anti-Pentecostal Argument." In *Aspects of Pentecostal-Charismatic Origins*, edited by Vinson Synan, 99–122. Plainfield, NJ: Logos International, 1975.

Warfield, Benjamin B. *Counterfeit Miracles*. 1918. Reprint, London: Banner of Truth, 1972.

Williams, George H., and Edith Waldvogel. "A History of Speaking in Tongues and Related Gifts." In *The Charismatic Movement*, edited by Michael P. Hamilton, 67–71. Grand Rapids: Eerdmans, 1975.

Williams, J. Rodman. *Renewal Theology: God, the World & Redemption*. Grand Rapids: Zondervan, 1990.

5

Montanism

Precursor of the Contemporary Charismatic Movement?
Feminist Aspirations?

ESTHER YUE L. NG

Introduction

TO MANY CONTEMPORARY CHRISTIANS, the term Montanism sounds unfamiliar, and they may well doubt the value of devoting time and effort to treat it in a collection of essays on the Holy Spirit. However, a self-professed "life-long Pentecostal" and Professor of Church History has written that "Montanism can be viewed as an instructive proto-type of the modern Pentecostal and Charismatic movements complete with their prophetic claims, words, challenges, actions, discernment, and backlash."[1] This evaluation is shared to a certain extent even by Chinese scholars with no charismatic inclinations. Thus the Chinese church historian Wing-Hung Lam prefaced his discussion of Montanism by describing it as "a charismatic movement that arose within the traditional church during the second century."[2] In view of the rapid proliferation of Pentecostal and Charismatic

---

1. Robeck, "Montanism and Present Day 'Prophets'," 413–29. Thus, also, Stanley M. Burgess calls Tertullian "the Church's first important Pentecostal theologian," and F. Dale Bruner traces the ancestral line of the Pentecostal Movement through the Montanists (cited in Thiselton, *Holy Spirit*, 182–83, 311, respectively).

2. Lam, *Christian Theology in Development*, 65. (The work is in Chinese; English

churches worldwide, it would be instructive to see what lessons we can learn from the movement and history of Montanism even now.

Furthermore, several female prophets played a key role in the Montanist movement. One of them even claimed that Christ appeared to her in the form of a woman and gave her an important revelation. For this reason, many feminists today attach great significance to Montanism and claim that it elevates the status of women.[3] Is this view justified? Is a charismatic view of spiritual gifts always conducive to the advancement of women's standing? This too will be explored in this chapter.

In the following, we will give a historical overview of the origin of Montanism and trace the reasons adduced by the orthodox church to reject this movement, especially in its early stage. We will then outline the diverse views of present-day scholars regarding the interaction of Montanism with the early orthodox church, followed by an analysis of the strengths and weaknesses of such views and their underlying presuppositions. Finally we will attempt to draw lessons from past history.

The Rise and Decline of Montanism

Historical Sources

Since the documents and writings stemming from the founders of Montanism are no longer extant, our knowledge of the movement comes primarily from authors of the early catholic church, such as Eusebius (c. 265–339 AD; see *Ecclesiastical History*, 4–5) and Epiphanius (315–403 AD; see *Panarion* 48). As they basically wrote against Montanism in the fourth century over one and a half centuries after the rise of its founder Montanus (in mid-second century), their portrayal of Montanism has been viewed by some modern scholars as untrustworthy, having employed inaccurate sources and being biased in their outlook.[4] However, no matter whether Eusebius and Epiphanius were careful to check their sources, scholars generally agree that these two fathers cited works of their predecessors,[5] and there

---

translation of the text by the present author.)

3. See, e.g., Huber, "Women and the Authority of Inspiration," 89; Schüssler Fiorenza, *In Memory of Her*, 300–1. Likewise, speaking of Montanism's emancipatory attitude towards women, see Peter Lampe in Tabbernee and Lampe, *Pepouza and Tymion*, 133.

4. Thus, Bauer, *Orthodoxy and Heresy*, 134, 137; Aune, *Prophecy in Early Christianity*, 313; Huber, "Women and the Authority of Inspiration," 48–49, 52–56.

5. Thus Eusebius (*Ecclesiastical History*, hereafter *EH*) cited the works of an anonymous person (5.16–17), Apollonius (5.18), and Serapion (5.19). He also mentioned writings by Claudius Apollinaris (4.27), Miltiades (5.17.1), Rhodo (5.13), and Gaius

is historical value in their writings. In addition, apart from Eusebius and Epiphanius, other early church fathers have commented on Montanism in their writings. Some of them belonged to the second and third centuries (e.g., Clement of Alexandria, Origen, Hippolytus, Firmilian of Caesarea), while others came from the fourth and fifth centuries (e.g., Jerome, Theodoret, Basil of Caesarea, Augustine). Furthermore, the famous church father Tertullian of Carthage (c. 160–220 AD) later espoused Montanism, and his works defending its tenets and practices have survived till now. Moreover, there exist inscriptions which may shed further light on historical Montanism. Therefore, with sufficient caution and critical judgement, it still seems feasible to depict the history and characteristics of Montanism with some measure of objectivity.

Origin and Decline

According to the anonymous writer cited by Eusebius, as a recent convert to the Christian faith, Montanus came from the village of Ardabav[6] in Phrygia around 170 AD.[7] Some fourth century writers referred to him as a former priest of Apollo and stated that he was a castrated man.[8] Besides Montanus, two female prophets came into prominence, namely, Maximilla and Priscilla. As they originated from Phrygia, the church fathers antagonistic to them referred to their adherents as Phrygians or Cataphrygians. They, however, regarded themselves as advocates of the New Prophecy, claiming that the Paraclete (Holy Spirit) came to them with such power that they were constrained to utter prophecies. According to the account in Epiphanius,[9] either Priscilla or the later Quintilla claimed that once when she was asleep in Pepuza, Christ appeared to her in the form of a woman and told her that Jerusalem would one day descend in that holy place. Perhaps for this reason,

---

(6.20.3). See Heine, *Montanist Oracles and Testimonia* (cited hereafter as *MO*). For the anonymous source cited by Epiphanius, see *MO*, 29–51. See also Amidon, *Panarion of St. Epiphanius*, 170–72 (=*Panarion* 48.7.1–48.13.1).

6. Besides Eusebius, see also Theodoret, cited in *MO*, 169, #136.

7. Eusebius (*EH* 5.16.7) stated that Montanus arose when Gratus was the proconsul of the province of Asia. Epiphanius, on the other hand (*Panarion* 48.1.2), mentioned that Montanus came to prominence during the nineteenth year of the Roman emperor Antonius Pius, i.e., in the 50s of the second century. Contemporary scholars tend to accept the view of Eusebius, but others favor the dating by Epiphanius. For a detailed discussion of the dates, see Trevett, *Montanism*, 26–45.

8. *MO*, 123, #89, quoting *Debate of a Montanist and an Orthodox Christian*; Jerome, quoted in *MO*, 149, #106.

9. Epiphanius, *Panarion* 49.1; see *MO*, 5, #11.

they gave Pepuza (and the neighboring town Tymion) the name New Jerusalem, and asked followers to gather there.[10] In addition to such features, Montanists allegedly emphasized the value of martyrdom, promoted new fasts, ate only dry foods at certain times, and prohibited remarriage after the death of a spouse.[11] Their teaching spread rapidly not only to neighboring areas but also to Gaul, North Africa and Rome.

At the same time, opponents to the New Prophecy abound, and gave various reasons for doing so. In addition to objecting to their novel ascetic practices and stringent requirements, an early anonymous anti-Montanist author and Apollonius (cited by Eusebius) castigated them for their profligacy (collecting money and worldly living), and for their uncontrolled ecstasy and frenzied speech, finding such behavior contrary to biblical precedents of prophets, and even alleging that they were possessed by the devil, not by the Holy Spirit (see discussion below).

For whatever reason, many local church synods decided that the New Prophecy was a heresy to be cast out of the church. It is true that some believers in Gaul attempted to intervene and promote acceptance of the New Prophecy, writing a letter to the bishop of Rome in the process. It is also true that, for a while, the bishop of Rome was ready to accept the new prophets, and even sent out a conciliatory letter. However, according to Tertullian, with the coming of Praxeas from Asia to Rome rehashing the views of anti-Montanist predecessors, the bishop of Rome changed his mind, recalled his letter and rejected the prophets.[12] After the conversion of the Roman emperor Constantine to Christianity, he issued an edict that prohibited the meeting of Montanist believers.[13] Subsequently, the adherents of the New Prophecy became an illegal sect. In 550 AD, Bishop John of Ephesus confiscated the Montanist church building at Pepuza and burned the bones

---

10. Eusebius (*EH* 5.18.2) citing the work of Apollonius; see *MO*, 23, #24.

11. This can be readily seen from Tertullian's defense of Montanists; see his *Concerning Flight under Persecution* 9.4; *The Soul* 55.5 (*MO*, 7, #14: on martyrdom); *On Fasting* 1 (*MO*, 83, #57: on new fasts); *Monogamy* 14.3–7; 15.1–3 (*MO*, 81, 82, #55, 56: prohibition of second marriage). Some modern scholars (such as William Tabbernee) reject the charge of voluntary martyrdom. However, Polycarp knew of at least one Phrygian (likely Montanist) named Quintus who volunteered himself but later gave up martyrdom (see *MO*, 13, #20).

12. Tertullian, *Against Praxeas*, 1, in *MO*, 89, #63.

13. For reports of early councils, see *MO*, 17, #23 (Anonymous); *MO*, 103, #80 (letter by Firmilian of Caesarea); *MO*, 179, #147 (*Libellus Synodicus*). For the efforts by the church of Gaul, see Eusebius, *EH* 5.3.4 (*MO*, 13, #21). See also Tertullian, *Against Praxeas* 1 (*MO*, 89, #63). For the edict of Constantine, see Eusebius, *Life of Constantine* 3.64–66 (*MO*, 109, #84).

of Montanus, Maximilla and Priscilla there.[14] With this, Montanism either merged with the catholic church or vanished in history.

Various Contemporary Perspectives

The early catholic church generally judged Montanism to be a heresy or at least a schismatic movement, but modern-day scholars hold diverse views on the development of early Catholicism and are accordingly diverse in their assessment of this movement.

In the first place, though not necessarily agreeing entirely with the direction of the early catholic church, certain scholars are of the opinion that she was correct in the way she treated Montanism. Some of them agree that Montanism was indeed a theological heresy that deserved to be expunged. Others agree that Montanists were possibly charlatans. Still others regard them as being heavily influenced by pagan practices in Phrygia, thus deviating from traditional Christian praxis.[15]

Secondly, other scholars think it is understandable that the early catholic church rejected the extremism of Montanist praxis even though it did not amount to a heresy doctrinally, because it challenged the authority of the catholic church and was detrimental to her efforts to curb the onslaught of various heresies such as Marcionism and Gnosticism. Yet, from hindsight, these scholars see the rejection of the New Prophecy as "damaging and regrettable." Some would connect this rejection with the general decline of true prophecy in the church.[16]

Finally, according to many scholars, Montanism was a genuine spiritual movement, perceived either as a movement of renewal or of innovation. In the former case, it is generally held that, by the second century, the catholic church had lost the former vitality of the Spirit-infused life and became a fossilized and patriarchalized institution of monarchical bishops and subordinate clergy. Montanism arose in such a milieu in protest as a renewal movement that emphasized spontaneous spiritual gifts (such as prophetic utterances and visionary experiences), purity in life, an earnest longing for the return of Jesus Christ, and courageous martyrdom.

---

14. Trevett, *Montanism*, 231–32; Tabbernee, *Fake Prophecy and Polluted Sacraments*, 424.

15. Farnell, "Montanist Crisis," 235–62. Regarding Montanist prophets as being akin to wandering charlatans, see Schöllgen, "Der Niedergang des Prophetentums in der Alten Kirche," 97–116. For scholarly disputes about possible pagan influence on Montanism, see note 48 below.

16. See, for example, Wright, "Why Were the Montanists Condemned?," 15–22; Nestler, "Was Montanism a Heresy?," 67–78.

Moreover, Montanism permitted women to express their spiritual gifts freely, irrespective of their sex.[17] Somewhat in contrast to this view, after a career-long study of Montanism, William Tabbernee comes to the conclusion that Montanism "may tentatively be defined as an innovative prophetic movement intent on bringing Christianity into line with what it believed to be the ultimate revelation of the Spirit through the New Prophets."[18] No matter whether the movement was one of renewal or innovation, the early orthodox church fathers found it intolerable and sharply attacked Montanism, possibly resorting to rhetorical exaggeration and even character assassination at times.[19]

From our brief account here, it is evident that we need to explore further the historical development of church institution, women's participation in ministry, and the manifestation of charismatic gifts before we can fully answer the questions posed in the title of this chapter: Was Montanism a "charismatic movement" in the early church and a fulfillment of feminist aspirations?

A Critique of the Various Positions and Historical Lessons

1. Development of Church Institution in the Early Church

To many scholars (Protestants in particular), during the apostolic era, the gifts of the Holy Spirit (including prophecy and glossolalia [speaking in tongues]) came upon believers in general, and there were no fixed office-bearing leaders; owing to the delay of the Parousia (Jesus' second coming), by the second century the charismatic gifts and dynamism that characterized the early days waned and faded, and the church became institutionalized and fossilized.[20]

However, more and more scholars rightly point out that churches in New Testament times already possessed structure and organization. Thus

---

17. Thus Aune, *Prophecy in Early Christianity*, 313; Trevett, *Montanism*, 195. However, she does recognize that Polycarp, Irenaeus, and the catholic martyrs cannot "be dismissed simply as bureaucrats of a worldly and institutionalised catholic Church" (*Montanism*, 148). See also next section and note 20.

18. Tabbernee, *Fake Prophecy and Polluted Sacraments*, 424.

19. See Bauer, *Orthodoxy and Heresy*, 145; Huber, "Women and the Authority of Inspiration," 39, 54.

20. See especially Käsemann, "Ministry and Community," 63-94; Banks, "From Fellowship to Organization," 79-89.

the church of Philippi had overseers and deacons (Phil 1:1), and other churches established by Paul likewise.[21] In fact, spiritual gifts may very well co-exist with fixed offices of ministry, just as there were prophets associated with the temple in Old Testament times.[22]

In addition, even in the movement that emphasized the work of the Paraclete and the age of the New Prophecy, there certainly existed a rank of leaders. Early in the movement, besides the prophets Montanus, Maximilla and Priscilla, there was an administrator (ἐπίτροπος), the first one being named Theodotus.[23] After Tertullian espoused the New Prophecy, he did not repudiate the institution of bishops and deacons in the catholic church.[24] In fact by the fourth century, Montanist churches may have even surpassed the catholic church in their tiers of leadership, including Patriarch, κοινωνός (companion/partner), bishop, and deacon.[25] Judging from these titles, it seems wrong and simplistic to claim that Montanism arose as a protest movement against the institutionized hierarchy of the catholic church.

2. Women's Status

If institutional hierarchy was not the bone of contention, what about the dispute over women? Was Montanism such an advocate of women leadership that caused a backlash in the early catholic church intent on curbing this movement by attacking its female prophets?

On first blush, this seems a reasonable view. In fact, according to certain scholars, the main prophetic oracles from Montanism passed on in history were attributed to Maximilla and Priscilla. These women were therefore the real leaders while Montanus was just responsible for the execution and administration of the Montanist church. Furthermore, both the anonymous writer and Apollonius cited by Eusebius castigated the female prophets and claimed that certain individuals of the catholic church attempted several times to exorcise the evil spirit within Maximilla but were thwarted by her supporters. Thus the female prophets rather than Montanus bore the brunt

---

21. Thus, Campbell, *Elders*, 16–17; Nardoni, "Charism in the Early Church," 646–62.

22. Forbes, *Prophecy and Inspired Speech*, 250; Fung, "Ministry in the New Testament," 154–212 (especially 163–77).

23. Anonymous, in Eusebius, *EH* 5.16.14 (*MO*, 19, #23).

24. Mattei, "Regards inactuels sur une Église en mutation," 275–87.

25. Jerome, "Epistle to Marcella," 41:3 (*MO*, p. 151, #106). For three inscriptions of the deceased Christian men bearing the title of κοινωνός , see Tabbernee, *Montanist Inscriptions and Testimonia* (hereafter cited as *MIT*), 491, 510, 514 (# 80, 84, and 85, respectively).

of attacks from church leaders.[26] Moreover, adherents of Montanism indeed appealed to Galatians 3:28, 1 Corinthians 11:5 as well as the historical succession of female prophets in support of Montanist women uttering prophecies and serving as overseers and elders.[27]

Nevertheless, on further analysis this view appears one-sided. First of all, as noted by Christine Trevett, oracles of Montanus also survived, and primary sources about this movement generally refer to Montanus as the founder of the movement. Besides, such sources likewise attacked the greed and deception of the male leaders within Montanism (including Montanus, Themiso, Alexander), and reported of attempts by leaders of the catholic church to expel the unclean spirit residing in Montanus.[28] In addition, the church fathers did not reject the movement merely on account of the sex of the female prophets. In fact, the apostolic fathers highly respected the contribution of women in their midst (see, for instance, Grapte in Hermas; Alsace and Tavia in Ignatius's epistles).[29] According to Origen, Didymus and the Anonymous Orthodox (fourth century), there were female prophets also in the catholic church (e.g., the four daughters of Philip, and the extra-biblical Ammia), but they would not speak out publicly in assemblies.[30] Judging from such statements, the problem with Montanism was not that they venerated female prophets but that their ways contravened biblical teaching and traditional praxis.

Furthermore, after Tertullian accepted the New Prophecy, even though he regarded the prophecies of Maximilla and Priscilla as sayings of the Paraclete, he apparently did not accept women taking on clerical roles. In addition, according to him, there was a woman in his church who regularly saw visions during worship services and would afterwards share her visions with some church leaders (including Tertullian himself) for them to evaluate whether such visions were genuine and acceptable.[31] Judging from such descriptions, at least in the Montanist circle to which Tertullian

26. Jensen, *God's Self-Confident Daughters*, 167.

27. *Debate of a Montanist and an Orthodox Christian* (*MO*, 125, #89); Epiphanius, *Panarion* 49.2-3 (*MO*, 133-35, # 94). Thus in Trevett's opinion (*Montanism*, 195), Montanism regarded the fulfillment of Joel 2:28-29 as the rationale for women assuming various roles.

28. Trevett, *Montanism*, 160-61.

29. Hermas, Visions 2.4.3. See a discussion in Gryson, *Ministry of Women in the Early Church*, 14; Ignatius, *Letter to Polycarp* 8:2.

30. Origen, *Catenae on Paul's Epistles to the Corinthians* 14.36 (*MO*, 99, #77); Didymus, *On the Trinity*, 3.41.3 (*MO*, 145-47); *Debate of a Montanist and an Orthodox Christian* (*MO*, 125, #89).

31. Tertullian, *On the Soul*, 9.4 (*MO*, 71, #41); Gryson, *Ministry of Women in the Early Church*, 19.

belonged in Carthage, being a female prophet did not imply membership in the leadership structure of the church. As for ordinary female believers in Montanist churches, their status might have been analogous to their counterparts in catholic churches and likewise less than the standing of male believers.[32] In fact, according to the analysis of some scholars, when Tertullian wrote the treatise requiring virgins (not just married women) to wear veils in church assemblies, he already espoused Montanism.[33] To be sure, it has been argued with some plausibility that the Montanism which existed in North Africa was a modified version, or Tertullian played a significant role in shaping it.[34] Nevertheless, the Montanist situation in Carthage at least shows that the prominence of women leadership in roles other than as prophetesses was not integral to the movement.

3. Prophetic Speech/Oracles

1) Spiritual Gifts in the Early Church

As mentioned in the above discussion on the institutionalization of the early church, modern scholars often allege that vibrant gifts of the Holy Spirit declined in the second century church such that Montanus started a protest movement. However, this view too is problematic.

Actually, if we turn to the writings of the apostolic fathers, we discover the following: Ignatius claimed that he knew of the mistakes of the schismatics as revealed to him by the Spirit, Hermas recorded visions and divine oracles; the Didache presupposed itinerant prophets. Later, Irenaeus claimed that believers still uttered prophecies and saw visions as inspired by the Spirit. In Carthage, visions and prophecies persisted even in the time of Cyprian the bishop of Carthage (c. 200–258 AD).[35] Even when leaders

---

32. Trevett, *Montanism*, 197. However, it seems female martyrs for Christ during persecutions (such as Perpetua and Felicitia) enjoyed esteem that surpassed that of male clergy. See Jensen, *God's Self-Confident Daughters*, 115; Tabbernee, "Perpetua, Montanism and Christian Ministry," 421–41 (433–34).

33. See Dunn, "Rhetoric and Tertullian's *De Virginibus Velandis*," 1–30 (25–29); Gryson, *Ministry of Women in the Early Church*, 19.

34. Thus, Powell, "Tertullianists and Cataphrygians," 139–53; Trevett, *Montanism*, 75; Alexander and Smither, "Bauer's Forgotten Region," 178–79. In any case, while Tertullian was reproached for his alignment with the New Prophecy on some matters, he was still highly respected in the catholic church. Tertullian later dissociated himself from the Cataphrygians, and started his own congregations, but these Tertullianists were later won over by Augustine; see Praedestinatus 1.26, 86 (*MO*, 171, #137; 173–74, #138); Augustine, *Heresies*, 86 (*MO*, 165, #129).

35. Ignatius, *To the Philadelphians* 7; Hermas, "Mandates 11"; *Didache* 13:1;

of the catholic church opposed the New Prophecy, they presupposed the reality of spiritual gifts. Thus the anonymous writer quoted by Eusebius stated that "the apostle is of the opinion that the prophetic gift must be in the whole church until the final coming [of Jesus]." Likewise, Origen's rebuttal of the validity of Montanist prophetesses assumed the continued existence of prophets and prophetesses.[36]

As for the gift of glossolalia, a statement from Chrysostom hints that it had disappeared by the fourth century. However, the words of Irenaeus clearly indicate that believers could speak in tongues in the second and third centuries.[37] If Mark 16:9–21 is a later addition from the second century (as most textual critics believe), then verse 17 seems to reflect the persistence of charismatic phenomena at that time: "And these signs will accompany those who believe: In my name they will drive out demons; they will speak in new tongues." (NIV)

Furthermore, to explain the earlier reception of Montanist writings by many Christians, Eusebius wrote, "for the many other wonders of the divine charisma still being accomplished up to that time in various churches caused many to believe that those men [Montanus, Alcibiades and Theodotus] also prophesied."[38]

Judging from such data, it is evident that "extraordinary" spiritual gifts did not cease in the second century; nor were they confined to church leaders and barred from "lay Christians."[39]

2) The Manner of Prophetic Utterance

According to the writings of church fathers (such as Miltiades, the Anonymous, Epiphanius, Didymus) and Tertullian's later treatises, the catholic church objected to the manner in which Montanus and his followers delivered prophetic speech. To the orthodox writers, biblical prophets were fully conscious and self-controlled when they delivered their prophecies, whereas Montanist "prophets" were in the grips of frenzied, uncontrollable,

---

Irenaeus, *Against Heresies* 5.6.1. For other examples, see Forbes, *Prophecy and Inspired Speech*, 247n63. For the situation in North Africa, see Robeck, *Prophecy in Carthage*, especially 204–5.

36. The Anonymous, see *EH* 5.17.4 (*MO*, 21, #23); Origen (see n. 30).

37. Chrysostom, *Homilies on 1 Cor. No.* 29; for a discussion on this, see Forbes, *Prophecy and Inspired Speech*, 83.

38. *EH* 5.3.4 (*MO*, 13, #21).

39. Schöllgen, "Der Niedergang des Prophetentums in der Alten Kirche," 100, against the view of Ash, "Decline of Ecstatic Prophecy," 227–52.

extraordinary ecstasy (παρεκστάσις), babbling and uttering strange things.⁴⁰ As for the Montanist protagonists, they countered such arguments by citing biblical passages which mention ἐκστάσις or similar terms to prove that Peter too didn't know what he was saying as he witnessed Christ's transfiguration and the presence of Moses and Elijah (Luke 9:33); later Peter was likewise out of his senses when he fell into a trance.⁴¹

Some contemporary scholars tend to accept the Montanist rebuttal that there were biblical precedents of ecstasy being "out of the senses" and so judge the orthodox heresiologists to have lost the argument.⁴² However, it is noteworthy that the early church fathers were careful to distinguish the various meanings of the word ἐκστάσις: excessive amazement (as when Peter saw Moses and Elijah appearing on the Mount of Transfiguration), madness (such as the state of Montanist prophets), temporary unconsciousness in sleep (as in the case of Adam when God created Eve from his side). These church fathers pointed out that in none of the biblical precedents cited by Montanists were the persons involved in a frenzied state. To the contrary, these and many other biblical precedents show that even when these persons saw visions, their mind and reason were under control and they were aware of their surroundings.⁴³ To be sure, the church fathers did not mention the case of pre-classical prophets and their disciples: when they were inspired and spoke by the Spirit, they seemed unaware of their surroundings (see 1 Sam 19:19–24). Nevertheless, it remains true that when the vast majority of biblical prophets delivered their prophecies, they were self-controlled, and Paul certainly stated that "the spirits of prophets are subject to the control of prophets. For God is not a God of disorder but of peace." (1 Cor 14:32–33)⁴⁴

---

40. Eusebius, *EH* 5.17.1 (Miltiades); 5.16.7, 5.17.2 (Anonymous); see *MO*, 15, 21, #23; Epiphanius, *Panarion* 48.1.3–48.7.8 (*MO*, 31–39, #26); Didymus, "Fragments from the Exposition of Didymus on the Acts of the Apostles 10.10"; *MO*, 147, #104. Some modern scholars have argued that the babbling of Montanist prophets mentioned by the church fathers may have been instances of glossolalia; see Latourette, *History of Christianity*, 1:128; Kydd, *Charismatic Gifts*, 33–34; Palma, cited by Nestler, "Was Montanism a Heresy?," 69. However, there is insufficient basis to claim the Montanists engaged in glossolalia. See Forbes, *Prophecy and Inspired Speech*, 160–61, and further discussion on note 47 in this chapter.

41. Tertullian, "Against Marcion" 4.22, (*MO*, 69, #40).

42. Wright, "Why Were the Montanists Condemned?," 16–17.

43. Epiphanius, *Panarion* 48.1.4 (4), in *MO*, 35. For a similar list of meanings of the word ἐκστάσις, see Didymus, "Fragments from Exposition on Acts of the Apostles 10.10" (cited in *MO*, 147, #104): the trance caused by wonder, the state of being outside the senses being led to spiritual things, and to be deranged.

44. Thiselton, *First Epistle to the Corinthians*, 1143–45; Fee, *God's Empowering Presence*, 250; Kydd, *Charismatic Gifts*, 33–34; Garland, *1 Corinthians*, 661–62.

To prove that Montanist prophecy was unbiblical and so spurious, Epiphanius cited the following oracle from Montanus: "Behold, man is like a lyre, and I flit about like a plectron; man sleeps, and I awaken him; behold, it is the Lord who changes the hearts of men and gives men a heart." According to Epiphanius, Maximilla also said, "I am compelled to come to understand the knowledge of God whether I want to or not."[45]

To certain contemporary scholars, such sayings merely emphasized God's sovereignty in inspiring prophecy in contrast to human passivity and are therefore unobjectionable. Indeed, on the basis of these two isolated sayings, one cannot forthrightly decide whether Montanist prophecy was contrary to the manner in which the Holy Spirit inspired biblical prophets. Nevertheless, the source cited by Epiphanius also described Montanus "who undertakes things that are frightening (τὰ δεινὰ μεταχεριζόμενος), and often abuses himself and those near him in a frightening manner (δεινῶς χρώμενος). For he is ignorant of what he utters and does, since such a man has fallen into an ecstasy of folly (ἐκστάσις ἀφροσύνης)."[46] From this description, it seems likely that when Montanus entered a state of frenzy, not only were his words strange, but his motions were so violent that he himself and people nearby were physically endangered. This behavior then differed from the manner in which biblical prophets (including prophets mentioned in 1 Sam 19:19–24) spoke when inspired by the Spirit. In view of the violent motions, the unintelligible speech can hardly be equated with the biblical phenomenon of glossolalia, contrary to the view of some modern scholars.[47] In fact, such frenzied behavior resembled spirit possession in the mystery cult of Dionysius, while the intelligible sayings attributed to the Montanist prophets are comparable to the oracles of Delphi.[48] If Montanus was indeed

---

45. See *Panarion* 48.4.1 and 48.13.1, cited in *MO*, 3, #3; *MO*, 4, #8.

46. *Panarion* 48.5.8, cited in *MO*, 37, #26.

47. William Tabbernee regards the ὑποκριται, who objected to orthodox attempts to exorcise Maximilla (Eusebius, *EH* 5.19.3; *MO*, 27, #25) as interpreters of glossolalia legitimating her speech (*Fake Prophecy and Polluted Sacraments*, 95–96). While it is true the word ὑποκριται occasionally bore the meaning of "interpreters" (of visions and speech), there is no indication whatsoever in the context to suggest such a meaning. Rather, similar to Irenaeus's usage of *in hypocrisi* (*Against Heresies* 3.11.12, cited in *MO*, 53, #27), the word should be translated "hypocrites."

48. For a description of Hellenistic religions, see Forbes, *Prophecy and Inspired Speech*, 146–47. For a discussion on Eusebius, *EH* 5.16.9(ἐκφρονως ἀκαίρως ἀλλοτρίπως), see Forbes, *Prophecy and Inspired Speech*, 161. See also Aune, *Prophecy in Early Christianity*, 19–22, 33–34. For a vivid account of frenzied ecstatic behavior typical of wandering prophets and priests, see Schölligen, "Der Niedergang des Prophetentums in der Alten Kirche," 113.

a former priest of Apollo and castrated (devotee of Cybele) as alleged by catholic fathers, such behavior may be understandable.[49]

3) The Content of Prophetic Speech

According to some church fathers, Montanism should be rejected because certain prophecies made by Maximilla were never fulfilled. Thus Eusebius cited the anonymous author that she had prophesied of the coming of wars and anarchy, but there were no general or local wars in the 13 years since her death; even Christians enjoyed peace. Epiphanius, on his part, noted that Maximilla had declared, "After me there will no longer be a prophet, but the end." Yet 290 years had elapsed since then with kings coming and going, and the world persisted.[50] The nonfulfillment of prophecy was, therefore, one reason why the catholic church regarded Maximilla as a false prophet.[51] Nevertheless, it is noteworthy that the argument of nonfulfillment of prophecy played a minor role in the numerous charges against Montanism.

More often, the church fathers decried the content of Montanist prophecies (as with the manner of utterance) as at variance with the consistent teaching of the Scriptures. For instance, with regard to Maximilla's prophecy that no prophet would succeed her, the anonymous author cited by Eusebius stated that "the apostle [Paul] is of the opinion that the prophetic gift must be in the whole Church until the final coming" (cf. Eph

---

49. Scholars differ widely on the issue whether Montanus was impacted by pagan influences. Some are of the opinion he inherited the orthodox theological tradition of the Apocalypse of John and the writings of Ignatius; see, e.g., Trevett, "Apocalypse, Ignatius, Montanism," 313–38. Similarly, William Tabbernee denied pagan influence in the early period of Montanism; see *Fake Prophecy and Polluted Sacraments*, 122–23. Others accept the portrayal of the church fathers and are convinced of his pagan background (cult of Apollo); thus Daunton-Fear, cited in Stewart-Sykes, "Original Condemnation of Asian Montanism," 10n53; also Hirschmann, *Horrenda Secta*; Tabbernee and Lampe, *Pepouza and Tymion*, 144.

50. Eusebius, *EH* 5.16.19; Epiphanius, *Panarion* 48.2.4–7; see *MO*, 19, #23; 29–31, #26 respectively.

51. On the criterion of fulfillment of true prophecy, contemporary scholars debate whether the New Testament understanding differed from the Old Testament. According to Wayne Grudem, the fact that prophecy had to be evaluated and could be interrupted in 1 Cor 14 and 1 Thess 5:19–21 suggests revelations from NT prophets may err and do not necessarily imply absolute divine authority, as distinct from OT prophets. See his *Gift of Prophecy*, 75, 81–83, 145. Farnell ("Montanist Crisis"), however, sees in the orthodox attack on the nonfulfillment of Montanist prophecies an indication that the NT and the early church did not deviate from OT teaching on the testing of prophets.

4:11; 1 Cor 1:7; 13:8–12).[52] Besides, the catholic church cited the prophecy of Paul that "in the last days difficult times will arise, . . . [s]ome will depart from sound teaching, giving heed to erring (spirits) and teachings of demons, forbidding to marry and commanding to abstain from food which God created for us to receive with thanksgiving" (cf. 1 Tim 4:1, 3).[53] Related to this is the observation that Montanists evidently exalted the alleged new revelations conveyed to them by the Holy Spirit, claiming that they possessed the New Prophecy. According to the church fathers, Montanist followers even claimed that the prophecy they possessed surpassed the preaching of Jesus and the apostles, for Jesus had said that the Paraclete would teach certain truths which the apostles were unable to bear at that point of time.[54] In fact, the claim that the new Jerusalem would descend on Tymion-Pepousa was based, not on the Scriptures, but on a vision witnessed by Priscilla or Quintilla.

Thus the dispute between the catholic church and Montanism involved the question of the authenticity of prophetic oracles as well as the issue of salvation history. In other words, it dealt with the criteria for the discernment of divine revelation and with the course of progressive revelation. To the catholic church (as represented by Hippolytus), the Paraclete already came at Pentecost (and not for the first time in Montanus); the final revelation about Jesus Christ was complete with the writings by the apostles, and the Apocalypse written by the apostle John was the final piece of such writings; all writings subsequent to John could not possess the same authority. The canon and the rule of faith originating from the apostles constituted the norm to adjudicate between orthodoxy and heresy; the many writings by Montanist authors were to be evaluated by this norm as well.[55] According to this understanding, even if there was a need of genuine prophecy, it would not add anything new to the content of faith. If so, after Tertullian accepted the New Prophecy, how did he defend its novel views and practices?

Tertullian's method was to make a distinction between doctrine and practice. The former (as encapsulated by the Apostle's Creed) was unnegotiable and unalterable, while the latter (articles of discipline and life)

---

52. Eusebius, *EH* 5.17.4; see *MO*, 21, #23.

53. Epiphanius, *Panarion* 48.8. 6–8, 48.9.1–10 (*MO*, 39, 41, #26); Origen, *On First Principles* 2.7.3 (*MO*, 95, 97, #73).

54. See the rebuttal in Hippolytus, *Refutation of All Heresies* 8.19, (*MO*, 57, #32); Pseudo-Tertullian, *Against All Heresies* 7 (*MO*, 59, #34); Theodoret, *Compendium of Heretical Falsehoods* 3.1 (*MO*, 169, #136); Praedestinatus 1.26 (*MO*, 171, #137).

55. Hippolytus, *On Antichrist*, 47–48; see Lam, *Early Church*, 70. See also Hippolytus, *Refutation of All Heresies* 8.19 (*MO*, 57, #32). For another analysis of Hippolytus's view, see Williams, "Hippolytan Reactions to Montanism," 131–37.

admit new revisions gradually brought about by the Paraclete by God's grace.[56] Thus, just as Jesus removed the Mosaic concession to divorce, the Paraclete removed second marriage in the New Prophecy.[57] Tertullian further points out the Montanist practice of eating dry foods during two weeks a year (except for Sabbaths and Sundays) differs fundamentally from the heretics (such as Marcion and Tatian) who teach perpetual abstinence from certain foods; Montanists should not, therefore, fall under the condemnation in 1 Tim 4:3.[58]

Tertullian's defense of the New Prophecy's prohibition of second marriage and the practice of eating dry foods during prescribed times sounds persuasive. Nevertheless, is it really possible to maintain a clear-cut separation between doctrine and practice?[59] In fact, in Tertullian's writings, the new teaching of the Paraclete had encroached upon the sphere of doctrine. For example, Tertullian claimed that the New Prophecy "has predicted that an image of the city [of the New Jerusalem] will appear as a sign before the manifestation of its presence." He also recounted the vision of a Christian sister in which a soul was exhibited to her in bodily form. In the same treatise *On the Soul*, he mentioned how the martyr Perpetua saw only martyrs in her vision of Paradise, and how the Paraclete (through the New Prophecy) frequently taught that "the soul pays some penalty in Hades, without violation of the fullness of the resurrection through the flesh also." Moreover, according to the Paraclete, the blood of the martyrs "is the complete key of Paradise."[60] Such new teachings obviously did not merely pertain to discipline in daily living but belong to the doctrine of eschatology. It is true that the early church fathers did not attack such views but focused more on refuting the Montanist practice of extreme asceticism and its advocacy of voluntary martyrdom. However, they observed astutely that the Montanist acceptance and welcome of the new Prophecy (especially revelations that contradicted biblical teaching) were not based on solid principles and would certainly lead to abuse and grave errors.[61]

56. Tertullian, *The Veiling of Virgins* 1 (*MO*, 63, 65, #36).

57. Tertullian, *Monogamy* 14.3.7 (*MO*, 81, #55).

58. Tertullian, *Fasting* 15 (*MO*, 87, #62).

59. On the distinction between the two and its bearing on the definition of heresy, see Nestler, "Was Montanism a Heresy?," 75. Nester personally finds it difficult to separate the two.

60. See respectively Tertullian, *Against Marcion* 3.24; *On the Soul* 9.4; 55.4–5; 58.8 (*MO*, 69, #39); *MO*, 71, #41; *MO*, 71, #42; *MO*, 73, #43.

61. While it is generally acknowledged that Priscilla or Quintilla prophesied about the future descent of the New Jerusalem in Pepuza, Tertullian was silent on this point, either because he was unaware of it, or because he was not convinced of its veracity. On

Furthermore, some church fathers noted that certain sects of Montanism regarded the Father of the universe as also the Son, thus lapsing into the Modalistic Monarchianism of Noetians.[62] Probably related to this observation is an oracle attributed to Montanus stating that "Neither angel nor envoy, but I the Lord God the Father have come." Likewise Maximilla presumably said the following: "I am pursued like a wolf from the sheep. I am not a wolf. I am Lord, and spirit, and power"; "hear not me, but hear Christ."[63] To some contemporary scholars or persons in the charismatic movement, such a way of speaking in first person merely implies that the speaker regards himself as the mouthpiece of God and not as God himself. Thus the early church fathers should not have denounced Montanism on the basis of such oracles. However, no matter how Montanus and Maximilla regarded their relationship with God, their oracles probably created some misunderstanding in the hearers such as confusing the persons of the Trinity, and giving the impression to ignorant people that Montanus was God incarnate. In fact, the fourth century church father Basil alleged that the Pepuzans attributed the name Paraclete to Montanus and Priscilla, and that they were baptized into the Father and the Son and Montanus or Priscilla.[64] The information provided by Basil seems reliable, for a fourth century Christian inscription from Numidia said "Flavius Avus, the domestic (*domesticus*) has completed what he promised in the name of the Father, and of the Son, and of the lord Muntanus (an alternate spelling of Montanus)." Another inscription bore the following words: "By order of the blessed Muntanus, Purpurius has provided (this pillar) through the handiwork of Donatus."[65]

---

the other hand, Tertullian clearly believed in a future millennial kingdom on earth (see *Against Marcion* 3.24, in *MO,* 67, 69, #39), while it is unsure whether chiliasm featured in the New Prophecy. See works cited in note 34.

62. See Hippolytus, *Refutation of All Heresies* 10.25–26 (*MO,* 57, #33); Pseudo-Tertullian, *Against All Heresies* 7 (*MO,* 59, #34).

63. See respectively Epiphanius, *Panarion* 48.11 (*MO,* 3, #2); Eusebius, *EH* 5.16.17 (*MO,* 3, #5); Epiphanius, *Panarion* 48.12.4 (*MO,* 5, #7).

64. Basil of Caesarea, *Epistle* 188.1 (*MO,* 129–31, #92).

65. *Corpus of Latin Inscriptions,* vol. 8, 1 n. 2272 (*MO,* 165, #131). According to William Tabbernee, the name Muntanus actually refers to an African Christian martyr and not the founder of Montanism (*MIT,* 445–52). However, in view of the singular "name" and the linkage of Muntanus to the Father and the Son, it is unlikely he was treated as a mortal man. Besides, the martyr Muntanus was only one among others in the *Passio* of Montanus and Lucius in Africa Proconsularis (Burns and Jensen, *Christianity in Roman Africa,* 25). Thus most scholars take the name Montanus in this inscription to refer to the founder of Montanism (Trevett, *Montanism,* 219). For a discussion of another inscription that mentioned Muntanus, see *MIT,* 536–39. Once again, Tabbernee sees a reference to the venerated martyr. However, it is far more likely Montanus, the alleged

4) The Fruit of the Prophets

As mentioned above, the leaders of the early catholic church denounced the licentious and worldly conduct of the Montanist prophets, thereby revealing them as false prophets. However, many contemporary scholars distrust and explain away the lurid descriptions from the heresiologists. How then should one interpret this kind of negative portrayal that is fair to both the historical accusers and the accused?

First of all, judging from extant writings, not all church fathers of the catholic church attacked the profligate private lives of the Montanist prophets and adherents. At least Tertullian did not address such charges after he espoused the New Prophecy.[66] Therefore, when the early church fathers made derogatory remarks about Montanist prophets, perhaps they were not doing so without grounds. It is possible that such conduct did constitute an important reason among others that led to the church fathers' rejection of Montanism.[67]

Secondly, among church fathers of the catholic church, those who wrote most on the unchristian conduct of Montanist prophets seemed to know them in person. The anonymous author cited by Eusebius was one such person, writing fourteen years after the death of Maximilla. It is noteworthy that when he was uncertain of the reliability of some piece of information, he would openly express his reservation. For instance, he repeated the story that both Montanus and Maximilla were said to have hung themselves separately. He also recounted the report that the first ἐπίτροπος Theodotus was once lifted up in a spurious ecstasy and then thrown down, dying miserably. Then he added the disclaimer that he did not personally see the events and could not be certain that the three really died this way.[68] Other writers also voiced out their uncertainties regarding their sources. Thus Epiphanius was unsure of the exact name of the Montanist prophet (whether Priscilla or Quintilla) who saw Christ coming to her in female form. He was likewise unsure whether it was Priscillians or Quintillians who had the abominable practice of mixing infant blood with flour in their eucharist, etc. Jerome, for his part, declined to comment on the latter practice in his letter to Marcella, evidently not wanting to go beyond credible evidence.[69]

Paraclete himself (rather than Montanus the deceased saint), "ordered" Purpurius to erect a commemorative pillar.

66. Wright, "Why Were the Montanists Condemned?"
67. Aune, *Prophecy in Early Christianity*, 229.
68. Eusebius *EH* 5.16.13–15 (*MO*, 19, #23).
69. See Epiphanius, *Panarion* 49.1; 48.14 (*MO*, 133, #94); *MO*, 131, #93; Jerome, *Epistle* 41, *To Marcella* (*MO*, 151, #106 [4]). For a brief defense of Epiphanius's credibility, see Hartog, *Orthodoxy and Heresy*, 199.

Another author who wrote a lengthy account on the conduct of early Montanist leaders forty years after Montanus arose was Apollonius, the bishop of Ephesus. In this he reported that Montanus appointed revenue collectors; their so-called prophets and martyrs collected money even from the poor, the orphans, and the widows; the first prophetesses left their husbands; Priscilla received gold and silver and expensive clothes; Maximilla's male consort Alexander was condemned by Aemilius Pompinus, proconsul in Ephesus, for the robberies he committed, a crime recorded in the public archive of Asia; the Montanist prophets dyed their hair, painted eyelids, loved ornaments, played at dice-boards with dice, and lent money at usury.[70] Some of these allegations may be explained differently and more charitably: the collection and lending of money might have been administrative measures, and the prophetesses might have deserted their husbands to devote themselves to their new-found faith. However, the imprisonment of Alexander is harder to explain away. Thus it does not seem justified to brush aside entirely the charges raised by Apollonius and brand them as character assassination. Some of the Montanist prophets might really have been greedy charlatans preying upon gullible people.[71]

It is also possible that a number of the allegations against the prophets are attributable to influences from paganism that may be less repugnant morally. Thus Vera Hirschmann has demonstrated a number of parallels between Montanism and the pagan cults: the collection of money from adherents (including widows and children) similar to pagan voluntary associations that provided funeral services to members, the calling of married prophetesses "virgins," the existence of administrators called κοινωνοι, ecstatic prophecy, rigoristic practices, prominent female roles, etc.[72] The demand for money, costly garments and painting of the eyes, too, may have other pagan precedents.[73] Even the alleged prominence of Montanist women in leadership might have been borrowed from the cultural milieu: numerous inscriptions from Asia Minor showed that women served as public priestesses, civic officeholders bearing various titles, and as patrons of

---

70. Eusebius, *EH* 5.18 (*MO*, 23–27, #24).

71. Schöllgen, "Der Niedergang des Prophetentums in der Alten Kirche."

72. For a concise summary, see Hirschmann, *Horrenda Secta*, 139–43.

73. In Miletus (276/5 BC) the rules of ritual stipulated that "whenever a woman wishes to perform an initiation for Dionysius Bacchius . . ., she must pay a piece of gold to the priestess at each biennial celebration." A letter c. 245 B.C. from Egypt requested the recipient send a named flautist and a named eunuch (with various musical instruments) for a women's festival, and wanted the latter to wear his most elegant clothing. See Lefkowitz and Fant, *Women's Life in Greece and Rome*, 273–74, #384, 387, respectively.

various voluntary associations in Roman times.[74] Moreover, according to Epiphanius, owing to the alleged revelation of Christ concerning Pepuza, the Quintillians/Pepuzians and Priscillians even at his time had women and men initiated at Pepuza, claiming that "if they wait, they may behold the Christ."[75] This attitude towards a special site reminds one of pagan beliefs concerning the shrines of deities such as Asclepius.

Such "worldly behavior" might not have characterized all the Montanist prophets everywhere all the time. Judging from the writings of church fathers and some inscriptions, a more common phenomenon is the tendency of Montanists (including Tertullian) to describe those who rejected the New Prophecy as "psychics" (ψυχικός) and themselves as "spiritual people" (πνεματικός), pure like the ancient Nazirites.[76] This sense of higher spirituality and superiority over other Christians was certainly detrimental to church unity.

5) *The Spirit of the Prophets*

In addition to the "charlatan" interpretation and "pagan influence" interpretation, contemporary scholars have employed other sociological models to understand the conflict between the early catholic church and Montanism, e.g., as a political struggle of those in authority striving to protect their interest against dissidents, or as a rejection by urban dwellers (believers within the catholic church) of the manner of prophecy by rural believers (Montanist).[77]

While these approaches have some explanatory power, they fail to discuss a crucial metaphysical element in the arguments of the early church: the church fathers might very well agree that Montanist prophecies did not originate from the prophets themselves but were spirit-inspired;

---

74. For a sample of such titles, see MacMullen, "Women in Public," 213; Boatwright, "Plancia Magna of Perge," 249–72; Kearsley, "Women in Public Life," 189–211.

75. *Panarion* 49.1–3 (1) (in *MO*, 133, #94). It is noteworthy that the passage goes on to say, "For the thought of those who do not retain the anchor of the truth, but deliver themselves to one who carries them about for any cause whatever, is subject to Bacchic frenzy." Epiphanius thus compared the heresy to the cult of Dionysius.

76. Clement of Alexandria, *Stromata* 4.13.93.1 (*MO*, 95, #71); Origen, *On the Epistle to Titus* (*MO*, 9, #19); Tertullian, *Monogamy* 1.1–7 (2,3) (*MO*, 77, #51). This practice is also attested by inscriptional evidence: at least four inscriptions use the word πνεματικός or its feminine form for the deceased Christian (see *MIT*, 63, 86, 93, 95).

77. Stewart-Sykes, "Original Condemnation of Asian Montanism." Similarly, Robert Williams on Hippolytus's rejection of Montanism as contrary to scholastic exegesis; see his "Hippolytan Reactions to Montanism."

however, the church fathers decided on the basis of the unbiblical manner and content of their prophetic speech and their conduct that they were inspired not by the Holy Spirit but by the devil himself. According to the anonymous writer cited by Eusebius, the first Montanist ἐπίτροπος Theodotion entrusted himself to the spirit of deceit; likewise, the source of Epiphanius and Origen both said that the founders of Montanism fulfilled the prophecy of Paul (in 1 Tim 4:1, 3) by giving heed to erring spirits and the teachings of demons; Firmilian of Caesarea similarly concluded that it was the spirit of error that inspired Montanus and Priscilla, and then went on to say that "those who lay claim to their false prophecy against the faith of Christ cannot have Christ."[78]

Such statements by the catholic church fathers were not merely spoken to vilify and demonize their opponents, but were actually accompanied by concrete actions. An anonymous author cited by Eusebius stated that some esteemed bishops (including Zoticus and Julian) tried to refute the spirit in Maximilla but were prevented by her supporters (the party of Themiso); according to Eusebius, the bishop of Ephesus Apollonius reported the same incident, and Serapion the bishop of Antioch sent an epistle by Apolinarius bishop of Hierapolis with autograph signatures of a large number of other bishops, one of whom stated that Sotas in Anchialus wanted to cast out the demon in Priscilla, but was prevented by the hypocrites.[79] However, another attempt at exorcism succeeded: according to Firmilian of Caesarea, once a woman appeared as a prophetess able to perform certain portentous deeds and utter predictions, and even celebrated Eucharist and baptized many; but later a brother strong in faith and courage managed to reveal the wickedness of the spirit and presumably cast it out.[80]

Presuppositions Underlying Various Contemporary Views

If the early church fathers were so convinced of the demonic origin of Montanism, why are contemporary scholars so unwilling to take their words

---

78. *EH* 5.16.14 (*MO*, 19, #23); Epiphanius, *Panarion* 48.8.7 (*MO*, 41, #26); Origen, *On First Principles* 2.7.3 (*MO*, 95#73); Firmilian of Caesarea, cited in Cyprian, *Epistle* 74.7 (*MO*, 101, #80).

79. *EH* 5.16.17 (*MO*, 19, #23); *EH* 5.18.5 (*MO*, 25, #24); *EH* 5.19.3 ("Letter of Serapion," in *MO*, 27, #25).

80. Firmilian of Caesarea, in Cyprian, *Epistle* 74.10 (*MO*, 103–5, #81). Since Firmilian was discussing Montanists prior to this passage, scholars generally think this miracle-working woman was a Montanist believer (see Schüssler Fiorenza, *In Memory of Her*, 301).

seriously and offer various other reasons instead to explain their rejection of the New Prophecy? Here I would suggest that, just as biblical scholars have their presuppositions in the exegesis of biblical texts, historians too look at their literary and epigraphic sources with presuppositions related to their past experiences and mental horizons. In this particular instance, three particular presuppositions come to my mind: 1) the legacy of the Enlightenment that no longer believes in spirits (angels or demons) directly acting upon human beings; 2) the impact of Walter Bauer's thesis that Christian orthodoxy was merely the victor rewriting history and ruthlessly suppressing the losers who may actually have been saintly and admirable; and 3) the conviction of equality for all and championship of women leadership.

Taking the three in reverse order, it is easy to understand why many contemporary scholars, especially those with feminist aspirations, would look with favor upon a historical movement that seems to eschew hierarchy and apparently allows women to exercise their spiritual gifts freely. We have already examined these two views above and found the historical picture not as rosy as imagined.

As for the legacy of Walter Bauer, it suffices here to say that his thesis has been closely scrutinized and found wanting. Especially cogent is the observation that the early church fathers refuted various heresies not as armchair theologians or power-greedy churchmen, but as shepherds of their flock undergoing state persecution for being Christians. To see their efforts at curbing heresy as power struggle seems anachronistic.[81] However, H. de Soyres had asked poignantly, "was the 'Spirit' which Tertullian preached, and for which Perpetua died, the Father of lies, or was it the Spirit of God?" This same question continues to puzzle scholars.[82] To be sure, the account of the martyrdom of Perpetua and Felicitas shows admirable piety and true Christian devotion. However, scholars have rightly demonstrated that the account itself (if not the introductory remarks of the redactor too) does not come from a Montanist background. It is, rather, characteristic of North African Christianity in general at that time, and the two martyrs have been fondly celebrated by the catholic church.[83] Equally certain, the New Proph-

81. See various essays in Hartog, *Orthodoxy and Heresy*, especially 208; Köstenberger and Kruger, *Heresy of Orthodoxy*, 41–67.

82. Cited in Trevett, *Montanism*, 1, at the beginning of her monograph, but left unaddressed, stating (on 149) that it is not for historians to address the question posed by Soyres. There is no doubt, however, in David Wright's mind, that "[t]he most attractive face of Montanism is glimpsed in the prologue and epilogue of the *Passion of Perpetua* . . ." This sentence follows immediately after his judgment that the rejection of the New Prophecy was damaging and regrettable (see "Why Were the Montanists Condemned?," 21).

83. To be sure, there are scholars who view Perpetua and Felicitas as Montanist

ecy had Tertullian as a terrific advocate, a writer with theological acumen and great rhetorical skill, and he was greatly impressed by the Montanist teaching of chastity and discipline. However, as mentioned above, it is not certain how typical he was as a Montanist adherent, and he might have been temperamentally predisposed to the legalistic rigorism of Montanism. It is also possible that the purity advocated by Priscilla had less to do with moral purity in general and more to do with sexual abstinence in order to have visionary experiences: "Purification produces harmony," she prophesied, "and they see visions, and when they turn their faces downward they also hear salutary voices, as clear as they are secret."[84]

With regard to the present scholarly assessment of Montanism, it is instructive to compare this with the current rejection of the cult of Eastern Lightning (or Church of the Almighty God) by Chinese churches as an analogous case. To be sure, the two differ greatly in many aspects, notably in the latter's attack on the Scriptures, denigration of the doctrine of Trinity, and belief in the presence of God's militant final kingdom even now. However, there are some similarities that merit a comparison.[85] Just as a Montanist prophet reported of Christ appearing in female form to her in their hometown, we have Eastern Lightning claiming that Christ has returned in the form of a woman (Yang Xiangbin) in a certain city in China. Just as Montanists wrote treatises claiming that the New Prophecy excels previous revelations by Christ and the apostles, so the male founder (Zhao Weishan) and the female Christ of Eastern Lightning have allegedly written new and superior revelations from God. Just as Montanists expected the world to end soon, so do present-day believers of the Eastern Lightning. Just as early heresiologists from different regions attacked the deception and dubious conduct of Montanist prophets, so in the present day we have writers in China, Hong Kong, Taiwan and elsewhere who are knowledgeable of different cults denouncing the beliefs and practices of Eastern Lightning (including sexual seduction, kidnapping, brainwashing, coercion, and even murder). Just as numerous early church leaders attached their signatures

---

Christians. See Butler, *New Prophecy and "New Visions"*; Tabbernee, "Perpetua, Montanism, and Christian Ministry," 421–41. In their opinion, it was the Catholic editors who dropped the original (allegedly Montanist) introduction in later editions of the *Passio*. However, the original manuscript tradition and the almost canonical legacy of her account in Augustine's day point to the conclusion that the account was not Montanist but typical of North Africa. See Moreschini and Norelli, *Early Christian Greek and Latin Literature*, 358; Robeck, *Prophecy in Carthage*, 87–94, 202.

84. Tertullian, *Exhortation to Chastity* 10 (*MO*, 67, #37), in connection with the prohibition of second marriages.

85. Among many reports, see Wu (吴道宗), "Eastern Lightning (東方閃電所「閃」出來的問題)," 18–27; www.chinesetheology.com/EasternLightning.htm.

to a letter penned by Apolinarius against the Montanist prophets, we see a declaration against the contemporary cult of Eastern Lightning appearing in the March 2, 2013, issue of a newspaper in Taiwan (*Chinese Christian Tribune*) signed by more than fifty leaders of various denominations and Christian organizations. In the case of Eastern Lightning, the testimony of church leaders and heresiologists is generally accepted because there is no doubt about their trustworthiness; but in the case of Montanism, contemporary scholars treat the reports of the early church fathers with the "hermeneutics of suspicion." Very likely a presumption of the untrustworthiness of the early church fathers (following Walter Bauer) underlies much of the study of the early church, Montanism included.[86]

But perhaps the greatest obstacle to contemporary scholars taking the reports of early church fathers seriously is that most of them lack experience in dealing with the realm of spirits. Here scholars exposed to traditional folk religions clearly have an advantage. It is actually not unusual for people heavily involved in folk religions to be possessed by spirits that would convulse them, making them unaware of the surroundings, and enable them to foretell the future and perform extraordinary deeds. Some may even "hear voices" that urge them to kill themselves. Even if such a possessed person converts to Christianity, the spirit(s) residing in him may still be lurking inside. Attempts to exorcise the spirits in the name of Jesus often succeed, though it is possible for them to return to a person who persists in sin.[87] To students of Montanism coming from such a context, the accounts of the ancient heresiologists are credible while the Montanist prophets are really suspect.

Conclusion

In the early period of the emergence of the New Prophecy, the catholic church did not immediately repudiate it entirely: Irenaeus the bishop of Lyons apparently attempted to bring the church together; by the time of Origen, there was still discussion whether Montanism should be seen as

---

86. It has been said that "Bauer's professed neutral critical method too frequently slips into the role of defense lawyer of apologist for the heretics rather than impartial judge of the evidence" (Hartog, *Orthodoxy and Heresy*, 11). In his reading of the ὑποκρται, of the name Montanus in inscriptions, and his denial of pagan influence on early Montanism, it seems Tabbernee too is more like a defense lawyer than an impartial judge.

87. For the phenomena of spirit possession in different cultures, see Tippett, "Spirit Possession," 143–74; Keener, "Spirit Possession," 215–36. For cases that converted even psychiatrists to a belief in demon possession, see Instone-Brewer, "Jesus and the Psychiatrist," 133–48; Peck, *Glimpses of the Devil*.

a schism or a heresy.[88] Nevertheless, the opposition party eventually won out in the catholic church, and contemporary scholars have offered various reasons for this victory.

After a careful analysis of such views, the present author is of the opinion that anti-supernaturalist, Bauerian and feminist presuppositions have led many scholars astray. In fact, Montanism was not a protest movement against the gradual institutionalization of the catholic church. Neither did the movement venture to advance the leadership role of women. Consequently, the catholic church did not ruthlessly oppose the movement to defend her own prerogatives or to suppress women. The catholic church in fact made the right decision in view of the numerous problems present in Montanist prophecy: violent and harmful ecstatic behavior, the New Prophecy's denigration of the teaching of Christ and the apostles, the unverifiable and even extremist doctrinal statements, unfulfilled prophecies, inappropriate and arrogant conduct, etc. all cast doubt on the allegedly divine origin of their prophecy.

Nevertheless, it should be noted that, while the early catholic church rejected Montanism, she did not claim that supernatural spiritual gifts had ceased after the apostolic age. If the theory of cessationism championed by some modern scholars were the consensus of the second century church, the catholic church would only need to point to the impossibility of any genuine new prophecy instead of going to such lengths to refute it.

Today, adherents of the Pentecostal/Charismatic Movement would do well to reconsider their practice of claiming Montanism as their precursor. Moreover, as the church in general deals with the controversial issue of charismatic gifts as well as the proliferation of cults that claim to have received new revelations, hopefully she would learn from the assessment of Montanism in the early church. Only then can we "be built up until we all reach unity in the faith and in the knowledge of the Son of God and become mature, attaining to the whole measure of the fullness of Christ. Then we will no longer be infants, tossed back and forth by the waves, and blown here and there by every wind of teaching and craftiness of people in their deceitful scheming" (Eph 4:13–14).

Bibliography

Alexander, David C., and Edward L. Smither. "Bauer's Forgotten Region: North African Christianity." In *Orthodoxy and Heresy in Early Christian Contexts: Reconsidering the Bauer Thesis*, edited by Paul Hartog, 166–92. Eugene, OR: Pickwick, 2015.

---

88. Origen, *On the Epistle to Titus* (*MO*, 9, #19)

Amidon, Philip R., trans. and ed. *The Panarion of St. Epiphanius, Bishop of Salamis: Selected Passages*. New York: Oxford University Press, 1990.

Ash, James L., Jr. "The Decline of Ecstatic Prophecy in the Early Church:" *Theological Studies* 37 (2016) 227–52.

Aune, David E. *Prophecy in Early Christianity and the Ancient Mediterranean World*. Grand Rapids: Eerdmans, 1983.

Banks, Robert. "From Fellowship to Organization: A Study in the Early History of the Concept of the Church." *Reformed Theological Review* 30 (1971) 79–89.

Bauer, Walter. *Orthodoxy and Heresy in Earliest Christianity*. Edited by Robert A. Kraft and Gerhard Krodel. Mifflintown, PA: Sigler, 1996.

Boatwright, Mary T. "Plancia Magna of Perge: Women's Roles and Status in Roman Asia Minor." In *Women's History and Ancient History*, edited by Susan Pomeroy, 249–72. Chapel Hill: University of North Carolina Press, 1991.

Burns, J. Patout, Jr., and Robin M. Jensen. *Christianity in Roman Africa: The Development of its Practices and Beliefs*. Grand Rapids: Eerdmans, 2014.

Butler, Rex D. *The New Prophecy and "New Visions": Evidence of Montanism in "The Passion of Perpetua and Felicitas."* Washington, DC: Catholic University of America Press, 2006.

Campbell, R. Alastair. *The Elders: Seniority within Earliest Christianity*. Studies of the New Testament and its World. Edinburgh: T. & T. Clark, 1994.

Daunton-Fear, A. "The Ecstasies of Montanus." *Studia Patristica* 17 (1982) 648–51.

Dunn, Geoffrey D. "Rhetoric and Tertullian's *De Virginibus Velandis*." *Vigiliae Christianae* 59 (2005) 1–30.

Epiphanius. *The Panarion of St. Epiphanius, Bishop of Salamis: Selected Passages*. Translated and edited by Philip R. Amidon. New York: Oxford University Press, 1990.

Farnell, F. David. "The Montanist Crisis: A Key to Refuting Third-Wave Concepts of NT Prophecy." *The Master's Seminary Journal* 14 (2003) 235–62.

Fee, Gordon D. *God's Empowering Presence: The Holy Spirit in the Letters of Paul*. Peabody, MA: Hendrickson, 1994.

Forbes, Christopher. *Prophecy and Inspired Speech in Early Christianity and its Hellenistic Environment*. Wissenschaftliche Untersuchungen zum Neuen Testament. 2 Reihe, 75. Tübingen: Mohr/Siebeck, 1995.

Fung, Ronald. "Ministry in the New Testament." In *The Church in the Bible and the World: An International Study*, edited by D. A Carson, 154–212. Exeter: Paternoster, 1987.

Garland, David E. *1 Corinthians*. Baker Exegetical Commentary on the New Testament. Grand Rapids: Baker Academic, 2003.

Grudem, Wayne. *The Gift of Prophecy in the New Testament and Today*. Westchester, IL: Crossway, 1988.

Gryson, Roger. *The Ministry of Women in the Early Church*. Collegeville, MN: Liturgical, 1980.

Hartog, Paul A., ed. *Orthodoxy and Heresy in Early Christian Contexts: Reconsidering the Bauer Thesis*. Eugene, OR: Pickwick, 2015.

Heine, Ronald E. *The Montanist Oracles and Testimonia*. Patristic Monograph Series 14. Macon, GA: Mercer University Press, 1989.

Hirschmann, Vera-Elisabeth. *Horrenda Secta: Untersuchungen zum frühchristlichen Montanismus und seinen Verbindungen zur paganen Religion Phrygiens*. Historia-Einzelschriften 179. Stuttgart: Franz Steiner, 2005.

Huber, Elaine C. "Women and the Authority of Inspiration: A Reexamination of Two Prophetic Movements from a Christian Feminist Perspective." PhD diss., Graduate Theological Union, 1984.

Instone-Brewer, David. "Jesus and the Psychiatrist." In *The Unseen World: Christian Reflections on Angels, Demons and the Heavenly Realm*, edited by Anthony N. S. Lane, 133–48. Grand Rapids: Baker, 1996.

Jensen, Anne. *God's Self-Confident Daughters: Early Christianity and the Liberation of Women*. Translated by O. C. Dean Jr. Louisville: Westminster John Knox, 1996.

Käsemann, Ernst. "Ministry and Community in the New Testament." In *Essays on New Testament Themes*, edited by Ernst Käsemann, 63–94. London: SCM, 1964.

Kearsley, R. A. "Women in Public Life in the Roman East." *Tyndale Bulletin* 50 (1999) 189–212.

Keener, Craig S. "Spirit Possession as a Cross-Cultural Experience." *Bulletin for Biblical Research* 20 (2010) 215–35.

Köstenberger, Andreas J., and Michael J. Kruger. *The Heresy of Orthodoxy: How Contemporary Culture's Fascination with Diversity Has Reshaped Our Understanding of Early Christianity*. Wheaton, IL: Crossway, 2010.

Kydd, Ronald. *Charismatic Gifts in the Early Church*. Peabody, MA: Hendrickson, 1984.

Lam, Wing-Hung. *Christian Theology in Development: The Early Church*. Hong Kong: China Graduate School of Theology, 1990.

Latourette, Kenneth Scott. *A History of Christianity*. Vol. 1, *Beginnings to 1500*. Rev. ed. 2 vols. New York: Harper & Row, 1975.

Lefkowitz, Mary R., and Maureen B. Fant. *Women's Life in Greece and Rome: A Source Book in Translation*. Baltimore: Johns Hopkins University Press, 1992.

MacMullen, Ramsay. "Woman in Public in the Roman Empire." *Historia* 29 (1980) 208–18.

Mattei, Paul. "Regards inactuels sur une Église en mutation: Tertullien et les paradoxes de son ecclésiologie." *Revue des Sciences Religieuses* 75 (2001) 275–87.

Moreschini, Claudio, and Enrico Norelli. *Early Christian Greek and Latin Literature: A Literary History*. Translated by Matthew J. O'Connell. Vol. 1, *From Paul to the Age of Constantine*. 2 vols. Peabody, MA: Hendrickson, 2005.

Nardoni, Enrique. "Charism in the Early Church since Rudolph Sohm: An Ecumenical Challenge." *Theological Studies* 53 (1992) 646–62.

Nestler, Erich. "Was Montanism a Heresy?" *Pneuma* 6 (1984) 67–78.

Peck, M. Scott. *Glimpses of the Devil: A Psychiatrist's Personal Accounts of Possession, Exorcism, and Redemption*. New York: Free Press, 2005.

Powell, Douglas. "Tertullianists and Cataphrygians." *Vigiliae Christianae* 41 (1987) 139–53.

Robeck, Cecil M., Jr. "Montanism and Present-Day 'Prophets.'" *Pneuma* 32 (2010) 413–29.

———. *Prophecy in Carthage: Perpetua, Tertullian, and Cyprian*. Cleveland: Pilgrim, 1992.

Schöllgen, Georg. "Der Niedergang des Prophetentums in der Alten Kirche." In *Prophetie und Charisma*, edited by Ingo Baldermann et al., 97–116. Jahrbuch für biblische Theologie 14. Neukirchen-Vluyn: Neukirchener, 1999.

Schüssler Fiorenza, Elisabeth. *In Memory of Her: A Feminist Theological Reconstruction of Christian Origins*. London: SCM, 1984.

Stewart-Sykes, Alistair. "The Original Condemnation of Asian Montanism." *The Journal of Ecclesiastical History* 50 (1999) 1–22.
Tabbernee, William. *Fake Prophecy and Polluted Sacraments: Ecclesiastical and Imperial Reactions to Montanism*. Supplements to Vigiliae Christianae 84. Leiden: Brill, 2007.
———. *Montanist Inscriptions and Testimonia: Epigraphic Sources Illustrating the History of Montanism*. Patristic Monograph Series 16. Macon, GA: Mercer University Press, 1997.
———. "Perpetua, Montanism, and Christian Ministry in Carthage c. 203 C.E." *Perspectives in Religious Studies* 32 (2005) 421–41.
Tabbernee, William, and Peter Lampe. *Pepouza and Tymion: The Discovery and Archaeological Exploration of a Lost Ancient City and an Imperial Estate*. Berlin: De Gruyter, 2008.
Thiselton, Anthony C. *The First Epistle to the Corinthians: A Commentary on the Greek Text*. New International Greek Testament Commentary. Grand Rapids: Eerdmans, 2000.
———. *The Holy Spirit: In Biblical Teaching, through the Centuries, and Today*. Grand Rapids: Eerdmans, 2013.
Tippett, Alan R. "Spirit Possession as It Relates to Culture and Religion: A Survey of Anthropological Literature." In *Demon Possession: A Medical, Historical, Anthropological, and Theological Symposium; Papers Presented at the University of Notre Dame, January 8–11, 1975, under the Auspices of the Christian Medical Society*, edited by John W. Montgomery, 143–74. Minneapolis: Bethany Fellowship, 1976.
Trevett, Christine. "Apocalypse, Ignatius, Montanism: Seeking the Seeds," *Vigiliae Christianae* 43.4 (1989) 313–338.
———. *Montanism: Gender, Authority, and the New Prophecy*. New York: Cambridge University Press, 1996.
Williams, Robert Lee. "Hippolytan Reactions to Montanism: Tensions in the Churches of Rome in the Early Third Century." *St Pat* 39 (2006) 131–37.
Wright, David F. "Why Were the Montanists Condemned?" *Themelios* 2 (1976) 15–22.
Wu, Daniel Tao Chung (吳道宗). "Eastern Lightning and the Problems Revealed (東方閃電所「閃」出來的問題)." *Spirit Wind* 535 (2017) 18–27.
"東方閃電/全能神教會：關於這異端邪教的相關網站." http://www.chinesetheology.com/EasternLightning.htm.

6

The Holy Spirit

*Retrieving the Patristic Pneumatology
of the Fourth Century*

Loe Joo Tan

Introduction

To assert that the doctrine of the Holy Spirit has gained a position of significance and prominence especially over the past century is to state the obvious. Across the confessional spectrum, churches—ranging from mainline Protestant to Catholic, evangelical to Pentecostal—have rediscovered that an understanding of the person and work of the Spirit is not only critical for corporate growth and the task of missions, but also for a deeper relationship with God. Amos Yong has argued that this resurgence in interest in pneumatology is part of the particular gift of the Pentecostal movement to the global church.[1] In addition, much has been made of the rise of the "pacific century" for the Chinese church, i.e., that the next century of church growth will come mainly from Asian churches, especially churches in China. If these two ideas are to be believed, then a proper understanding of the doctrine of the Spirit will be indeed foundational to the continued growth of the Chinese church. At the same time, there is a need to be circumspect about growing trends in the development of pneumatology worldwide, particularly as witnessed

---

1. Yong, *Spirit Poured Out*, 28.

in the growth of the neo-Charismatic movement. Many of the issues facing the church today regarding the Spirit are not new; they have arisen since its beginning in Roman times, whether under persecution or later under the Constantinian order. These include not just the deity of the Spirit, but his relationship to the Father and the Son, as well as his universal work within other peoples and his particular ministry within the church. It is therefore appropriate, when exploring the doctrine of the Spirit from a Chinese perspective, to take a step back to retrieve some of the historical and theological resources already at our disposal. Within church history, the fourth century in particular has manifested an intense period of discussion about the ministry and person of the Spirit. This chapter will therefore attempt to bring some of these issues to light and to elaborate on the pertinent contributions of the Patristic fathers, in particular Athanasius, Basil of Caesarea, Gregory of Nazianzus, and Gregory of Nyssa.[2]

The Divine and Distinct Spirit

In recent decades, scholarly work in the field of patristic studies has been inspired to a large extent by the work of Lewis Ayres and Michel Barnes who have both argued for a "Pro-Nicene" theology undergirding the fourth century theological debates.[3] Much of this is a reaction to the assertion of systematic theologians, who, influenced by the work of De Régnon, have tended to rely on a simplistic East/West divide in the development of their trinitarian theology.[4] Nonetheless, even dissenters of this view do agree upon one thing; that the earliest theological discussions that occupied the attention of the church fathers were not pneumatological in nature but rather theological (Theology Proper) and christological. Early Christian thinkers struggled mightily to reconcile the strong monotheism they had inherited from Judaism and incorporate the New Testament depiction of Christ being as fully divine as the Father. Not surprisingly, there was initially strong opposition toward seeing Christ as divine; the most famous of which was Arius of Alexandria, whose ideas, as Ayres and Barnes have ably argued, should actually be seen as part of a larger trajectory of "Eusebian theology"; named after

---

2. For a concise introduction to the theological and historical background of Athanasius and the three Cappadocians, see Young and Teal, *From Nicaea to Chalcedon*, 24–28.

3. Ayres, *Nicaea and its Legacy*, 236–40; Barnes, "Fourth Century," 56–57.

4. For a discussion of De Régnon's work in its context, see Hennessy, "An Answer to de Régnon's Accusers," 179–97.

its two chief proponents, Eusebius of Caesarea and Eusebius of Nicomedia.[5] While the 325 Council of Nicaea did resolve several christological issues, when it came to the person of the Spirit, its Creed only admitted a terse "*We believe in the Holy Spirit.*"[6] It took the efforts of the post-Nicene fathers, especially Athanasius and the Cappadocian fathers,[7] to lay out a more systematic defense of the deity of the Spirit that culminated in the final version of the Creed promulgated at the 381 Council of Constantinople and augmented for the section on the Spirit with the familiar expression today, "*the Lord and Giver of life, who proceeds from the Father, who with the Father and the Son together is worshiped and glorified, who spoke by the prophets.*"[8] Hence, controversy and subsequent consensus regarding the Spirit were really only manifested toward the end of the fourth century. During the post-Nicaea period, two main pneumatological works stood out to refute arguments against the deity of the Spirit: Athanasius's *Ad Serapion*, and Basil of Caesarea's *On the Holy Spirit*.[9] Both bishops had expended considerable energy earlier to defend the deity of the Son during the christological debates, and it is not surprising therefore, to find some of those same arguments employed to defend the Spirit's divinity. As a case in point, we note how in Basil's earliest theological work, *Contra Eunomium*, he had argued for the deity of the Son vis-à-vis the Father. He writes,

> But if community of *ousia* is taken to mean that both (i.e., Father and Son) are seen as having an identical principle of being, then it is confessed that light is also the being of the Only begotten, and whatever principle of being one ascribes to the Father is attributed also to the Son: if that is taken to be the meaning of community of *ousia*, then we accept the doctrine.[10]

---

5. Besides the work of Ayres and Barnes, other helpful accounts of the events of the fourth century can be found in Behr, *Nicene Faith*; Hanson, *Search for the Christian Doctrine of God*.

6. An account of the events leading up to the Council of Nicaea can be found in Kelly, *Early Christian Doctrines*, 223–56.

7. Prestige has located the trinitarian formula of "one being three persons" (*mia ousia treis hypostaseis*) as coming in particular from the combined efforts of the Cappadocians rather than Augustine as commonly believed (Prestige, *God in Patristic Thought*, 233).

8. For a comparison between the 325 Creed of Nicaea (N) and the 381 Creed of Constantinople (C), see Kelly, *Early Christian Creeds*, 205–30, 332–67.

9. For a detailed study of Athanasius and Basil's life and ministry, see Fedwick, *Church and the Charisma*; Anatolios, *Athanasius*.

10. Basil, *Contre Eunome*, 43; translation mine. An English version has since been released: Basil, *Against Eunomius*.

Here, Basil is reasoning that given the closeness and community of the Father-Son relationship, whatever principle of *ousia* (being) that one ascribes to the Father should also be attributed to the Son in order to ensure the *homoousios* (same being) of the Son with the Father. This maneuver became one frequently employed, by not only Basil, but also Athanasius and subsequently Hilary of Poitiers and Augustine, to assert that the Son is as fully divine as the Father. However, when it comes to the question of the Spirit, it leaves unanswered the status of the relationship between him and the Father. In fact, an unintended corollary of the previous assertion could be that the Spirit-Father relationship be viewed as similar to the relationship between the Son and the Father, leading to a possible conclusion that the Spirit is another Son. Secondly, at this stage of doctrinal development, there was an unresolved problem that resides in the correlative nature of the Father-Son relationship, i.e., the Father is father because He is father of the Son, and the Son similarly so because he is the son of the Father. This seems to rule out any room for the Spirit to be conceived in the same manner since scriptural descriptions of him as the "Spirit of God" and the "Spirit of Christ" (Rom 8:9) do not seem sufficiently distinctive enough to warrant seeing him as a separate *hypostasis* (person) as the two other Persons. Indeed, such was the point made by the heretics of the late fourth century known as the *Pneumatomachi*, or Spirit-Fighters, who, while accepting the co-divinity of Father and Son, argued that the Spirit could not be at the same level as the Father and Son, for they could not envisage his distinctiveness from them and subscribed instead to a form of binitarianism.

The immediate task of the church fathers, therefore, was to establish simultaneously the distinctiveness and deity of the Spirit. As an initial attempt, Athanasius sought to assert the distinctiveness of the Spirit in his pneumatological treatise using the familiar image language that he had earlier used to assert the deity of the Son. Thus, Athanasius writes that, "[t]he Spirit is said to be, and is, the *image* of the Son" (emphasis added).[11] By image language, Athanasius was utilizing the scriptural assertion of Christ being the "image of God" to argue that Christ is an expression of God's being (and hence equally divine), rather than merely an expression of God's activity. While this strategy worked well for the Son, it was quickly seen as less convincing for the Spirit, because scripture simply did not employ the same image language for the Spirit. Recognizing this, Basil decided not to employ the same strategy of image language and instead chose only to assert that "the relation of the Spirit to the Son is the same as that of the Son to the Father."[12]

---

11. Athanasius, *Letters to Serapion Concerning the Holy Spirit*, I.24.
12. Basil, *On the Holy Spirit*, 17.43.

This reticence is noteworthy since, as Aghiorgoussis has reasoned, not only was there no scriptural basis for Athanasius's formulation, but more importantly, it could potentially violate the doctrine of divine monarchy in which the Father is the source of the monarchy. Aghiorgoussis further argues that Basil views the human person as the image of God (the Father), and never as the image of the Son or the Spirit, and contrasted this with Augustine's view of man as the image of the Trinity.[13] For Basil, the distinctiveness of the Spirit does not lie in him being the image of the Son but rather in a relation of Spirit-Son that is analogous to the Son-Father relations. Further analysis by Hildebrand showed that in his formulation, the Spirit is not only *not* the Image of the Son but also should be seen rather as the light in which the Image is illuminated.[14] Image is therefore not merely a depiction of a prototype, but also its manifestation.[15] This provides the basis for access to the Son; that it is through the Spirit that one reaches the Son, and through the Son, one sees the Father. Thus, Basil writes that, "natural goodness, inherent holiness and royal dignity reaches from the Father through the Only Begotten to the Spirit"[16] and the Spirit is called the light that illuminated the Image while he himself can never be seen.[17]

While the distinctiveness of the Spirit compared to Father and Son may be settled, questions remain about his divinity. Here, like Athanasius, the Cappadocian father left no doubt about his thoughts on this matter, as a quote from *On the Holy Spirit* shows,[18]

> The Holy Spirit, too, is numbered with the Father and the Son, because He is above creation, and is ranked as we are taught by the words of the Lord in the Gospel, "Go and baptize in the name of the Father and of the Son and of the Holy Ghost." He who, on the contrary, places the Spirit before the Son, or alleges Him to be older than the Father, resists the ordinance of God, and is a stranger to the sound faith, since he fails to preserve the form of doxology which he has received, but adopts some new fangled device in order to be pleasing to men.[19]

---

13. Aghiorgoussis, "Applications of the Theme 'Eikon Theou,'" 270.

14. Hildebrand, *Trinitarian Theology of Basil*, 185.

15. For a discussion of Basil's usage of the term "image" as a sign of God, see Aghiorgoussis, "Image as 'Sign,'" 19–54.

16. Basil, *On the Holy Spirit*, 18.47.

17. Aghiorgoussis, "Image as 'Sign,'" 267.

18. Gribomont has provided an outline of the structure of this treatise. See Gribomont, "Intransigence and Irenicism," 124–28.

19. Basil, *St. Basil*, Letter 52.4.

Basil therefore asserts that the Spirit is ranked above creation in the same manner that the Father and Son are, and that he shares in the same Name based on the Great Commission of Matthew 28:19–20. Any endeavor to place the three Persons on different footings is seen as contrary to Scripture and to be rejected by the church. Later, Basil would also clarify how the Spirit is both distinct from the Father and Son, and yet as divine as them at the same time. Earlier on, he had argued that the Spirit leads us to knowledge of the Son who in turn reveals the Father. Much hinges on the analogical relation between the Son and the Spirit. Basil resolves any potential danger of seeing the Spirit as a second Son and thereby makes him a "brother" to Christ by referring to the Spirit as "of God" not in the sense of begetting but of *proceeding* as in the breath of the Father's mouth,

> [T]he Spirit is described to be of God, not in the sense that all things are of God, but because He proceeds from the mouth of the Father, and is not begotten like the Son. Of course, the "mouth" of the Father is not a physical member, nor is the Spirit a dissipated exhalation, but "mouth" is used to the extent that it is appropriate to God.[20]

By identifying procession, based on John 15:26, as that act proper to the Spirit within the immanent Trinity, this very operation of proceeding is thus differentiated from that of the begetting of the Son, which leads to the conclusion that the Spirit is distinct from the Son, but also divine since he proceeds from the "mouth" of the Father. In effect, through the work of Basil and earlier, Athanasius, several different relations between the Father and Son and between the Son and Spirit have been highlighted, which then allowed for the subsequent conception of the Three as equally divine and yet distinct from one another.[21]

---

20. Basil, *On the Holy Spirit*, 18.46.

21. We note, as many authors have commented, that the church father did not use the phrase *homoousios* for the Holy Spirit in his works, the phrase that was used to denote the co-deity of the Son and the Father. Hildebrand attributes Basil's alternate usage of *homotimos* because it did not have the technical connotations of *homoousios* (*Trinitarian Theology of Basil*, 95). Zizioulas considers that Basil believed in the full deity of the Spirit but eschewed the term because he was averse to *ousia* language (*Communion and Otherness*, 184). Nonetheless, it is clear, at least to Gregory of Nazianzus, that Basil did hold to the divinity of the Spirit but had merely delayed using the term because he knew his enemies were watching for this (Gregory of Nazianzus, "Oration 43," 43.68–69).

The Inseparability of the Spirit with the Son and Father in Worship

As has been recognized in our discussion so far, in attempting to address the question of the deity and distinctiveness of the Spirit, both Athanasius and Basil had come to the same conclusion, that it is impossible to do so without giving an account of his relationship with the Father and the Son. In fact, without exception, all the church fathers found it inconceivable that any account of the Spirit can be provided in isolation from that of the Father and Son, and nowhere is this more apparent than when it comes to practical worship. Gregory of Nyssa, Basil's younger brother,[22] reasons that the Father, Son, and Spirit are inseparable in worship in his attempt to argue for the deity of the Spirit against another group of Spirit-deniers, the Macedonians.[23] Nyssa argues that the only way one could worship the Father is through worshipping the Son, and one can only worship the Son through the Holy Spirit. Hence, worship of all three is inseparable,

> But you will say, "When I think of the Father it is the Son (alone) that I have included as well in that term." But tell me; when you have grasped the notion of the Son have you not admitted therein that of the Holy Spirit too? For how can you confess the Son except by the Holy Spirit? At what moment, then, is the Spirit in a state of separation from the Son, so that when the Father is being worshipped, the worship of the Spirit is not included along with that of the Son?[24]

Besides worship, even the very conception of the three Persons cannot be separated. For example, any conception of the Son leads inevitably to that of the Spirit and vice versa, for the two are so intertwined that they are always associated with the other,

> [T]he thought of 'unction' conveys the hidden meaning that there is no interval of separation between the Son and the Holy Spirit. For as between the body's surface and the liquid of the oil nothing

---

22. Gregory of Nyssa took over the mantle of leadership for theological orthodoxy after the demise of his elder brother. For a study of his life and works, see Gregory of Nyssa, *Life of Moses*, 1–23; also see Meredith, *Gregory of Nyssa*.

23. While some scholars have argued the Macedonians are essentially the same as the *Pneumatomachi*, Hanson has cautioned that the connection remains unproven. (See Hanson, *Search for the Christian Doctrine of God*, 762).

24. Gregory of Nyssa, "On the Holy Spirit," 2.5.324.

intervening can be detected, either in reason or in perception, so inseparable is the union of the Spirit with the Son.[25]

Lucian Turcescu has astutely remarked that this passage by Gregory of Nyssa effectively asserts that any confession of the divinity of the Son must necessarily include a confession of the divinity of the Spirit.[26] For Basil, similarly, the inseparability of the Three can be seen not only in worship, but from the initial acts of creation as well. When the angels were first created, all three Persons work together such that "the ministering spirits exist by the will of the Father, are brought into being by the work of the Son, and are perfected by the presence of the Spirit."[27] This inseparable operation of the Trinity is also seen in the context of general creation, "When you consider creation, I advise you to first think of Him who is the first cause of everything that exists: namely, the Father, and then of the Son, who is the creator, and then the Holy Spirit, the perfector."[28] Salvation history also bears witness to the inseparability of the Son and the Spirit who acted together to carry out the will of God, "In the first place, the Lord was anointed with the Holy Spirit, who would henceforth be inseparably united to His very flesh . . . After His baptism, the Holy Spirit was present in every action He performed."[29]

Nonetheless, while the works of the Three are inseparable and apparent, this does not imply that one can understand the Trinity, for the divine being is incomprehensible and hence the patristic father always retained a reverence for the activities of the Trinity,

> For in learning that He is beneficent, and a judge, good, and just, and all else of the same kind, we learn diversities of His operations, but we are none the more able to learn by our knowledge of His operations the nature of Him who works . . . Indeed the substance is one thing which no definition has been found to express.[30]

This understanding of the inseparability of the Trinity is one of the key features of Pro-Nicene theology, and as Ayres has noted, can be found in the writings of Basil of Ancyra, Hilary of Poitiers, and in Athanasius's

---

25. Gregory of Nyssa, "On the Holy Spirit," 2.5.321; Basil, *On the Holy Spirit*, 11.27.
26. Turcescu, *Gregory of Nyssa and the Concept of Divine Persons*, 113.
27. Basil, *On the Holy Spirit*, 16.38.
28. Basil, *On the Holy Spirit*, 16.38.
29. Basil, *On the Holy Spirit*, 16.39.
30. Gregory of Nyssa, "On the Holy Trinity," 2.5.329.

Ad Serapion.[31] The inseparability of the three Persons in the Godhead led Nyssa to conclude that in all of their external operations, they are of one will and one accord,

> Since then the Holy Trinity fulfils every operation in a manner similar to that of which I have spoken, not by separate action according to the number of the Persons, but so that there is one motion and disposition of the good will which is communicated from the Father through the Son to the Spirit (for as we do not call those whose operation gives one life three Givers of life, neither do we call those who are contemplated in one goodness three Good beings, nor speak of them in the plural by any of their other attributes); so neither can we call those who exercise this Divine and superintending power and operation towards ourselves and all creation, conjointly and inseparably, by their mutual action, three Gods.[32]

Nyssa's reasoning is this: the unity of being in the Godhead can be seen that there is a single will of God communicated from the Father through the Son to the Spirit. This has led some scholars to question the exact nature of this unity. Christopher Stead poses the question thus: should any divine operation be seen as one to which each Person *contributes* or *completes*?[33] If it were the former, it would imply the contribution of each Person is incomplete without the others, whereas in the latter it could suggest the other two persons are redundant since one alone would suffice. Stead argues that while both possibilities can be seen in various parts of the writings of the fathers, he leans more towards the "contributory" model and suggests its drawbacks may be mitigated by presupposing the divine Persons are perfectly united in will and knowledge.[34] As another possible solution to the issue of the unity of divine will, Bradshaw has suggested an analogy with a single gift given under the name of a husband and wife in which each completes the act of giving the gift yet the gift is given in the names of both.[35] Finally, Prestige has noted that the thought of the Cappadocians as a whole does lie in the "triplicity of equal *hypostaseis*" rather than an identity of the *ousia*, which "came second in order of prominence" for them, and suggests this explains why they may sometimes have been charged with tritheism even though they were clearly

---

31. Ayres, *Nicaea and its Legacy*, 214.

32. Gregory of Nyssa, "On 'Not Three Gods,'" 2.5.334; For a discussion of the structure and argument of this treatise by Nyssa, see Ayres, "Not Three People," 445–74.

33. Stead, *Philosophy in Christian Antiquity*, 185.

34. Stead, *Philosophy in Christian Antiquity*, 186.

35. Bradshaw, *Aristotle East and West*, 160–61.

monotheists.[36] In either case, all agreed that the unity of divine will was central to the thought of the fathers, and that this means the inseparability of the Three may be reconciled with their distinctiveness.

The Spirit's Work in Deification

One of the most distinguishing features of fourth century theology was the development of the idea of *theosis* or *theopoiesis* (deification), or literally, becoming god. While the idea itself had its antecedent roots in the fathers of the preceding centuries, the fourth century witnessed a developed understanding of the work of the Spirit in the transformation of the human person. Kärkkäinen has summarized that deification reflects the deepest desire of humanity—to live in union with God.[37] To appreciate the nuances inherent within the patristic usage of term, Normal Russell has proposed a threefold framework based on a detailed study of the metaphor of deification in early Christian history.[38] These basic approaches, i.e., (1) nominal, (2) analogical, and (3) metaphorical, form a continuum that expresses different kinds of relationships between the human and divine, and are helpful in understanding patristic intention behind this seemingly theologically extravagant claim. The first category, *nominal*, signifies a direct relation between the word *theosis* and a title of honor, such as when Scripture uses the word 'gods' to human beings. The second, *analogical*, carries the idea of the nominal further, e.g., when Moses was seen as a "god" to Pharaoh in the relative sense that a wise man would seem like one to a fool. The *metaphorical* usage of the term is characterized in two different ways; (a) an *ethical* understanding that sees deification as accomplished through ascetic efforts to achieve Godlikeness (or *homoiosis*), and (b) a *realistic* approach that suggests human beings may be transformed through participation, or *methexis*, in God. The latter idea further contains two aspects; *ontological*, i.e., when human nature is transformed "in principle by the Incarnation," or *dynamic*, when the appropriation of the realistic benefits of deification are done "through the sacraments of baptism and the Eucharist."[39] In sum, we may see the concept of deification as analogous with the idea of sanctification in modern theology, with the caveat that the patristic fathers did not demarcate this as solely the work of the Spirit but understood it trinitarianly. Given Russell's extensive survey,

---

36. Prestige, *God in Patristic Thought*, 242–43. Prestige himself did not think the Cappadocian fathers had lapsed into tritheism.
37. Kärkkäinen, *One with God*, 1–3.
38. Russell, *Doctrine of Deification*, 1–3.
39. Russell, *Doctrine of Deification*, 4–15.

the concept of deification by Athanasius and Gregory of Nazianzus will be analyzed with the help of this typology.

For Athanasius, the chief term he employed to describe the process of "becoming God" was *theopoiesis* rather than *theosis*. Thus, in *On the Incarnation*, Athanasius writes that Christ "was made man in order that we might be made God."[40] Similarly, in a letter to Adelphus, he states "He (Christ) has become Man, that He might deify us in Himself."[41] Russell has described Athanasius's thinking here as essentially following the Irenaean *Tauschformel* or "exchange formula," i.e., "the Son of God being made the Son of man, that through Him we may receive the adoption,—humanity sustaining, and receiving, and embracing the Son of God."[42] For John Meyendorff, *theopoiesis* was the main argument with which Athanasius had employed to counter Arius's claim, i.e., if Christ was less than divine, he would not be able to assist man in his desire to become like God,[43] while T. F. Torrance similarly argues the point that for Athanasius, *theopoiesis* is synonymous with adoption as sons of God in Christ.[44] In terms of the Spirit, Athanasius sees him as the principal actor in this process given that his role as the *Holy*, or as the deifying Spirit.[45] Deification is hence a trinitarian process that could not happen if the status and role of the Spirit is diminished in any way.

Anatolios has further noted that in Athanasius's view, deification is when the invisible God becomes visible and knowable through Christ's humanity so that "at this point . . . God's nearness to humanity reaches the point of humanity's deification."[46] He notes that Athanasius believes that in this process, the human attributes of Christ are transformed and oriented towards the divine, and "not simply juxtaposed to the divine."[47] The deifica-

---

40. Athanasius, "On the Incarnation of the Word," 54.3. A more recent translation can be found in Athanasius, *On the Incarnation*, 167.

41. Athanasius, "Letters," Letter 60.4.

42. Russell, *Doctrine of Deification*, 169; See also Irenaeus of Lyons, "Against Heresies," 3.16.3; The christological orientation of Athanasius's view of *theosis* has also been noted in a detailed analysis of his soteriology by Hess, who detected at least eight closely related motifs, all of which are centered around the theme of salvation wrought by the work of Christ, including renewal, participation, union to the Logos, and being perfected in Christ (Hess, "Place of Divinization," 369–74); Osborn too concurred that Athanasius's understanding of the work of salvation was christologically directed and that he perceives it not as an abstract principle but that Christ "really became what we are" in order to save us (Osborn, *Irenaeus of Lyons*, 88).

43. Meyendorff, *Byzantine Theology*, 33.

44. Torrance, *Trinitarian Faith*, 264–65.

45. Berthold, "Procession of the Spirit in Athanasius," 125–31.

46. Anatolios, *Athanasius*, 38.

47. Anatolios, *Athanasius*, 151.

tion of general humanity by Christ is therefore a transforming dynamic in which human "passibility is rendered impassible."[48] Thus Athanasius can say that "the Word was not impaired in receiving a body, that He should seek to receive a grace, but rather He deified that which He put on, and more than that, 'gave' it graciously to the race of man."[49] For creation as a whole, its participation in the power of the word also renders it safe from collapsing back into its inherent nothingness from which it came.[50] Habets has also reasoned that deification as understood by Athanasius includes the inauguration of salvation in justification and the entire sanctification and the life of faith, repentance, worship, and the sacraments; i.e., an encapsulation of the Christian life.[51] In short, Athanasius's concept of deification therefore seems to encompass both ethical and realistic facets; the latter referring to the participation in the life of God, and the former the required subjugation of passions and the practice of virtue.[52]

In slight contrast to Athanasius who emphasized the realistic aspects of deification, Basil's close collaborator, Gregory of Nazianzus's[53] focus was the imitation of Christ through ascetic endeavors.[54] Like Athanasius, Nazianzus saw deification as an exchange that encompasses our entire relationship with Christ.[55] The primary means by which this deifying work is initiated in the life of the believer is through the work of the Spirit that begins with baptism. Thus, Winslow describes that, for Nazianzus, baptism is "the operative locus of the deifying economy of the Holy Spirit and as such provides for the individual what was made available to all men by the economy of the Incarnate Logos."[56] Unlike Athanasius however, the church father was more careful in delineating the metaphorical difference between

48. Anatolios, *Athanasius*, 151.

49. Athanasius, "Against the Arians," 1.42.

50. Anatolios, "Soteriological Significance of Christ's Humanity," 270.

51. Habets, *Theosis in the Theology of Thomas Torrance*, 80. T. F. Torrance himself understands *theosis* not so much as "divinization" of humanity but rather a re-creation of "our lost humanity, for it lifts us up in Christ to enjoy a fullness of human life" (Torrance, *Trinitarian Faith*, 189).

52. Bradshaw has observed that the Greek conception of *theosis* need not connote any ontological participation in the being of God but only in his activities and operations (*energeia*) (Bradshaw, *Aristotle East and West*, 177).

53. An account of their close relationship throughout their lifetime is found in Rousseau, *Basil of Caesarea*, 258–63.

54. Russell, *Doctrine of Deification*, 214. For a comprehensive study of Gregory of Nazianzus's concept of *theosis*, see Winslow, *Dynamics of Salvation*; also see Beeley, *Gregory of Nazianzus*, 116–21.

55. Torrance, *Trinitarian Faith*, 180–81.

56. Winslow, *Dynamics of Salvation*, 34.

the ethical and realistic aspects of deification. For Nazianzus, the deifying work of the Spirit does not obliterate the gap between uncreated and created nature, and Christopher Beeley has described Gregory as extremely judicious in guarding against the view that deification meant becoming God in any ontological sense.[57] In Nazianzus's thought therefore, all ontology is differentiated into two clearly distinguished categories, either divine or creaturely, and a fundamentally insurmountable chasm remains between the two. Therefore, in his address to a group of bishops describing his preferred terms for the Trinity, Gregory states,

> Let us speak and think of the Unbegotten and the Begotten and the One who Proceeds, if you will agree to let me coin some words . . . Let us speak of a creature as being "of God"—for that is a great thing when said of us, after all!—but never as being God. Only then will I accept that a creature is God, when I too may literally become God! This is the point: if something is God, it is not a creature, for the creature is classed with us, who are not gods. But if it is a creature, it is not God, for it began in time.[58]

Nazianzus's point is clear. While one may be in the process of deification that began through baptism, ultimately we are only gods ethically. In this, he was echoing the view of Clement of Alexandria who argued that we become like God "not in essence (for it is impossible for that, which is by adoption, to be equal in substance to that, which is by nature)."[59] As Winslow summarized, Nazianzus strongly rejected the notion that in deification the distinction between Creator from the creature can be overcome, and argues instead for a potential for growth towards fulfilled creatureliness.[60] Therefore, in terms of the work of the Spirit in deification, the Cappadocian father's concept may have closer resonance with scripture than the bishop of Alexandria.

Conclusion

This chapter has discussed three main contributions that the patristic fathers of the fourth century have made to pneumatology and that may be helpful in our times. Firstly, both Athanasius and Basil of Caesarea, in opposition to

---

57. Beeley, "Holy Spirit in Gregory Nazianzen."

58. Daley, *Gregory of Nazianzus*, Oration 42.17, 148.

59. Clement of Alexandria, "Stromata," 2.17. Clement made these comments under the assertion that "no disciple is above his master."

60. Winslow, *Dynamics of Salvation*, 186–88.

the *Pneumatomachi*, have successfully maintained that the Spirit is both distinct and fully divine, with concomitant implications for the doctrine of the Trinity. In contrast, the history of theology has shown how the church often suffers from an implicit binitarianism by ignoring the person and work of the Spirit, and it is here that the coherent vision of the fathers may be illuminating. Secondly, the Spirit was recognized by Basil and Nyssa as inseparable in operations from the other two Persons, and that only a consideration of the work of all Three in totality in worship and creation could do justice to the witness of scripture. Such a formulation may help guard against our modern attempts to carve out a separate economy for the Spirit such that he is seen as working independently of the Father and Son. Finally, the deifying work of the Spirit shows that his primary task remains the transformation of lives of believers into the ethical likeness of God through becoming Christlike, and serves to remind us that this process of life-change is more critical and fundamental than any other manifestations or gifts of the Spirit that may be the flavor of the month in our times.

Bibliography

Aghiorghoussis, Maximos Metr. "Applications of the Theme '*Eikon Theou*' (Image of God) According to Saint Basil the Great." *The Greek Orthodox Theological Review* 21 (1976) 265–88.

———. "Image as 'Sign' (*Semeion*) of God: Knowledge of God through the Image According to Saint Basil." *The Greek Orthodox Theological Review* 21 (1976) 19–54.

Anatolios, Khaled. *Athanasius: The Coherence of His Thought*. London: Routledge, 2004.

———. "The Soteriological Significance of Christ's Humanity in St Athanasius." *St Vladimir's Theological Quarterly* 40 (1996) 265–86.

Athanasius. "Against the Arians." In *Athanasius: Select Writings and Letters*, edited by Archibald Robertson, 303–447. Nicene and Post-Nicene Fathers of the Christian Church, Second Series, 4. Edinburgh: T. & T. Clark, 1989.

———. "Letters." In *Athanasius: Select Writings and Letters*, edited by Archibald Robertson, 575–78. Nicene and Post-Nicene Fathers of the Christian Church, Second Series, 4. Edinburgh: T. & T. Clark, 1989.

———. *The Letters of Saint Athanasius Concerning the Holy Spirit*. Translated by Cuthbert R. B. Shapland. London: Epworth, 1951.

———. *On the Incarnation*. Translated by John Behr. Popular Patristics Series 44. Yonkers, NY: St. Vladimir's Seminary Press, 2011.

———. "On the Incarnation of the Word." In *Athanasius: Select Writings and Letters*, edited by Archibald Robertson, 31–67. Nicene and Post-Nicene Fathers of the Christian Church, Second Series, 4. Edinburgh: T. & T. Clark, 1989.

Ayres, Lewis. *Nicaea and its Legacy: An Approach to Fourth-Century Trinitarian Theology*. Oxford: Oxford University Press, 2004.

———. "Not Three People: The Fundamental Themes of Gregory of Nyssa's Trinitarian Theology as Seen in *To Ablabius: On Not Three Gods*." *Modern Theology* 18 (2002) 445–74.
Barnes, Michel René. "The Fourth Century as Trinitarian Canon." In *Christian Origins: Theology, Rhetoric, and Community*, edited by Lewis Ayres and Gareth Jones, 47–67. New York: Routledge, 1998.
Basil. *Against Eunomius*. Translated by Mark DelCogliano and Andrew Radde-Gallwitz. Washington, DC: Catholic University of America Press, 2011.
———. *Contre Eunome, suivi de Eunome, Apologie*. Paris: Cerf, 1982.
———. *On the Holy Spirit*. Translated by David Anderson. Crestwood, NY: St. Vladimir's Seminary Press, 1980.
———. *St. Basil: Letters and Select Works*. Edited by Philip Schaff. Translated by Blomfield Jackson. Nicene and Post-Nicene Fathers of the Christian Church, Second Series, 8. Edinburgh: T. & T. Clark, 1989.
Beeley, Christopher A. *Gregory of Nazianzus on the Trinity and the Knowledge of God: In Your Light We Shall See Light*. Oxford Studies in Historical Theology. New York: Oxford University Press, 2008.
———. "The Holy Spirit in Gregory Nazianzen: The Pneumatology of Oration 31." In *God in Early Christian Thought: Essays in Memory of Lloyd G. Patterson*, edited by Andrew B. McGowan and Lloyd G. Patterson, 151–62. Supplements to Vigilae Christanae 94. Leiden: Brill, 2009.
Behr, John. *The Nicene Faith*. Vol. 2. 2 vols. Formation of Christian Theology 2. Crestwood, NY: St. Vladimir's Seminary Press, 2004.
Berthold, George C. "The Procession of the Spirit in Athanasius." *Studia Patristica* 41 (2006) 125–31.
Bradshaw, David. *Aristotle East and West: Metaphysics and the Division of Christendom*. Cambridge: Cambridge University Press, 2004.
Clement of Alexandria. "The Stromata." In *The Writings of the Fathers Down to A.D. 325*, edited by Alexander Roberts and James Donaldson, 299–568. Ante-Nicene Fathers 2. Peabody, MA: Hendrickson, 1995.
Daley, Brian. *Gregory of Nazianzus*. Early Church Fathers. London: Routledge, 2006.
Fedwick, Paul Jonathan. *The Church and the Charisma of Leadership in Basil of Caesarea*. Toronto: Pontifical Institute of Mediaeval Studies, 1979.
Gregory of Nazianzus. "Oration 43." In *Cyril of Jerusalem, Gregory Nazianzen*, translated by Charles Gordon Browne and James Edward Swallow, 395–422. Nicene and Post-Nicene Fathers of the Christian Church, Second Series, 7. Edinburgh: T. & T. Clark, 1989.
Gregory of Nyssa. *The Life of Moses*. Translated by Abraham J. Malherbe and Everett Ferguson. Classics of Western Spirituality. New York: Paulist, 1978.
———. "On 'Not Three Gods.'" In *Gregory of Nyssa: Dogmatic Treatises; Select Writings and Letters*, translated by William Moore and Henry Austin Wilson, 331–36. Nicene and Post-Nicene Fathers of the Christian Church, Second Series, 5. Edinburgh: T. & T. Clark, 1989.
———. "On the Holy Spirt." In *Gregory of Nyssa: Dogmatic Treatises; Select Writings and Letters*, translated by William Moore and Henry Austin Wilson, 315–25. Nicene and Post-Nicene Fathers of the Christian Church, Second Series, 5. Edinburgh: T. & T. Clark, 1989.

———. "On the Holy Trinity, and of the Godhead of the Holy Spirit." In *Gregory of Nyssa: Dogmatic Treatises; Select Writings and Letters*, translated by William Moore and Henry Austin Wilson, 326–30. Nicene and Post-Nicene Fathers of the Christian Church, Second Series, 5. Edinburgh: T. & T. Clark, 1989.

Gribomont, Jean. "Intransigence and Irenicism in Saint Basil's 'De Spiritu Sancto.'" In *In Honor of Saint Basil the Great*, edited by S. M. Clare, 109–36. Still River, MA: St. Bede's, 1979.

Habets, Myk. *Theosis in the Theology of Thomas Torrance*. Farnham, UK: Ashgate, 2009.

Hanson, Richard Patrick Crosland. *The Search for the Christian Doctrine of God: The Arian Controversy 318–381*. Edinburgh: T. & T. Clark, 1998.

Hennessy, Kristin. "An Answer to de Régnon's Accusers: Why We Should Not Speak of 'His' Paradigm." *Harvard Theological Review* 100 (2007) 179–97.

Hess, Hamilton. "The Place of Divinization in Athanasian Soteriology." *Studia Patristica* 26 (1993) 369–74.

Hildebrand, Stephen M. *The Trinitarian Theology of Basil of Caesarea: A Synthesis of Greek Thought and Biblical Truth*. Washington, DC: Catholic University of America Press, 2007.

Irenaeus of Lyons. "Against Heresies." In *The Apostolic Fathers, Justin Martyr, Irenaeus*, edited by Alexander Roberts and James Donaldson, 315–567. Ante-Nicene Fathers 1. Peabody, MA: Hendrickson, 2001.

Kärkkäinen, Veli-Matti. *One with God: Salvation as Deification and Justification*. Collegeville, MN: Liturgical, 2004.

Kelly, J. N. D. *Early Christian Creeds*. London: Continuum, 2006.

———. *Early Christian Doctrines*. San Francisco: HarperSanFrancisco, 1978.

Meredith, Anthony. *Gregory of Nyssa*. New York: Routledge, 1999.

Meyendorff, John. *Byzantine Theology: Historical Trends and Doctrinal Themes*. 2nd ed. New York: Fordham University Press, 1987.

Osborn, Eric Francis. *Irenaeus of Lyons*. Cambridge: Cambridge University Press, 2001.

Prestige, George L. *God in Patristic Thought*. London: SPCK, 1964.

Rousseau, Philip. *Basil of Caesarea*. Berkeley: University of California Press, 1994.

Russell, Norman. *The Doctrine of Deification in the Greek Patristic Tradition*. Oxford: Oxford University Press, 2004.

Stead, Christopher. *Philosophy in Christian Antiquity*. Cambridge: Cambridge University Press, 1994.

Torrance, Thomas F. *The Trinitarian Faith: The Evangelical Theology of the Ancient Catholic Church*. Edinburgh: T. & T. Clark, 1988.

Turcescu, Lucian. *Gregory of Nyssa and the Concept of Divine Persons*. Oxford: Oxford University Press, 2005.

Winslow, Donald F. *The Dynamics of Salvation: A Study in Gregory of Nazianzus*. Cambridge, MA: Philadelphia Patristic Foundation, 1979.

Yong, Amos. *The Spirit Poured Out on All Flesh: Pentecostalism and the Possibility of Global Theology*. Grand Rapids: Baker Academic, 2005.

Young, Frances M., and Andrew Teal. *From Nicaea to Chalcedon: A Guide to the Literature and its Background*. Grand Rapids: Baker Academic, 2010.

Zizioulas, John D. *Communion and Otherness: Further Studies in Personhood and the Church*. Edited by Paul McPartlan. London: T. & T. Clark, 2006.

Cultural/Pastoral-Theological Perspective

7

The Logos and Pneuma of Creation

A Cross-Cultural Reading of Romans 8 and the Inspirited World

K. K. Yeo

Introduction

THE LANGUAGE IN ROMANS 8 contains rich Pauline metaphors that are indicative of feeling, emotion, and spirit. Due to my cultural interest in understanding the cosmos in terms of a spirit of communion—a spirit that fosters interconnectedness among members of creation—this chapter explains my reading of Romans 8 culturally using two key concepts: 1) "*dao-de*" (道德) or "the logic of morality" that speaks of human beings who themselves are responsible members of the ecological system, and; 2) passion of edification, a mutual honoring in the life of the crucified Christ. The intention is to explore the continuity of thought between Pauline theology and the Chinese *dao* (道). I will use both the Confucianist and *daoist* understandings to speak of human beings as part of the created world and to speak of creation as an animated and spiritual world.[1]

---

1. For more, see Yeo, *Musing with Confucius and Paul*. On the relationship between human spirit and God's Spirit, see Alexander, *Humanity of Christ*.

Spirit(s) and Creation:
Paul and Chinese Worldviews

An initial reading of Romans 8 seems to suggest that, besides the language of mind (φρόνημα, 8:6, 27) and will (ἑκοῦσα, 8:20; see also 1 Cor 9:17), Pauline metaphors in the text include those of feeling, emotion, and spirits: fear (φόβον, 8:15, 3:18, 13:3, 7; see also 1 Cor 2:3; 2 Cor 5:11, 7:1, 5, 11, 15; Eph 5:21, 6:5; Phil 2:12; 1 Tim 5:20); crying out (κράζομεν, 8:15; 9:27; see also Gal 4:6); spirit of adoption (πνεῦμα υἱοθεσίας, 8:15, 23; see also 9:4; Gal 4:5; Eph 1:5); suffering together (συμπάσχομεν, 8:17; see also 1 Cor 12:26); eager expectation (ἀποκαραδοκία, 8:19; see also Phil 1:20); groaning (συστενάζει, 8:22); and birth pangs (συνωδίνει, 8:22). The intention of this chapter is to examine Romans 8, and to propose a thesis that all the terms mentioned above speak of both the rationality and the trans-rationality of the "animated creation" or "inspirited creation," just like the Spirit of God "intercedes in sighing unutterable" (ὑπερεντυγχάνει στεναγμοῖς ἀλαλήτοις, 8:26). Indeed, Romans 8:19 uses the word "creation" to signify the nonhuman world as Paul writes, "the creation waits with eager longing for the revealing of the children of God"—with "children of God" meaning humanity as created by God rather than enslaved by the imperial logic of domination and manipulation. While I agree with Joseph Fitzmyer that Paul's usage of "creation" (ἡ κτίσις) in 8:19 is about the "nonhuman" world,[2] I see this usage as a particular reference to differentiate humanity from the nonhuman aspect of God's creation. But I see also Paul's inclusive usage in his theology speaking of the interconnectedness between human and nonhuman entities of the whole creation. In other words, Paul "envision[s] creation as an animate being on par with humanity, for he claims that it also will receive 'the freedom of the glory of the children of God' [8:21]."[3]

Paul may have written the Epistle to the Romans in Greek, but his theological understanding is quite Hellenistic-Jewish and, therefore, closer to oriental thought than to Greco-Roman.[4] The Jewish worldview shares many more commonalities with primitive cultures, such as Chinese and Native American, in that they also perceive creation to be dynamic and spiritual, rather than static and materialistic.[5]

---

2. Fitzmyer, *Romans*, 506. See Paul's usage of this term in Rom 1:20, 25; 8:19, 20, 21, 22, 39; 2 Cor 5:17; Gal 6:15; Col 1:15, 23.

3. McGinn, "Feminists and Paul in Romans 8:18–23," 25.

4. See Torrance, *Theology in Reconciliation*, 27–28.

5. Jay B. McDaniel's models on the relationship between nature/creation and human beings can provide multiple lenses for reading Paul, and most of those models within the Christian traditions do not favor a domination hermeneutic. The first is

It is not necessary to make Paul into a Chinese, for that would be anachronistic, but my point is to show that Paul in Romans 8 does have a dynamic view of creation as a life force that is capable of yearning, sighing, and expressing passion or suffering—a similar worldview as that of the ancient Chinese. Yearning and sighing are not simply anthropocentric metaphors, but reveal the pain and suffering of creation when the power of sin and death corrupt its beautiful and good nature.

The Dao Connecting Heaven, Creation, and Human

The *dao*, in Paul's way of understanding the matrix of creation, is the *dao* that connects intimately heaven, creation, and human beings. Though Daoism and Confucianism have different understandings of *dao*, in that Daoism speaks of the life force and freedom of the cosmos whereas Confucianism speaks of the moral fiber of the cosmos, both see *dao* connecting heaven, earth, and human beings. I will focus first on the Confucianist understanding of *dao*: heavenly *dao* and humanly *dao*.

Confucianist thought perceives the purpose of being humans as living in a harmonious relationship with *dao*, the cosmic principle. Analects 4:8 reads, "Knowing *dao* in the morning, one can die in the evening,"[6] suggesting that one ought to know *dao* before one's death so that, in knowing *dao*, one can live in accordance with the cosmic principle. *Dao* is the way of life, or the vision of life to be understood and practiced. It is referred to as *"tiandao"* (the Way of Heaven, 天道) in *Analects* 5:13 or *"rendao"* (the Way of

---

a Celtic model (Irish saints in the early Middle Age) that sees nature as a medium through which communion with the Spirit is possible. The second is a fertility model (Hildegard and nature mystics) that sees the Divine in the fertility of earth processes. The third is a friendship model (Francis of Assisi and the desert fathers) that sees the possibility of befriending all creatures for communion, companionship, and compassion. The fourth is a covenantal model that sees God's love for all creation. The fifth is a sacramental model (Orthodox traditions) that sees the sacramental dimension of all creation and, thus, the redemptive process of all. The sixth is a history of creation or evolutionary model (Irenaeus, Teilhard de Chardin, Thomas Berry, process theologians). See McDaniel, *With Roots and Wings*, 119–20. On my previous work on Pauline theology and Native American cultures, see Yeo, "Christ and the Earth," 179–218.

6. See Chen, *Lunyu Duxun Jiegu (Confucian Analects)*, 50. Yearley explains this verse, "To hear about the *dao* in the morning leads one to be able to face death in the evening with an attitude that can be described in related but different ways: contentment [Waley], or acceptance [Ivanhoe], or a lack of regret [Legge], or a not minding of it [Brookses], or a knowing that it is all right to die [Dawson], or perhaps more problematic, a knowing that you have not lived in vain [Lau]" (Yearley, "Existentialist Reading of Book 4 of the *Analects*," 263, 271–72n39).

Humanity, 人道) in *Analects* 15:29, both of which speak of the same nature that heaven and humans share. Therefore, human beings live in accordance with the principles of heaven and humanity.

The word "*tiandao*" occurs once in the *Analects* (5:13), and it is one of two texts (the other is 17:2) in which *xing* (human nature, 性) also appears.⁷ Stephen A. Wilson's reading of the *Analects* 5:13 regarding *tiandao* and human nature is illuminating, and explains the *dao* that connects heaven, humanity, and cosmos/earth:

> What makes the particular way of life Confucius advocates optimally humane (i.e., what makes human human (*xing*) is humane or *ren* 仁) is its expressing perfectly the place of human beings within the context of society, societies within the context of the larger world, and the larger world within the context of what Fingarette calls the "Cosmic *Dao*" [or '*tiandao*']. That is to say, the consummation of humaneness is not merely "fitting in" or being a fully socialized, graceful, and avid participator in society. At least for Confucius, it is virtue, and virtue has everything to do with what one takes to be the nature of human beings and their proper place within their physical and/or metaphysical environment.⁸

Similarly, a Confucianist scholar Mou Zongsan interprets the intrinsic connection between the outer transcendence of heaven (*tian*) and the inner transcendence of human nature (*xing*) as the Confucian ideal,⁹ vis-à-vis the bond that makes virtue cultivation a union with cosmic *dao*. That is to say, the unity of heaven and human (*tianren heyi*, 天人合一) and the unity of heaven and human in virtue (*tianren hede*, 天人合德) are fulfillments of the mandate of Heaven (*tianming*, 天命) through moral cultivation of *ren* (humaneness, 仁). Consequently, in Confucian thought, there is no dichotomy between humanity (*ren*) and cosmos (*tiandi*, 天地), implying a perichoretic relationship between the human and nonhuman worlds.

The word *rendao*, which appears in *Analects* 15:29, can be translated as "'a way of becoming consummately and authoritatively human.'"¹⁰ As 15:29 expounds, to become fully human is for the "person . . . to broaden the way (*dao*), and not [simply] the way (*dao*) that broadens the person.'"¹¹ In other

---

7. On various readings of the commentary tradition, see Ivanhoe, "Whose Confucius?," 119–33.
8. Wilson, "Conformity, Individuality," 99.
9. Mou, *Zhongguo Zhexue De Tezhi (Special Features of Chinese Philosophy)*, 52.
10. Ames and Rosemont, *Analects of Confucius*, 45.
11. Ames and Rosemont, *Analects of Confucius*, 46.

words, *rendao* (way of humanity) is part and parcel of the cosmic *dao* that "is transcendent, in the sense that it continues to exist even when it is not being actively manifested in the world, but it requires human beings to be fully realized (as humans)."[12]

The greatest Daoist philosopher, Laozi writes in *Daodejing*: "*Dao* produced Oneness. Oneness produced Duality. Duality evolved into trinity, and trinity evolved into the myriad things."[13] The word *dao* may correspond to *logos* (word, reason, thing, etc.) in Greek, but certainly transcends a rationalistic understanding of the *logos*. *Dao* is self-generative; it is the metamorphosis of a self-contained universe. In both classical cultures of the Chinese and the Greek, *dao* (cosmic principle), *tianli* (cosmic order), and *logos* were used to designate the creative principle or wisdom that generates a way of life that is harmonious and fulsome. *Dao*, understood in Chinese culture as "the Way," often means the concrete expression of the Transcendent. Therefore, the realization of moral order by humanity reflects the cosmic order (*tianli*) immanent within them. Just like *tian*, *dao* is also eternal in its existence and creative in its power; humanity as part of the cosmos participates in this *dao* that is perpetual and self-sustaining.

Thus, the dialectical relationship between *dao* (Way) and *de* (morality) encompasses the intertwined relationship between theology and ethics, which in turn is based on the union between *tian* (Heaven) and *ren* (humanity), that is, *tianren heyi* (union between heaven and humanity).

Against the semantic worldview of the Confucianist and Daoist understandings of *dao*, I read the theology of Romans 8 morally, and I read the virtue of Chinese worldview theologically.

Paul's View of Inspirited Creation and Incarnated Christ

The apostle Paul in Romans 8 employs a wide range of metaphors for salvation of the created world.[14] A concentration of metaphors describes creation as inspirited and animated with life—from which each member finds its own life form but also out of which members complement one another. Paul is not writing a thesis on natural science, but a theological science of creation aiming at the purposeful goal and soteriological logic of God's creation of the whole cosmos. Romans 8 implies that God loves and values creation, so

---

12. Slingerland, *Confucius Analects*, 186.
13. Translation of Bodde, "Harmony and Conflict," 23.
14. As has been shown by Beker, *Paul the Apostle*, 256–60; and Becker, *Paul*, 407–11.

much so that redemption of the created and human worlds is the principal platform of God's sacrificial love.

Unfortunately, too much of the traditional Western understanding of natural theology has been dualistic, in the sense that, God and creation, nature and supernature, are perceived to be in opposition to one another, and worse, if perceived as one dominating over the other. Alister E. McGrath critiques such "essentially dualist framework . . . [of] implicit assumption of ontological bipolarity . . . [that affirms] the transcendent can be accessed via the mundane, the eternal through the temporal, or the supernatural through the natural."[15] He writes,

> Nature and supernature are not to be thought of as two separate worlds, but as different expressions of the same reality. The doctrine of the incarnation affirms the capacity of the natural to disclose the divine, both on account of its status as the *divine creation,* and as the object of *God's habitation.* The point was stressed by John of Damascus, in his controversy with those who held that material or physical objects could not be vehicles of divine disclosure or revelation.[16]

Similarly, ecophilosophers, such as R. Avens and H. Skolimowski,[17] have been deliberating a "new gnosis"[18] of inspirited metaphysical principle as a way to overcome Kantian or Cartesian mind-body dualism. Donald E. Davies writes that human beings "are ontologically inseparable from the parabolic 'body of nature,' thus participating in its primordial rhythms by our embodiment. We are grounded in and to the earth, its rhythmic periodicities, and the meta-temporal fluctuations of a larger, more subtle Nature."[19]

Both created and human worlds, distinct yet intimately related entities, face the same enemy—death or futility, from which they need to be saved—although Paul qualifies that the futility of nonhuman creation is "not of its own will" (οὐχ ἑκοῦσα; 8:20). This suggests that 1) there is innate goodness in nonhuman creation; 2) the "fall" of nonhuman creation is not by its own volition; and 3) the futility of the human world is one of its own will. Death is the destructive force that makes creation fall short of God's purpose, desire, and glory. Futility, likewise, is the destruction of creation's purpose, the frustration of creation's effort to be itself alone, rather than the ability to find fulfillment in the Creator and, therefore, in his cosmic *dao.* The power of sin

---

15. McGrath, *Open Secret*, 14.
16. McGrath, *Open Secret*, 14–15.
17. Skolimowski, *Eco-philosophy*, taken from Davis, "Human/Nature," 106.
18. Avens, *New Gnosis*; taken from Davis, "Human/Nature" 106.
19. Davis, "Human/Nature," 106.

and death breaks and makes both human and nonhuman worlds, causing them to be less than who they are as they fall out of relationship with their Creator and, therefore, with one another. The solidarity between humanity and creation was originally destined to find joy in the Creator and enjoyment of his creation. Now, after the falling out of that relationship, their solidarity is none other than their groaning and suffering together (Rom 8:19–22). Human and nonhuman worlds are co-sufferers, for "the earth is in the same predicament as human beings: it is weak, suffering, subject to futility and death, and waiting for redemption from God."[20]

Romans 8:20 states that "the creation was subjected to futility, not of its own will by the will of the one who subjected it." Robert Jewett argues that the subjection in 8:20 does not come from God the Creator, but from humans who "play God and ended up ruining not only their relations with each other but also their relation to the natural world."[21] In light of Paul's use of the divine passive οὐχ ἑκοῦσα ("was subjected") and the term ματαιότητι ("emptiness, vanity, fruitlessness"), and φθορᾶς ("corruption"), Jewett is convinced that Paul in Romans 8 "has in mind the abuse of the natural world by Adam and his descendants. The basic idea is that the human refusal to accept limitations ruins the world."[22] He continues:

> Paul's audience could well have thought about how imperial ambitions, military conflicts, and economic exploitation had led to the erosion of the natural environment throughout the Mediterranean world, leaving ruined cities, depleted fields, deforested mountains, and polluted streams as evidence of this universal human vanity. That such vanity, enhanced by the Roman civic cult, was promising the restoration of the "golden age," "the age of Saturn," appears utterly preposterous in the light of this critical, biblical tradition.[23]

In the context of an imperfect creation (cosmos), Paul speaks of the sovereignty of God, regarding the comprehensiveness of God's purpose in the cosmos. One cannot miss the point in Romans 8 that the christological redemption is for *all creation*, including humanity and nature, both of whom are in bondage and suffering. That the Spirit, also known as God's presence, groans with creation and the church also points to the impartiality of God's love for all creation. In that sense, we can understand the crucified Christ as God in solidarity with creation in its suffering, using an intimate metaphor

20. Yeo, "Christ and the Earth," 201.
21. Jewett, *Romans*, 513.
22. Jewett, *Romans*, 513.
23. Jewett, *Romans*, 513.

of a woman and a child, birth pangs (συνωδίνει, 8:22).²⁴ In other words, it is the same divine Logos/*Dao* who creates *and* is immanently at work in creation to liberate creation from bondage, death, and futility. The divine Logos/*Dao* is fully embodied in the person of Christ, and therefore serves as *the analogy* between the Creator and the whole of creation—although affirming also the difference between Creator and creation. The word "analogy" (*analogia entis*) has been used in traditional Christian understanding to speak of God's presence in the world and yet not as part of the natural order itself—thus maintaining the ontological difference between God and creation while seeing the analogical correspondence.²⁵

Yet, any God-talk can swing to one side of the pendulum or the other. Romans 8:28 is often read anthropologically to the exclusion of nonhuman creation. However, Paul believes adamantly that "*all things* work together for good" (8:28). The word "all" (*panta*) in the Romans context includes weaknesses, suffering, adversity, brokenness, sin and depravity, or even the possible reality in first century of the bearing of the cross—all these not only experienced by humanity, but also by the *whole* of creation in the cosmic scale.²⁶ It is erroneous to think that salvation and the working out of good is just for Christians or believers, or only for humankind. We may infer from Paul's argument here that all things do not necessarily work together for good *on their own*, yet the book of Romans declares that *God's Spirit* is able to bring good *eventually* out of all things. That is the Christian hope.²⁷

God's Spirit enables the human and nonhuman worlds to have their own unique life-forms, but God's Spirit also enables their differentiated creatureliness to be interconnected to one another. This interconnection is one of solidarity rather than superiority, one of mutuality rather than hierarchy, one of interdependence rather than utilitarianism. Human beings are a significant part of creation, but they are not the only part, for the human world and the nonhuman world are in an ecology or empathic connection of mutual dependence and support. Thus, humankind is not to be envisioned as subjugating the earth, for humankind is not more skilled in self-preservation than the nonhuman world. In fact, humankind

---

24. See Elliott, "Creation, Cosmos, and Conflict," 153–54, on Roman subduing of women in contrast to Paul's view of "the real . . . invisible power of God . . . [on] reality [that] was stirring as palpably and irresistibly as the contractions of childbirth."

25. McGrath, *Open Secret*, 188–89.

26. The subject of Rom 8:28 is "all" (א C D F G K L P *al.*), not "God" (A B 81 *al.*), but the meaning of Paul in theism rather than naturalism is implicit in his theology; see discussion in Dunn, *Romans 1–8*, 481; Fitzmyer, *Romans*, 523; Byrne, *Romans*, 271–72.

27. Ziesler, *Paul's Letter*, 225.

is endowed with greater responsibility to care for others—for other people and for nonhuman creation.

We have seen that if there is any "subjugation" language used in Romans 8, what Paul might have thought of Genesis 1:28 is that it is about human responsibility of caring for the earth against the power of dominating sin and destruction. The words *rādā* (rule) and *kābaš* (dominion) of the earth in Genesis 1:28 are not about "pitiless subjugation and a contemptuous trampling underfoot"[28] of humanity over the earth. Rather, the metaphors should be read in terms of the human role in overcoming the chaotic universe and endangered world—along the earlier narrative of creation not so much *ex nihilo* (out of nothing) but *ex tumult* (out of tumults)—thus, saving and forming goodness out of *tohuwabohu* ("formlessness and void"). Andreas Schuele is correct in rendering the meaning of the two words in relation to violence and how as *imago Dei*, human beings are to care for the world:

> [T]he violence that is inherent in the world and threatens it from which within does indeed need to be "suppressed" and "subjugated." . . . Through the idea of human beings as the *imago Dei*, the history of civilizations becomes an integral part of the history of creation (Gen 10) . . . As such the *imago Dei* becomes a semantic correlate of other concepts such as love, intimacy, esteem, responsibility, care, and respect.[29]

Instead of subjugation of humans over the earth (*dominium terrae* theology), we see Paul's affirmation of the co-suffering of all creation, that is, the human and nonhuman worlds. For example, the cosmos groans with humanity in fallenness, because all are the same as they wait for eschatological salvation. There is no special privileging of human beings to the detriment of the cosmos. The Lakota people used the phrase *mitakuye oyasin* ("all my relations") to refer to the interconnectedness of every member of the creation with one another.[30] And McGinn writes of Romans 8, "in this process of living with the creation, human beings may make claims on the earth and its creatures, but the earth and its creatures also make claims on humanity."[31]

In fact, if the word "soul" or "spirit" of humanity is used to denote the core of humanness, then the "sickness" or "brokenness" of the human soul/spirit will count on Christ and the help of others (creation) to mend it. Donald Alexander writes, "As the *executive director* of the soul, the life of the

28. Schuele, "Uniquely Human," 8.
29. Schuele, "Uniquely Human," 14.
30. Yeo, "Christ and the Earth," 202–3.
31. McGinn, "Feminists and Paul in Romans 8:18–23," 33.

person, the human is that dimension of human nature that enables persons to act and to react toward others (including nonhuman creation) in a manner that mirrors the spiritual and moral character of God."[32] It is significant to include nonhuman creation in the word "others" because of what Paul has expressed in Romans 8, linking God's Spirit with the whole creation in the matter of salvation of human and nonhuman worlds. Perhaps, in light of such understanding, we should envision the human spirit as not simply a connection to God, but also, in Alexander's words:

> an orientation, an openness to the world (whole creation), an *exocentric centeredness* or capacity that, while not divorced from our biologically conditioned life, nevertheless in depth and complexity reaches beyond it in encounters of personal relatedness. *To reach beyond* is intended to convey a personal capacity for self-transcendence; that is, to reach (go) beyond the givenness of the natural in the instinctual equipment of human creatureliness and their relations to their biological capacities, or to transcend the immediacy of the present, described as human *openness* to the world and to the future.[33]

Indeed, the cosmic salvation of Christ, as described in Romans 8, is inextricably connected with God's primordial goal of consummating the original purpose of creating the *whole* cosmos, contra the Roman new-age ideology of conquer and domination. The purpose of consummating God's creating act takes on an eschatological character of the *alpha* (the beginning point of creation) and the *omega* (the finality of creation) in Christ. It is Christ who has chosen to be God's very own means of creation, thus sovereignly transforming the fallen world through Christ. The goal (*telos*) of God's creating the whole cosmos is the ultimate purpose of God's justice in restoring *all creation, not just individuals,* to wholeness, thus bringing the *whole* creation into a loving and just/righteous relationship with God. Indeed, "The redemption of one is the redemption of the other."[34] The active roles played by human and nonhuman creation in the renewal of the whole cosmos is described by Jewett as a "circular reversal," in which "creation waits for renewal by the children of God, and at the same time aids in their liberation."[35]

The agency of Jesus Christ as the "firstborn" of all creation (Rom 8:28) cannot be missed in the Romans text. The christological hymn in Col

32. Alexander, *Humanity of Christ*, 30.
33. Alexander, *Humanity of Christ*, 31.
34. Yeo, "Christ and the Earth," 203.
35. Jewett, *Romans*, 515.

1:15–17 also speaks of the cosmic vocation of Jesus Christ and the cosmic ministry of the Holy Spirit. Jesus Christ is the Lord of life, in whom all things cohere and to whom all things tend (Col 1:16–17).

God's love and his way of valuing creation, obliges human beings as servants of God to love creation the way God does. The "sons of God" (τῶν υἱῶν τοῦ θεοῦ; 8:19) are given the mission to restore the natural world, as well as the human world, through the gospel of "the firstborn." Jewett writes,

> These converts take the place of Caesar in the imperial propaganda about the golden age, but they employ no weapons to vanquish foes . . . . As the children of God are redeemed by the gospel, they begin to regain a rightful dominion over the created world (Gen 1:28–30; Ps 8:5–8); in more modern terms, their altered lifestyle and revised ethics begin to restore the ecological system that had been thrown out of balance by wrongdoing (1:18–32) and sin (Rom 5–7).[36]

It is significant also to note in Paul's teaching that "sons of God" do not see the subjection of creation as simply a single event of the "fall" or primeval curse in Genesis 1–3, but an ongoing occurrence. In other words, the suffering of creation is somehow tied to the wrongdoings of humankind to creation. W. Foerster writes that, "The futility takes the form of temporality which offers both space for repentance and the possibility of offense."[37]

Romans 8 reveals the justice of God as "eco-justice" that affirms the value and interrelatedness of all forms of life—as all wait for redemption. Creation and the order of things will show humanity the way to be human. All have their places in the system of life, therefore, greedy self-interest alters and distorts the place of others and of the system, as well as ourselves. Plants and animals are vital parts of life's system, just as humans also are essential parts of the same system.

The sacrificial love of God for creation in Paul's theology speaks of the centrality of the solidarity of Christ's suffering. Paul's soteriology is not simply about a substitutionary atonement *for* human sin (Rom 3:25; 5:6–8; 8:32; 2 Cor 5:14–15; Gal 2:20; 3:13; 1 Thess 5:9–10),[38] but much more so—since humanity is a part of creation—about God's loving involvement with creation that takes the christological and pneumatic (Holy Spirit) form of suffering, in solidarity with, and in an immanent participation with the life and trials of

---

36. Jewett, *Romans*, 512. See also the similar thesis of Elliott, "Creation, Cosmos, and Conflict," 152–53; and Foerster, "Ktizō," 485.

37. Foerster, "Ktizō," 485.

38. On the debate of the words *hilasterion* ("expiation" or "propitiation") and *paresin* ("passing over" or "overlooking") in Rom 3:25, see Dunn, *Theology of Paul*, 212–18.

creation. This kind of solidarity and participation brings about the reconciliation of all with God and their restoration of glory as intended and created by God. The "triple sighing of creation, Christians, and the Spirit"[39] empowers the church (which is the Body of Christ and the immanent presence of Christ) to be and to do mission in the Spirit and in solidarity with creation. This solidarity, in turn, takes a christological form as sacrificial love for all creation and a rendition of their glory.

Conclusion: Creaturely Human and Inspirited Creation

The summary of our thesis below is an attempt to construct Christian Chinese theology regarding creation. The intertextual reading of two worldviews, Pauline and Chinese, encourages us to focus on elements that are commensurable in order to bridge and overcome the distance and even conflicts of the two worldviews. Both worldviews do share the view of "inspirited" souls for the freedom and personhood of human beings. Christians often practice and enjoy the mystical union of divine and human beings. Believing in the will of God/heaven, people can have their will of freedom; thus, the relationship between Creator and creation is understood via the incarnation, that is, the Word made flesh. It is the permeation and emanation of God's breath/Word in the world that guides and sustains it.

In the patristic tradition, Tertullian writes of the relationship between the human soul and nature:

> These testimonies of the soul are simple as true, commonplace as simple, universal as commonplace, natural as universal, divine as natural. I don't think they can appear frivolous or feeble to any one, if he reflect on the majesty of nature, from which the soul derives its authority. If you acknowledge the authority of the mistress, you will own it also in the disciple. Well, nature is the mistress here, and her disciple is the soul. But everything the one has taught or the other learned, has come from God—the Teacher of the teacher.[40]

In early Chinese traditions, it is to some extent the Confucianists, but mostly the Daoist philosophers (also the Yin Yang philosophers), whose idea of an organically related cosmos most interest me in making a connection

---

39. Schneider, "Stenazō," 1076.

40. Tertullian, *On the Testimony of the Soul*, 26. See also Allen, *Spiritual Theology*, ch. 8.

with Romans 8.[41] The second greatest Daoist philosopher, Zhuangzi, for example, argues that because all things (*wanwu* 万物) are organically related, therefore, through the process of mutual transformation (*hua* 化), all life forms will be united. Zhuangzi writes, "All the ten-thousand things and I are one" (chap. 1), speaking not only of physical union, but also of psycho-virtue communion with the cosmos. Zhuangzi uses metaphoric language to describe such joy and beauty in at-one-ment or harmony with the cosmos:

> If you were to climb up on the Way (*Dao*) and its Virtue (*De*) and go drifting and wandering (*you* [游]), neither praised nor damned, now a dragon, now a snake, shifting (*hua*) with the times, never willing to hold on to one course only. Now up, now down, taking harmony for your measure, drifting and wandering (*you*) with the ancestor of the ten thousand things, treating things as things, but not letting them treat you as a thing—then how could you get into any trouble? (chap. 20)[42]

Paul's theology on living with Word or *Dao*, with others and oneself, is that the Trinitarian life (Christ and God's Spirit) has initiated, enabled, and consummated the reality of the whole cosmos living fully in God, the Source of life. By receiving such gift/grace and blessing/benediction, humans will then be able to empathize with one another through the *perichoresis* of divine life—as Jesus, the Living Word, has demonstrated that sacrificial love for all on the Cross. The higher purpose of attaining union with the *Dao* or the Word is so that one identifies with the crucifixion of Christ and also comes into union with his resurrection—the matrix of God's creation.

Bibliography

Alexander, Donald L. *The Humanity of Christ and the Healing of the Dysfunction of the Human Spirit.* Eugene, OR: Wipf & Stock, 2015.

Allen, Diogenes. *Spiritual Theology: The Theology of Yesterday for Spiritual Help Today.* Lanham, MD: Cowley, 1997.

Ames, Roger T., and Henry Rosemont Jr. *The Analects of Confucius: A Philosophical Translation.* New York: Random House, 1998.

Avens, Roberts. *The New Gnosis: Heidegger, Hillman, and Angels.* Dallas: Spring, 1984.

Becker, Jürgen. *Paul: Apostle to the Gentiles.* Translated by O. C. Dean Jr. Louisville: Westminster John Knox, 1993.

---

41. See my Chinese monograph in reading the books of Zhuangzi and James intertextually: 《庄子与雅各》 [*Zhuangzi and James*]. On natural spirituality, see Hudson, *Natural Spirituality*, ch. 2.

42. Watson, *Complete Works of Chuang Tzu*, 209; English full text available online at http://www.terebess.hu/english/chuangtzu.html.

Beker, Johan Christiaan. *Paul the Apostle: The Triumph of God in Life and Thought*. Philadelphia: Fortress, 1994.

Bodde, Derk. "Harmony and Conflict in Chinese Philosophy." In *Studies in Chinese Thought*, edited by Arthur F. Wright, 19–80. Chicago: University of Chicago Press, 1953.

Byrne, Brendan. *Romans*. Edited by Daniel J. Harrington. Sacra Pagina Series 6. Collegeville, MN: Liturgical, 1996.

Chen, Shihchuan. *Lunyu Duxun Jiegu (Confucian Analects. A Revised Text and New Commentary)*. Hong Kong: Union, 1972.

Davis, Donald E. "Human/Nature: Toward a Critical Ecology." *The Humanistic Psychologist* 14 (1986) 105–12.

Dunn, James D. G. *Romans 1–8*. Word Biblical Commentary 38A. Dallas: Word, 1988.

———. *The Theology of Paul the Apostle*. Grand Rapids: Eerdmans, 1998.

Elliott, Neil. "Creation, Cosmos, and Conflict in Romans 8–9." In *Apocalyptic Paul: Cosmos and Anthropos in Romans 5–8*, edited by Beverly Roberts Gaventa, 131–56. Waco, TX: Baylor University Press, 2013.

Fitzmyer, Joseph A. *Romans: A New Translation with Introduction and Commentary*. Anchor Bible 33. New York: Doubleday, 1993.

Foerster, W. "Ktizō." In *Theological Dictionary of the New Testament*, edited by Gerhard Kittel and Gerhard Friedrich, translated and abridged by Geoffrey W. Bromiley, 481–86. Grand Rapids: Eerdmans, 1985.

Hudson, Joyce Rockwood. *Natural Spirituality: Recovering the Wisdom Tradition in Christianity*. Danielsville, GA: JRH, 2000.

Ivanhoe, Philip J. "Whose Confucius? Which Analects?" In *Confucius and the Analects: New Essays*, edited by Bryan W. Van Norden, 119–33. Oxford: Oxford University Press, 2002.

Jewett, Robert. *Romans: A Commentary*. Hermeneia. Minneapolis: Fortress, 2007.

McDaniel, Jay B. *With Roots and Wings: Christianity in an Age of Ecology and Dialogue*. Maryknoll, NY: Orbis, 1995.

McGinn, Sheila E. "Feminists and Paul in Romans 8:18–23: Toward a Theology of Creation." In *Gender, Tradition, and Romans: Shared Ground, Uncertain Borders*, edited by Cristina Grenholm and Daniel Patte, 21–36. New York: T. & T. Clark, 2005.

McGrath, Alister E. *The Open Secret: A New Vision for Natural Theology*. Malden, MA: Blackwell, 2008.

Mou, Zongsan. *Zhongguo Zhexue De Tezhi (The Special Features of Chinese Philosophy)*. Taipei: Xuesheng, 1998.

Schneider, J. "Stenazō." In *Theological Dictionary of the New Testament*, edited by Gerhard Kittel and Gerhard Friedrich, translated and abridged by Geoffrey W. Bromiley, 1076. Grand Rapids: Eerdmans, 1985.

Schuele, Andreas. "Uniquely Human: The Ethics of the *Imago Dei* in Genesis 1–11." *Toronto Journal of Theology* 27 (2011) 5–16.

Skolimowski, Henryk. *Eco-Philosophy: Designing New Tactics for Living*. New York: Boyers, 1981.

Slingerland, Edward, trans. *Confucius Analects: With Selections from Traditional Commentaries*. Indianapolis: Hackett, 2003.

Tertullian. *On the Testimony of the Soul.* Translated by Thomas Herbert Bindley. London: SPCK, 1914. http://www.tertullian.org/articles/bindley_test/bindley_test_05test.htm.

Torrance, Thomas F. *Theology in Reconciliation: Essays towards Evangelical and Catholic Unity in East and West.* London: Chapman, 1975.

Watson, Burton, trans. *The Complete Works of Chuang Tzu.* New York: Columbia University Press, 1968.

Wilson, Stephen A. "Conformity, Individuality, and the Nature of Virtue: A Classical Confucian Contribution to Contemporary Ethical Reflection." In *Confucius and the Analects: New Essays*, edited by Bryan W. Van Norden, 119–33. Oxford: Oxford University Press, 2002.

Yearley, Lee H. "An Existentialist Reading of Book 4 of the Analects." In *Confucius and the Analects: New Essays*, edited by Bryan W. Van Norden, 237–74. Oxford: Oxford University Press, 2002.

Yeo, K. K. "Christ and the Earth in Pauline and Native American Understandings." In *Cross-Cultural Paul: Journeys to Others, Journeys to Ourselves*, edited by Charles H. Cosgrove et al., 179–218. Grand Rapids: Eerdmans, 2005.

———. *Musing with Confucius and Paul: Toward a Chinese Christian Theology.* Eugene, OR: Cascade, 2008.

———.《庄子与雅各：隐喻生命，遨游天恩》. 上海: 华东师范大学出版社, 2012. [*Zhuangzi and James* (Shanghai: Huadong Shifan Daxue VI Horae, 2012)].

Ziesler, John A. *Paul's Letter to the Romans.* London: SCM, 1989.

8

An Analysis of the Conceptual Metaphor THE HOLY SPIRIT IS FIRE in Selected Mandarin Christian Songs

Kai-Wen Karen Yuan

Introduction

"The Holy Spirit's fire" (聖靈的火) and "the Spirit's fire" (靈火) are terms common in Mandarin Christian books and praise songs. In Chinese Christian book stores and seminary libraries, Mandarin Christian books entitled "The Spirit's Fire" or similar are readily available. A glance through translated works shows that publishers have discarded original titles in favor of titles such as "The Spirit's Fire" in Mandarin to highlight the Holy Spirit's role as addressed in those books. For example, CCM Publishers in Hong Kong use 《靈火力源》 (literally, "The Spirit's Fire, the Power Source")[1] for Leona Frances Choy's *Powerlines: What Great Evangelicals Believed about the Holy Spirit*;[2] KIANOS Pte Ltd. published Raymond J. Davis's story of missions in Ethiopia, *Fire on the Mountains*, as 《高山靈火：一個非洲土著集體歸主的當代神蹟》 (literally, "The Spirit's Fire on the Mountains: A Miracle of the Communal Conversion of an African Tribe").[3]

1. Unless specified as official versions, the literal translation of all Mandarin book titles and lyrics are my own.
2. 蔡麗安 (Leona Frances Choy), 《靈火力源》.
3. 戴理望 (Raymond J. Davis), 《高山靈火》.

A typical case is the Church Revival series from the Olive Foundation of Taipei, a collection of translated books about the reviving work of the Holy Spirit across the world. The series editor dropped the original English titles and introduced "fire" ("火") into each title. That methodical insertion gives a sense of unity to the series of translated works and at the same time reveals the editor's awareness that "fire" or "the Spirit's fire" signifies "revival." The following list shows the original titles and their Mandarin counterparts in the series:

The Argentine Story 《火從天降—阿根廷大復興》 (literally, "Fire from Heaven—The Argentine Revival"),

The Flaming Flame 《火的延燒—阿根廷大復興續篇》 (literally, "Spreading Fire—Sequel to the Argentine Revival"),

Revival Fires in Canada 《奔騰之火—加拿大復興實錄》 (literally, "Surging Fire—A Report of the Canadian Revival"),

The Korean Pentecost and the Sufferings Which Followed 《野火燎原—韓國大復興報導》 (literally, "Spreading Wildfire—A Report of the Korean Revival"),

When the Spirit's Fire Swept Korea 《靈火繼焚燒—韓國教會大復興續》 (literally, "The Spirit's Fire Keeps Burning—Sequel to the Korean Revival"),

Another Wave of Revival 《火浪湧來—艾蘇薩街復興始末》 (literally, "Falling Waves of Fire—A Report of the Azusa Street Revival"), etc.[4]

This practice of publishers of Mandarin translations books on this subject shows their preference for terms such as "the Spirit's fire" to emphasize the Holy Spirit's paramount role in missions and revivals. Such phrases also occur frequently in Mandarin Christian songs. From earlier works, such as Li Jingxiong's "Hymn to the Holy Spirit" (李景雄〈聖靈頌〉 and Bolun Yang's "May the Spirit's Fire Revive Me"(楊伯倫〈願那靈火復興我〉) to more recent ones such as the Stream of Praise's "Fire of Revival"(讚美之泉〈復興的火〉)and Hing-Chai Cheng's "The Holy Spirit's Fire"(曾興才〈聖靈的火〉), there are many examples of the apparently prevalent Chinese Christian thought that the Holy Spirit and fire are so closely connected

4. 愛德華·米勒 (Edward Miller),《火從天降》；愛德華·米勒 (Edward Miller),《火的延燒》； 高科爾 (Kurt E. Koch),《奔騰之火》；威廉·布雷爾與布魯斯·亨特 (William Blair and Bruce Hunt),《野火燎原》； 古約翰等人 (Jonathan Goforth, et al.),《靈火繼焚燒》； 法蘭克·巴特曼 (Frank Bartleman),《火浪湧來》.

that "the Spirit's fire" is almost a synonym for the Holy Spirit or His work. Interestingly, "the Holy Spirit's fire" and "the Spirit's fire" are not actual Biblical terms, whether in Mandarin or in the original Hebrew and Greek. The indicators of a connection between the Spirit and fire are the explicit and implicit uses of the metaphor of fire for the Holy Spirit.

The common Chinese Christian use of vocabulary referring to the Spirit as fire has motivated this short study. The primary purpose of this study is to investigate the theological implications of the terms and, by scriptural analysis, to ascertain whether the blanket use of those terms is justified. Since the Bible never employs those terms directly, we cannot conduct an analysis of the words themselves but must rather seek to analyze the concepts conveyed by them. So we apply conceptual metaphor theory to reveal how the Bible uses the metaphor of fire to refer to the Holy Spirit.

Based on scriptural analysis, we hope to be able to find a sound basis for the conceptual metaphor THE HOLY SPIRIT IS FIRE and its two sub-metaphors: THE HOLY SPIRIT'S JUDGMENT IS FIRE and THE HOLY SPIRIT'S REVIVAL IS FIRE.[5] We shall then select some Mandarin Christian songs and examine the use of the two sub-metaphors in their lyrics. Singing is a medium of Christians worship and song lyrics, in which authors express their theological views, will shape the thought of those who sing them. Lyrics may be assumed to influence the thought and the spirituality of individuals and congregations. In view of this, we hope in this study to be able to clarify the basis for the terms "the Holy Spirit's fire" and "the Spirit's fire" and their associated theological concepts. We hope that this contribution will help Chinese Christians to appreciate the full meaning of the Holy Spirit as fire in Mandarin Christian songs.

Introduction to the Conceptual Metaphor FIRE

Conceptual Metaphor Theory

Metaphor uses one thing to describe another.[6] According to the conceptual metaphor theory proposed by George Lakoff and Mark Johnson, metaphor is not just about aesthetics[7] and novelty[8] of language but about

---

5. This chapter follows the theorists of conceptual metaphor by using mnemonics to present the name of a conceptual metaphor. Take the conceptual metaphor LIFE IS A JOURNEY as an example: LIFE IS A JOURNEY is here not a sentence but the name of the conceptual metaphor in small capital letters (Lakoff, "Contemporary Theory of Metaphor," 207, 209; cf. Howe, *Because You Bear This Name*, 70).

6. Soskice, *Metaphor and Religious Language*, 15.

7. Aristotle, *Rhetoric of Aristotle*, III, x 1–xi 13, 1410b; cf. Richards, *Philosophy of Rhetoric*, 90.

8. Davidson, "What Metaphors Mean," 32–35.

the expression of concepts.⁹ Metaphor is omnipresent in our daily life as it shapes our language, perspective and behavior. We often process information into our cognitive system by means of metaphor.¹⁰ Metaphor is also an effective tool of communication. Through metaphor, we can explain or understand unfamiliar, difficult or abstract things by the use of familiar, understandable or tangible things.¹¹

A conceptual metaphor consists of a source domain and a target domain, the former representing a concrete thing familiar to us and easy to understand, the latter an abstract thing unfamiliar to us or hard to understand. The process by which an element of the source domain corresponds to and explains an element of the target domain in the conceptual system is called cross domain mapping. Take, for example, the conceptual metaphor LIFE IS A JOURNEY: its source domain is the concrete concept JOURNEY and its target domain is the abstract concept LIFE. Elements of the former, such as TRAVELLER, STARTING POINT, DESTINATION, OBSTACLES and CROSSROADS, are mapped on the latter as corresponding elements such as LIVING PERSON, BIRTH, DEATH, DIFFICULTIES and CHOICES.¹²

The basic conceptual metaphor, also known as the conventional conceptual metaphor, expresses a concept common to people of the same culture.¹³ Certain basic conceptual metaphors are universal, because people of all cultures share the same or similar experiences and concepts (e.g., fire, water, life). For example, the basic metaphor LOVE IS FIRE occurs in Mandarin, English and biblical Hebrew, all of which use the vocabulary of fire to express the concept of love. Yi Li, an ancient Chinese poet of Tang Dynasty, used the verse "愛如寒爐火" ("love as a furnace fire for cold days") in his poem 《雜詩》 ("A Poem") to compare love with the fire that warms on cold days. English uses verbs associated with fire to express the emotion of love, as in "He burned with love" and "that kindled love in his heart."¹⁴ The Song of Songs employs the terms "flashes of fire," "flame" and "cannot quench" to depict the intensity of love, "[F]or love is strong as death, jealousy is fierce as the grave. Its flashes are flashes of fire, the very flame of the Lord. Many waters cannot quench love, neither can floods drown it" (Cant. 8:6b–7a ESV).

9. Lakoff and Johnson, *Metaphors We Live By*, 6.
10. Lakoff and Johnson, *Metaphors We Live By*, 6.
11. Lakoff and Turner, *More than Cool Reason*, 18–19, 25–26, 35–39, 52.
12. Lakoff and Turner, *More than Cool Reason*, 3–6, 9–10, 60–61.
13. Lakoff and Turner, *More than Cool Reason*, 9, 53.
14. Kövecses, *Emotion Concepts*, 46. For further discussion of the conceptual metaphor LOVE IS FIRE in English and Mandarin, see Zhang, "FIRE and HUO," 46–48.

Having introduced conceptual metaphor theory, we now discuss the basic conceptual metaphor FIRE, which serves as a basis for our study of the conceptual metaphor THE HOLY SPIRIT IS FIRE in the Bible.

The Basic Conceptual Metaphor FIRE

The basic metaphor FIRE uses the characteristics of fire to explain various things. We review briefly the qualities of fire. Fuel, air and ignition combine to produce fire, and fire produces light and heat. Fire, to keep burning, needs fuel and air. Fire takes on different appearances at different stages. On starting, it grows from faint glow to bright blaze until, at some point, it dims and dies.[15] Before a fire has died, we can revive it by adding fuel and air. Fire plays an important role in our lives. It gives light and produces heat that can be used for, e.g., general warmth, cooking, working metal or incinerating refuse. Uncontrolled fire, however, can cause tremendous destruction.[16]

The ancient Israelites used fire in daily living and in religious rituals, including for cooking (Isa 44:15), offering sacrifices (Lev 1:2ff.), keeping warm (Isa 44:15; Jer 36:22; Mark 14:54, 67; Acts 28:2), illumination (Job 18:5; Jer 25:10; Matt 5:15), melting or purifying metals (Num 31:21–23; Ezek 22:20; 24:11) and burning down objects, cities and idols (Josh 6:24; 8:8; 11:11; Num 31:10; Deut 7:5; Jer 32:29; 36:23). The narrative in Judges 15:4–5 illustrates the power of fire to destroy on a large scale: Samson set fire to the Philistines' grains and olive orchards by sending into their fields 150 pairs of foxes with burning torches fastened on the tails of each pair. James 3:5b speaks of the ability of fire to spread, "How great a forest is set ablaze by such a small fire" (ESV). There is plenty of scriptural evidence of how the Israelites thought about fire. The authors of the Old and New Testament books used the common understanding of fire to convey profound and abstract theological truths including, notably for our purposes, truths about the Holy Spirit and His working.

The Conceptual Metaphor THE HOLY SPIRIT IS FIRE

The conceptual metaphor THE HOLY SPIRIT IS FIRE in the Bible uses the characteristics of fire to describe the characteristics of the Holy Spirit, including His manifestation and functions. Although the present study focuses on the Holy Spirit, we cannot deal with the Spirit of God without

---

15. Lakoff and Turner, *More than Cool Reason*, 31–32; Zhang, "FIRE and HUO," 32.
16. Kövecses and Lakoff, "Anger," 58–59; Zhang, "FIRE and HUO," 54–55.

considering the Trinity. It will be helpful for our understanding of THE HOLY SPIRIT IS FIRE to look at it in the broader context of the conceptual metaphor GOD IS FIRE. We therefore begin with GOD IS FIRE, followed by THE HOLY SPIRIT IS FIRE and its sub-metaphors THE HOLY SPIRIT'S JUDGMENT IS FIRE and THE HOLY SPIRIT'S REVIVAL IS FIRE.

The Conceptual Metaphor GOD IS FIRE

In the Old Testament, fire usually represents the divine manifestation. Ezekiel describes the appearance of the Lord in the form of a man whose waist and below was fire (Ezek 8:2). The Lord spoke to Moses from a burning bush (Exod 3:2ff.) and to the Israelites from the midst of the fire at Mount Horeb (Deut 4:12ff; 5:4ff.; 10:4). He led the Israelites in the wilderness by a pillar of fire at night (Num 14:14; Deut 1:33; Neh 9:12, 19). These examples show the closeness of the connection and the basis of the conceptual metaphor GOD IS FIRE.

The Lord manifested Himself in fire but also used fire to destroy people and objects. For example, during Elijah's ministry, the Lord twice sent fire from heaven to kill Baʿal's prophets and worshippers (1 Kgs 18:36–38; 2 Kgs 1:10–12; cf. Luke 9:54). The Lord in His wrath sent fire to destroy sinners (Num 11:1–3; 16:35). Deuteronomy 4:24 uses the metaphor "the Lord your God is a consuming fire" to describe the effects of his anger.

Deuteronomy 4:24 conveys the metaphor by describing the Lord as "a consuming fire" to express both His furious reaction against the Israelites for worshipping false gods and the destructive force that He deployed. The Hebrew for consuming fire, אֵשׁ אֹכְלָה (literally "devouring fire," with the adjectival participle אֹכְלָה from אכל ["to eat"] modifying אֵשׁ ["fire"]), expresses the power of divine fire by comparing it to the way in which a fire can totally consume its victim. In line with that thought of "devouring," Deuteronomy employs שמד ("to destroy") in Deuteronomy 9:3a, 8, 14, 19, 20, 25, and its synonyms אבד in 9:3b and שחת in 9:26, to emphasize the Lord's power to destroy. He had sought to destroy the rebellious Israelites and would later destroy the wicked Anakites. Here the conceptual metaphor GOD IS FIRE or, more specifically, GOD IS CONSUMING FIRE, describes the Lord's anger and destructive power.

Lakoff and Zoltán Kövecses propose the conceptual metaphor ANGER IS FIRE, referring to characteristic physical reactions to anger, viz. increased body heat and redness of face.[17] ANGER IS FIRE is found in the Old

---

17. Lakoff, *Women, Fire, and Dangerous Things*, 388–89; Kövecses and Lakoff, "Anger," 58–59.

Testament. Hebrew uses אַף (nose, nostril) in an expression for "anger."[18] An idiomatic expression, "the burning of the nose" (the verbal אַף חָרָה or the nominal חֲרוֹן אַף), uses the concept to describe intense anger.[19]

As well as the common "burning of the nose" or the like to describe the Lord's anger (e.g., Exod 4:14; 22:23; 32:10–12; Num 25:4; 32:14), the Old Testament also compares divine wrath with "devouring fire." For example, Isa 30:27 tells of the Lord venting His raging anger (בֹּעֵר אַפּוֹ) through His speech, "his lips are full of fury, and his tongue is like a devouring fire (כְּאֵשׁ אֹכָלֶת)" (ESV); Jeremiah 7:20 uses first a metaphor of water for the Lord's act of "pouring out" His anger and wrath (אַפִּי וַחֲמָתִי) on human beings, animals, trees and crops, and then the metaphor of fire for His anger that "will burn and not be quenched" (ESV). On certain occasions of judgment, the Lord's anger came with actual fire that destroyed not only objects but sinners as well (Num 11:1–3; 16:35). In His wrath, the Lord showed through fire His jealous reaction against the Israelites for idol worship and His punishment of the worshippers of false gods (Deut 32:22).

In this regard, the Lord's fire of anger is also "the fire of judgment." We can therefore say that the conceptual metaphor GOD IS FIRE signifies divine wrath and judgment as well as divine manifestation. So, when the Israelites came before the Lord, who revealed Himself as fire and spoke from fire, on the one hand, they were amazed at His glory and power and, on the other, responded with fear (Deut 5:24–25; 18:16). We often think of fire negatively because of its danger and destructive power. Little wonder that the Israelites did not dare to approach the Lord's blazing fire.

Overall, the conceptual metaphor GOD IS FIRE has several layers of meaning. It denotes God's appearance and presence and His anger and judgment. The conceptual metaphor GOD IS CONSUMING FIRE in particular expresses the Lord's jealous fury, His execution of judgment and the destructive power that that judgment brings. The Lord's fire of judgment is associated with the Spirit's judgment, which is also associated with fire. We look at this below under "The Conceptual Metaphor THE HOLY SPIRIT'S JUDGMENT IS FIRE."

From the biblical texts mentioned above, we see that the conceptual metaphor GOD IS FIRE involves a mapping of the concept from the source domain FIRE to the target domain GOD. The corresponding elements of the two domains include:

FLAME » GOD'S MANIFESTATION (appearance, presence, glory etc.),

---

18. *BDB*, 60a.
19. *HALOT*, 351.

LIGHT » GOD'S GUIDANCE,

CONSUMING FIRE » GOD'S EMOTIONS (anger),

THE POWER TO BURN » GOD'S JUDGMENT.

The arrowhead "»" refers to the direction of cross-domain mapping. A summary is given in Table 1. The Conceptual Metaphor GOD IS FIRE.

The use of the conceptual metaphor GOD IS FIRE continues in the New Testament, which also utilizes that image to describe the appearance of Christ and of the Holy Spirit (FLAME » CHRIST'S/SPIRIT'S MANIFESTATION). For example, Jesus will return "from heaven with his mighty angels in flaming fire" (2 Thess 1:7–8 ESV). The expression, "His eyes were like a flame of fire," occurs three times in Revelation in descriptions of the glorious manifestation of the eschatological Christ (Rev 1:14; 2:18; 19:12). As for the Holy Spirit, the account of Pentecost in Acts 2:1–4 describes His appearance as "divided tongues as of fire (διαμεριζόμεναι γλῶσσαι)" (Acts 2:3 ESV). Revelation 4:5 refers to the seven spirits of God as seven "lamps/torches of fire (λαμπάδες πυρὸς)."[20] With regard to the Holy Spirit, the Bible uses the image of fire to describe both His manifestation and His activity involving believers. We turn to now, as texts for further study, those scriptural passages that reflect the conceptual metaphor THE HOLY SPIRIT IS FIRE. They can be divided into two categories according to theme: (1) the Holy Spirit in judgment and (2) the Holy Spirit in revival. So we divide the conceptual metaphor THE HOLY SPIRIT IS FIRE into two sub-metaphors: THE HOLY SPIRIT'S JUDGMENT IS FIRE and THE HOLY SPIRIT'S REVIVAL IS FIRE.

Table 1. The Conceptual Metaphor GOD IS FIRE

Source Domain: FIRE	Target Domain: GOD	
Element	Element	Implication
FLAME	GOD'S MANIFESTATION	Appearance, presence, glory
LIGHT	GOD'S GUIDANCE	Instruction
REDNESS and HEAT	GOD'S EMOTIONS	Anger
BURN	GOD'S JUDGMENT	Punishment

20. The footnote of NIV renders "the seven spirits" as "the sevenfold Spirit."

The Conceptual Metaphor
THE HOLY SPIRIT'S JUDGMENT IS FIRE

Several scriptural passages use "fire" when talking of the Holy Spirit's judgment. We explore here how these texts employ that metaphor. The conceptual metaphor THE HOLY SPIRIT'S JUDGMENT IS FIRE consists of the source domain FIRE and the target domain THE HOLY SPIRIT'S JUDGMENT. The element THINGS BEING BURNED/HEATED in the source domain corresponds to the element PEOPLE/SIN in the target domain.

The conceptual metaphor THE HOLY SPIRIT'S JUDGMENT IS FIRE may have its roots in Isaiah 4:3–4, "And he who is left in Zion and remains in Jerusalem will be called holy, everyone who has been recorded for life in Jerusalem, when the Lord shall have washed away the filth of the daughters of Zion and cleansed the bloodstains of Jerusalem from its midst by a spirit of judgment and by a spirit of burning (בְּרוּחַ מִשְׁפָּט וּבְרוּחַ בָּעֵר, ἐν πνεύματι κρίσεως καὶ πνεύματι καύσεως)" (ESV). This passage states that the Lord will use "a spirit of judgment" and "a spirit of burning" to distinguish those who belong to Him from those who do not. He will make holy the one who remains in Jerusalem and is recorded for life, but will destroy the one who acts wickedly (cf. Isa 3:8–11).[21] The "spirit of judgment" and "spirit of burning" are instruments of divine judgment.[22] If we render רוּחַ/πνεῦμα as "the Spirit of God," then "the Spirit of burning (רוּחַ בָּעֵר)" is applying the conceptual metaphors THE HOLY SPIRIT IS FIRE and THE HOLY SPIRIT'S JUDGMENT IS FIRE, the latter emphasizing purification and sanctification by the Spirit's fire. The description of judgment and cleansing by divine fire echoes the closing message of Isaiah in 66:15, "For behold, the Lord will come in fire, and his chariots like the whirlwind, to render his anger in fury and his rebuke with flames of fire" (ESV).[23] This verse comprises three elements of the conceptual metaphor GOD IS FIRE, namely MANIFESTATION, EMOTIONS (anger) and JUDGMENT.

We now return briefly to that broader conceptual metaphor GOD IS FIRE and the narrower term, GOD'S JUDGMENT IS FIRE, to look at how the Bible uses the image of fire to convey concepts inherent in the theme of God's judgment.

First, God's fire involves cleansing. The concept of cleansing by fire comes from experience: people passed metal utensils through fire to clean

---

21. Brueggemann, *Isaiah 1–39*, 42–44.

22. Blenkinsopp views רוּחַ as God's instrument for judgment and translates "with a wind [spirit] of judgment and with a wind [spirit] of burning" as "with a fiery wind in the judgment" (Blenkinsopp, *Isaiah 1–39*, 202).

23. Blenkinsopp, *Isaiah 1–39*, 204.

them (Num 31:21–23); high temperature flame could remove dross from metal or ore and thus purify it (Job 28:1–2; Ezek 22:20; 24:11). Just as the process of refining could separate metal from dross, so could God's act of refining separate the obedient from the disobedient—God would preserve the former but destroy the latter. The structure of the conceptual metaphor GOD'S JUDGMENT IS FIRE consists of the element METALS/ORE in the source domain mapped onto (GOD'S) PEOPLE in the target domain and the element dross in the source domain mapped onto NOT GOD'S PEOPLE or SIN in the target domain.

In the case of Isaiah 4:3, despite its use of רחץ ("wash, wash off, away, bathe")[24] and דוח ("rinse, cleanse"),[25] which invoke the image of cleansing by water, "burning by fire" is used for the divine activity of purging. There are other biblical texts which express more clearly the concept of cleansing by fire through the conceptual metaphor GOD'S JUDGMENT IS FIRE. Malachi 3:1–5, for example, refers to the coming Lord (cf. Luke 3:16) as "a refiner's fire" and as "fuller's soap" (water metaphor), who, on the one hand, will cleanse the Levites so that "they will bring offerings in righteousness to the Lord" (ESV) and, on the other hand, will judge those who practice evil and do not fear the Lord. The Lord's judging fire will ultimately separate the good from the evil and those who fear Him from those who do not (cf. Mal 3:18). Those who survive the fire of judgment are God's people, who have been made clean (Mal 3:2–3) or have passed the divine trial (cf. Zech 13:9; 1 Cor 3:13).

Beside the image of refining fire, the image of burning chaff also conveys the conceptual metaphor GOD'S JUDGMENT IS FIRE, in which the element CHAFF of the source domain is mapped onto NOT GOD'S PEOPLE on the target domain. In line with the example from Malachi, and following the image of refiner's fire in chapter 3, chapter 4 uses the image of the burning of useless chaff to depict the divine fire's elimination of all the proud and wicked. Malachi 3–4 shows a double function of divine fire: to refine and to punish. God's judgment has a positive and a negative aspect—He uses fire to purify the righteous and fire to destroy sinners. Our use of "judgment" below will not be limited to its negative aspect.

Having discussed the broader conceptual metaphor GOD'S JUDGMENT IS FIRE, we return to THE HOLY SPIRIT'S JUDGMENT IS FIRE. In addition to Isaiah 4:3–4, which conveys the metaphor in the expression "the Spirit of burning," Matthew 3:11 and its parallel, Luke 3:16,[26] employ this same metaphor. Certain concepts in these two New Testament passages may allude to

24. BDB, 934.
25. HALOT, 216.
26. The parallel passage of the Gospel of Mark reads, "the baptism of the Holy Spirit" without mentioning "fire" (Mark 1:8).

the conceptual metaphor GOD'S JUDGMENT IS FIRE in the Old Testament. Those New Testament texts mention the prophecy of John the Baptist that the Messiah will come and baptize "with the Holy Spirit and fire." The Greek phrase for "with the Holy Spirit and fire," ἐν πνεύματι ἁγίῳ καὶ πυρί, has two nouns πνεύματι ἁγίῳ ("the Holy Spirit") and πυρί ("fire") governed by one preposition ἐν ("with"), indicating that the Messiah's baptism of "the Holy Spirit and fire" is one single baptism and not two separate baptisms.[27] To see how "the baptism with the Holy Spirit and fire" and "the Holy Spirit's judgment" are associated, we look more closely at the two passages.

In John the Baptist's message of conversion in Matthew 3:7-12, the noun "fire" occurs three times—once in each of verses 10, 11 and 12. Verses 10 and 12 use the metaphor of burning to express the Messiah's judgment and verse 11 states that "the coming one" "mightier than John"—the Messiah—will baptize with "the Holy Spirit and fire." We look first at verses 10 and 12, which seem easier to understand and which will certainly guide our interpretation of "the baptism of the Holy Spirit and fire" in 3:11. In 3:10, the statement that fire will burn down the tree that does not bear good fruit implies that the tree that bears good fruit will be spared destruction (cf. Matt 7:19). Similarly, the statement in 3:12 that the Messiah will burn up the useless chaff but save the wheat in the barn also connotes the notion of separation of two groups of people (Matt 13:24-30, 36-43; cf. Jer 23:28; Mal 4:1).[28] Those images of burning the fruitless tree and burning the unusable chaff suggest that punishment and refinement are two sides of the same coin. That echoes what we have seen with regard to GOD'S JUDGMENT IS FIRE in Isaiah 4:3-4. Just as God uses fire to eliminate sinners but purify the righteous, so will the Messiah distinguish between those who repent and those who do not, preserve the former and do away with the latter.

Some scholars see in the metaphor of fire in 3:10, 12 only the destruction of the unrepentant and overlook the corollary that the repentant are saved from destruction. That interpretation seems narrow and incomplete.[29] Our understanding is that 3:11 refers to both types of subject—the repentant and the unrepentant. Hence we perceive the Messiah's baptism of

---

27. Blomberg, *Matthew*, 80n68.

28. The metaphor of wheat and chaff is first used in Jer 23:28-29, where verse 28 uses a rhetorical question, "What is the chaff to the wheat?" (KJV), to distinguish them. The latter represents the false prophet, whose words are not from the Lord and without value, like chaff. The former represents the true prophet, who speaks for the Lord and whose words are full of power, like a fire that consumes and like a hammer that shatters a rock (v. 29).

29. For example, Gundry, *Matthew*; Davies and Allison, *Critical and Exegetical Commentary*, 1:317-18.

the Spirit and fire to be a baptism affecting everyone: bringing salvation to the repentant and punishment to the unrepentant.[30] Luke 3:1–18, which is parallel to Matthew here, supports this view.

The arrangement of the Lukan passage is slightly different. Between the themes of the burning of the tree without good fruit (Luke 3:9; par. Matt 3:10) and of the baptism of "the Holy Spirit and fire" (Luke 3:16; par. Matt 3:11), which is immediately followed by the metaphor of wheat and chaff (Luke 3:17; par. Matt 3:12), Luke inserts dialogues between John and the crowds, tax collectors and soldiers and describes people's expectations about the arrival of the Messiah (Luke 3:10–15). The common question to John from those three groups of people, "What shall we do?" shows a positive response to John's words and implies an intention to repent (Luke 3:10, 12, 14). John's audience, referred to as "you," probably includes not only the "brood of vipers" whom he identifies and rebukes—the Pharisees and the Sadducees—but also both groups, viz. those who hear and repent and those who hear but do not repent.[31] In this regard, the recipients of "the baptism of the Holy Spirit and fire" included in the "you," are both the repentant and the unrepentant. We can therefore see that "the baptism of the Holy Spirit and fire" is not limited to punishment but includes salvation. This view is consistent with the twofold function of divine judgment presented in the rest of the Gospel of Luke. Earlier than 3:16, Luke has mentioned several times the Messiah's salvific and punitive acts by the power of the Spirit (Luke 1:51–53, 71, 74; 2:34–35). All of those passages have in common the concept of separation: God will separate those who accept Him from those who reject Him. The former receive grace and the latter chastisement.[32]

The Matthean and Lukan parallels use "the baptism of the Holy Spirit and fire" for the Messiah's judgment, in which the Holy Spirit plays a part. John 16:7–11 says about the Holy Spirit's function in judgment that He comes to "convict the world (τὸν κόσμον) concerning sin and righteousness and judgment" (John 16:8 ESV). This verse hints at the Holy Spirit's "preliminary work" on unbelievers (John 16:9) in that some are moved by the Holy Spirit and accept Jesus (cf. 2 Cor 12:3) while others choose to reject Jesus and are condemned (John 16:9).[33] The Holy Spirit's role in saving the repentant and condemning the unrepentant as mentioned in the Gospels of Matthew, Luke and John corresponds well with the Old

---

30. Plummer, *Exegetical Commentary*, 29; Blomberg, *Matthew*, 80; Gibbs, *Matthew 1:1—11:1*, 157; cf. Nolland, *Luke 1—9:20*, 153.

31. Plummer, *Exegetical Commentary*, 28–29; Morris, *Gospel According to Matthew*, 62; Hagner, *Matthew 1–13*, 52.

32. Kienzler, *Fiery Holy Spirit*, 34–35.

33. Chafer, *Systematic Theology*, 3:222.

Testament's treatment of the Lord's acts of refining the righteous and destroying sinners. As mentioned above, in the conceptual metaphor God's judgment is fire, fire represents the double function of divine judgment. Similarly, "the baptism of the Holy Spirit and fire," applies the conceptual metaphor THE HOLY SPIRIT'S JUDGMENT IS FIRE.

Table 2. The Conceptual Metaphor GOD'S/THE HOLY SPIRIT'S JUDGMENT IS FIRE summarizes our discussion of judgment by God and by the Holy Spirit.

Table 2. The Conceptual Metaphor
GOD'S/THE HOLY SPIRIT'S JUDGMENT IS FIRE

Source Domain: FIRE	Target Domain: GOD/THE HOLY SPIRIT'S JUDGMENT	
Element	Element	Implication
THINGS BEING BURNED/HEATED:	PEOPLE/SIN:	
METALS/ORE	RIGHTEOUS ONES	Purification, sanctification, salvation
DROSS	SINNERS	Punishment
CHAFF	SIN	Elimination

The Conceptual Metaphor THE HOLY SPIRIT'S REVIVAL IS FIRE

The term "revival" is widely used and has multiple layers of meaning. Before we discuss the term, we must first clarify its use.[34] Earle E. Cairns defines "revival" as "the work of the Holy Spirit in restoring the people of God to a more vital spiritual life, witness, and work by prayer and the

---

34. The English verb "revive" means "wake up and live." Beougher, "Revival, Revivals," 831. Its approximate synonyms, expressing the notions of rebirth and renewal, are חיה and שוב in Hebrew, and ἀναζάω and ἀναθάλλω in Greek. Opperwall-Galluch, "Revive/Reviving," 178. Two places in the New Testament concerning rebirth and renewal involve the use of the water metaphor: In John 3, Jesus taught Nicodemus that rebirth means being "born of water and the Holy Spirit" (3:5–6, 8); Titus 3:5 interprets the believer's salvation experience as "by the washing of regeneration and renewal of the Holy Spirit." This chapter omits discussion of the aspects of rebirth and renewal, for they are not within the scope of our working definition of revival and they are mostly presented through the metaphor of water rather than of fire.

word after repentance in crisis for their spiritual decline."[35] We summarize this definition in the following main points: (1) revival is a work of the Holy Spirit, (2) the primary object is believers (evangelism is for unbelievers), (3) revival assumes previous spiritual decline, and (4) revival brings spiritual renewal and vibrant witness.[36] Charles G. Finney, in his Revival Fire, states that revival is not "fanatical excitement,"[37] but rather "manifest Divine influence,"[38] which goes through stages of "rise, progress, temporary decline, and again revival."[39]

The concept THE HOLY SPIRIT'S REVIVAL IS FIRE begins, we may say, at Pentecost with the descent of the promised Spirit in the form of fire. Acts 2:1–4 tells of the Holy Spirit appearing as fiery tongues descending from heaven on each of the believers, who then begin to speak in tongues and are filled with the Holy Spirit.[40] The indwelling Spirit then endows believers with the ability to bear witness to Jesus (Acts 1:8) and with gifts to build up the church (1 Cor 12:4–11; Rom 12:3–8; Eph 4:11; 1 Pet 4:10–11). The New Testament uses the image of fire to illustrate the operation of the Holy Spirit in believers, specifically by comparing His influence on believers to the intensity of fire. Such influence is dynamic, and dynamic change is reflected in the thriving of the spiritual life of believers. The change of status of the Holy Spirit's influence and of believers' spirituality is called "revival." In other words, "revival" denotes the Holy Spirit's influence on believers' spirituality, including their inner states of mind and outward actions. We can therefore establish the conceptual metaphor THE HOLY SPIRIT'S REVIVAL IS FIRE, which maps the source domain FIRE onto the target domain THE HOLY SPIRIT'S REVIVAL. In more detail, INTENSITY in the source domain is mapped as THE SPIRIT'S INFLUENCE on the target domain (INTENSITY » THE SPIRIT'S INFLUENCE) and THINGS BEING HEATED/BURNED in the source domain is mapped as BELIEVER'S SPIRITUALITY on the target domain (THINGS BEING HEATED/BURNED » BELIEVER'S SPIRITUALITY).

---

35. Cairns, *Endless Line of Splendor*, 22.

36. Beougher, "Revival, Revivals," 831. Timothy K. Beougher cites Carins's definition of revival and summarizes it into five points, of which this chapter lists only four and omits the item about "prayer and Bible reading" which is not immediately relevant to the conceptual metaphor THE HOLY SPIRIT'S REVIVAL IS FIRE.

37. Finney, *Revival Fire*, 32–37.

38. Finney, *Revival Fire*, 4.

39. Finney, *Revival Fire*, 4.

40. Dunn, *Acts of the Apostles*, 25. The concept of "filling" comes from the image of water or fluid, in which water or fluid represents the Holy Spirit and the container represents the believer (cf. Isa 44:3; Ezek 39:29; Joel 2:28; John 7:37–39; 1 Cor 12:13, etc.). One of the outward manifestations of filling with the Holy Spirit is the believer's boldness in preaching and serving.

In the New Testament, three verbs related to fire express the conceptual metaphor THE HOLY SPIRIT'S REVIVAL IS FIRE: ζέω ("be fervent" in Acts 18:25; Rom 12:11), ἀναζωπυρέω/ἀναζωπυρέω ("rekindle" in 2 Tim 1:6) and σβέννυμι ("extinguish" in 1 Thess 5:19). The first, ζέω, literally meaning "boil, seethe," is used figuratively to describe strong emotions (such as anger, love or desire) that become very intense or "hot."[41] We need to burn fuel to boil water, so fire plays a role in this image. Without a fire burning for long enough, the water cannot be heated to boiling point.[42] The Mandarin Bible translates ζέω as "火熱" (literally, "fiery hot," see e.g., Chinese Union Version [CUV], Chinese New Version [CNV], Chinese Contemporary Version [CCV]) in its translation, so emphasizing the high intensity.[43] The verb ζέω is used with τῷ πνεύματι to form ζέων τῷ πνεύματι in Acts 18:25 and τῷ πνεύματι ζέοντες in Romans 12:11 ("be fervent in the Spirit/spirit"). The noun τῷ πνεύματι may be associated with the Holy Spirit or the believer's spirit.[44]

"Be fervent in Spirit/spirit" is found in Romans 12:11, where Paul enumerates several attitudes that Christians should hold in their service to the Lord: "Do not be slothful in zeal, be fervent in spirit, serve the Lord" (ESV).[45] On the surface, "Be fervent in spirit" suggests that the burden of responding to Paul's exhortation falls primarily on believers. From the theological point of view, however, the believers' power to respond comes from the Holy Spirit (Acts 1:8).[46] Hence, "be fervent in Spirit" is probably the correct reading. In this vein, in the conceptual metaphor THE HOLY SPIRIT'S REVIVAL IS FIRE, the influence of the Holy Spirit is the fire and the things being burned or heated (fuel or water) are the believers' states of mind (e.g., enthusiasm). The Holy Spirit's fire heats up believers' emotions to boiling (HEAT » BELIEVER'S EMOTIONS) and, at the same time, transmits energy to them, thus empowering them to serve (ENERGY » EMPOWERMENT). "Fervent in spirit" also describes Apollos's positive response to instruction in the way of the Lord, "He had been instructed in the way of

---

41. BDAG, 426.

42. Cranfield, *Critical and Exegetical Commentary*, 634. Cranfield states that ζέω is generally used of water boiling but is also sometimes used of solids (e.g., copper) being red-hot.

43. In Rev 3:14–22, two words related to ζέω, viz. the adjective ζεστός (Rev 3:15) and the verb ζηλεύω ("be eager, earnest," Rev 3:19), echo the image of water with respect to its temperature. The Holy Spirit rebukes the lukewarm church of Laodicea as neither cold nor hot (οὐ ζεστὸς) and calls her to be fervent and repent (Rev 3:15–16, 19) (Oepke, "ζέω, ζεστός," 876–77; BDAG, 427).

44. Cranfield, *Critical and Exegetical Commentary*, 634; Bock, *Acts*, 591–92.

45. Cranfield, *Critical and Exegetical Commentary*, 634.

46. Oepke, "ζέω, ζεστός," 876.

the Lord. And being fervent in spirit, he spoke and taught accurately the things concerning Jesus, though he knew only the baptism of John" (Acts 18:25 ESV). Apollos's enthusiasm in teaching people about Jesus can be said to have been ignited by the fire of the Holy Spirit.[47]

Another verb close to "being fervent in spirit" in meaning is "rekindle" (ἀναζωοπυρέω/ἀναζωπυρέω).[48] "Rekindle" occurs in 2 Timothy 1:6, where Paul encourages Timothy, "Because of this I remind you to rekindle God's gift (ἀναζωπυρεῖν τὸ χάρισμα τοῦ θεοῦ), that you possess through the laying on of my hands" (NET). The word "rekindle" suggests a particular stage in the burning process: if we add fuel to a fire and blow air on it before it becomes too feeble or goes out, the flame can be restored to its original intensity. The expression "to rekindle God's gift" compares the operation of the Holy Spirit to that process. The object to be rekindled is God's gift within Timothy. That gift, distributed by the Holy Spirit (cf. 1 Cor 12:4, 11), epitomizes the work of the Holy Spirit in the believer.[49] Paul's use of "rekindle" may suggest that Timothy had been too timid to use his spiritual gift and therefore needed to be reminded (cf. 1:7) but there is no clear textual evidence for that theory. All we know for sure is that Paul encourages Timothy to continue using his spiritual gift.[50] The conceptual metaphor the Holy Spirit's revival is fire, expressed in the verbs "be fervent" and "rekindle," uses the concept of a flourishing fire to portray the believers' vibrant spirituality in response to the Holy Spirit's work in their lives.

The opposite of the thriving fire is the fire gone out, conveyed by the verb σβέννυμι ("extinguish").[51] "Do not extinguish the Holy Spirit (τὸ

---

47. Scholars hold different views on τῷ πνεύματι in Acts 18:25. The reference of the phrase to either the Holy Spirit or Apollos's spirit affects our understanding of Apollos's status as having received the Spirit or as not having received it. Dunn translates ζέων τῷ πνεύματι as "aglow with the Spirit"; Bock, in light of Acts 10:45–46, does not reject the possibility that τῷ πνεύματι could refer to the Holy Spirit. In his view, Acts 10:45–46 demonstrates the believer's reception of the Holy Spirit prior to baptism (Dunn, *Acts of the Apostles*, 250; Bock, *Acts*, 592). Against that, *BDAG* ("with burning zeal"), NET ("great enthusiasm"), and R. Kent Hughes ("with great fervor") regard ζέων τῷ πνεύματι as Apollos's spiritual fervor. Hughes argues Apollos did not receive the Holy Spirit until Acts 18:26. See *BDAG*, 426; Hughes, *Acts*, 247–48. Although it is reasonable to render ζέων τῷ πνεύματι as Apollos's zeal, the impetus for that zeal still originates in the Holy Spirit.

48. *BDAG*, 62–63.

49. Chafer, *Systematic Theology*, 3:362.

50. For a brief discussion of views on Timothy's spirituality deduced from the word ἀναζωπυρέω, see Mounce, *Pastoral Epistles*, 475–76.

51. The Greek verb σβέννυμι is used in the context of extinguishing fire (Matt 12:20; Heb 11:34) or putting out a light (Matt 25:8). Its metaphorical use is found only in 1 Thess 5:19 ("Do not quench the Holy Spirit" ESV) and Eph 6:16 ("extinguish all the flaming darts of the evil one" ESV).

πνεῦμα μὴ σβέννυτε)" (NET) in 1 Thessalonians 5:19 uses the image of a fire in danger of going out to refer to the influence of the Holy Spirit in an individual life.[52] Today's New International Version translates it as "Do not put out the Spirit of fire" and the International Standard Version uses "Do not put out the Spirit's fire," highlighting the use of the image. CUV paraphrases the verse as "不要消滅聖靈的感動" (literally, "do not extinguish the motivating influence of the Holy Spirit"), to clarify that it is not the Holy Spirit Himself that can be extinguished but rather His motivating influence, again applying the conceptual metaphor THE HOLY SPIRIT'S REVIVAL IS FIRE. This verse warns that believers can suppress or resist the work of the Holy Spirit in their hearts.[53]

It is worth noting that the three verbs "be fervent," "rekindle" and "do not extinguish" are in the present tense, emphasizing the progressive aspect of the actions—the fire must be kept burning.[54] "Be fervent" and "do not extinguish" have exhortatory and imperatival force. Corresponding verses can be translated as follows: "Be fervent [continually]" (Rom 12:11; cf. Rev 3:19) and "Do not [continually] extinguish the fire of the Holy Spirit" (1 Thess 5:19). In Timothy, "to rekindle" is grammatically not an imperative but an infinitive preceded by "I remind you" (present indicative), to express an ongoing result which Paul expects, "I remind you to [continually] rekindle God's gift that you possess" (2 Tim 1:6). The constant burning flame symbolizes the believer's constant and passionate commitment to serve. To the source domain therefore, we can add DURATION, corresponding to the BELIEVER'S COMMITMENT in the target domain, highlighting that aspect of service for the Lord.

The functions of the conceptual metaphor THE HOLY SPIRIT'S REVIVAL IS FIRE are several. Change in the fire's intensity represents change in the degree of the Holy Spirit's influence on believers and the fluctuation in their spirituality between thriving and decline. The heating of water to boiling serves to illustrate intensity of the believer's love for God and his/her commitment in serve Him.

---

52. Frame, *Critical and Exegetical Commentary*, 205.

53. Bruce, *1 & 2 Thessalonians*, 125. Bruce renders the image of fire in 1 Thess 5:19 as the Holy Spirit or his acts. The latter is specifically referred to as prophecy (cf. 1 Thess 5:20; also see Jer 20:9—"If I say, 'I will not mention him, or speak any more in his name,' there is in my heart as it were a burning fire shut up in my bones, and I am weary with holding it in, and I cannot." [ESV]). Also see Frame, *Critical and Exegetical Commentary*, 205. Frame argues the reference to the Holy Spirit here includes all aspects of his work, such as the giving of "a hymn, or a word of instruction, a revelation, a tongue or an interpretation" (1 Cor 14:26 NIV), in addition to prophecy.

54. Wallace, *Greek Grammar*, 518.

Table 3 summarizes the main points of the conceptual metaphor THE HOLY SPIRIT'S REVIVAL IS FIRE.

Table 3. The Conceptual Metaphor
THE HOLY SPIRIT'S REVIVAL IS FIRE

Source Domain: FIRE	Target Domain: THE HOLY SPIRIT'S REVIVAL	
Element	Element	Implication
INTENSITY	THE SPIRIT'S INFLUENCE	Strong or weak
STAGE –Extinguish –Rekindle	THE SPIRIT'S INFLUENCE	Being suppressed Spiritual gift being used
THINGS BEING HEATED	BELIEVER'S SPIRITUALITY	Thriving or decline
HEAT	BELIEVER'S EMOTIONS	Enthusiasm
ENERGY	BELIEVER'S SERVICE	Empowerment
DURATION	BELIEVER'S COMMITMENT	Continuity

The Use of the Conceptual Metaphor THE HOLY SPIRIT'S JUDGMENT IS FIRE in Mandarin Christian Songs

Below we list the lyrics of several Mandarin Christian songs chosen for their use of the conceptual metaphor THE HOLY SPIRIT IS FIRE. We seek to understand the views expressed in the lyrics and use the sub-metaphors, THE HOLY SPIRIT'S JUDGMENT IS FIRE and THE HOLY SPIRIT'S REVIVAL IS FIRE, as our rubrics for the investigation. The songs studied are either those with which I am familiar or those produced by online search per Mandarin phrases such as "聖靈的火" ("the Holy Spirit's fire") and "靈火" ("the Spirit's fire"). I use an illustrative sample of five songs; space prohibits a comprehensive survey.

"Hymn to the Holy Spirit" 〈聖靈頌〉
/Li Jingxiong (李景雄)

Li Jingxiong's "Hymn to the Holy Spirit" uses four natural phenomena, wind, water, fire, and light, one in each of four stanzas, to describe the Holy Spirit. The third stanza reads:

> 聖靈如火焰。
> 人情冷漠，勢利刻薄。
> 靈火熾熱熊熊，
> 事奉熱誠，相待厚情，
> 普世榮慶。

> The Holy Spirit is like fire.
> Relationships are cold, people are selfish and mean.
> The Spirit's fire is hot and blazing,
> believers are fervent to serve, and hospitable to others,
> which is widely glorified and celebrated.

> (副歌)
> 聖靈之光,
> 合乎神意,
> 表揚基督,
> 遍臨全地,
> 猶如在天。

> (Chorus)
> The light of the Holy Spirit,
> In line with God's will,
> To the praise of Christ,
> All over the earth,
> As in heaven.[55]

The first line, "The Holy Spirit is like fire" is taken up in the third line by the phrase "the Spirit's fire" which is an explicit example of the conceptual metaphor THE HOLY SPIRIT'S REVIVAL IS FIRE. Hence, "The Spirit's fire is hot and blazing" maps elements of the source domain HEAT and DURATION, onto the target domain as BELIEVER'S EMOTIONS and BELIEVER'S COMMITMENT respectively. The fire that is hot and blazing yields the strongest light and heat. With respect to the element HEAT, the "coldness" of human indifference stands in stark contrast to the "heat" of the Holy Spirit's flame and the "fervor" of believers. Heat from the Spirit's fire provides energy to empower

---

55. 李景雄, 〈聖靈頌〉。

believers to serve with "fervor" and warmth to show "hospitality." Among the indifferent and selfish, believers, by enthusiasm and hospitality, will stand out as admirable witnesses to Jesus Christ. With respect to DURATION, the hot, flaming fire expresses the Holy Spirit's lasting influence on believers and the resulting ongoing vitality of believers' commitment in service.

"May the Spirit's Fire Revive Me" 〈願那靈火復興我〉/Bolun Yang (楊伯倫)

Bolun Yang wrote this song in 1976. Its three stanzas and the chorus all begin with the line, "May the Spirit's fire that revives me revive again," which is the song's theme.

1. 願那復興我的靈火，重新再來一次復興我，
   起初的信心何處失落，我願悔改重新再得著。
   在明媚的春光裡，在幸福的生活中，
   我們陶醉，我們歡樂，早把主恩典忘記。

1. May the Spirit's fire that revives me revive again,
   Restore the faith which I have lost,
   I am willing to repent and regain it.
   In the lovely springtime, in the happy life,
   we live elated and captivated,
   having forgotten the Lord's grace.

2. 願那復興我的靈火，重新再來一次復興我，
   起初的希望何處失落，我願悔改重新再得著。
   在穩妥的事業裡，在迷人的笑聲中，
   我們遊戲，我們沉迷，早把主恩典忘記。

2. May the Spirit's fire that revives me revive again,
   Restore the hope which I have lost,
   I am willing to repent and regain it.
   In job security, in glamorous laughter,
   we have fun and indulge, having forgotten the Lord's grace.

3. 願那復興我的靈火，重新再來一次復興我，
   起初的愛心何處失落，我願悔改重新再得著。
   在艱苦的歲月裡，在百般的試煉中，
   我們禱告，我們儆醒，毋把主恩典忘記。

3. May the Spirit's fire that revives me revive again,
   Restore the love which I have lost,
   I am willing to repent and regain it.

> In difficult times, in various trials,
> we watch and pray, let us not forget the Lord's grace.
>
> (副歌)
> 願那復興我的靈火，重新再來一次復興我，
> 起初的信望愛何處失落，我願悔改現在就得著。
>
> (Chorus)
> May the Spirit's fire that revives revive me again,
> Restore the faith, hope and love which I have lost,
> I am willing to repent and regain them.[56]

The phrase "the Spirit's fire" under the theme of revival emphasizes INTENSITY and STAGE of the conceptual metaphor THE HOLY SPIRIT'S REVIVAL IS FIRE. Fire has the intensity to heat up or melt the coldest things, as the Spirit of God can reheat a heart which has grown cold in faith, hope and love. That is the spiritual change that the song asks for as revival. The lyrics sketch the several phases of the believer's spiritual progress, including temporary decline, awakening in crisis, repentance and a petition to the Holy Spirit (phases which correspond well with Cairns's and Finney's remarks on revival).

"Fire of Revival" 〈復興的火〉 /John Liu (劉榮神)

This song is from Album 6, Wonderful Creator, from the "Stream of Praise." The lyrics below are the official Mandarin and English versions. Its chorus attributes "revival's fire" to "Spirit desire." The official Mandarin version reads differently, rendering "Spirit desire" as "the Spirit's fire" ("聖靈的火"), thus equating "revival's fire" with "the Spirit's fire." The Mandarin version indicates more clearly the use of the conceptual metaphor THE HOLY SPIRIT'S REVIVAL IS FIRE.

> 1. 復興的火焰在燃燒，
>   讓我們響起勝利的號角，
>   傳揚耶穌基督的真道，
>   一起邁向合一的宣教。
>
> 1. Let the fire of revival blaze,
>   Let us sound the victorious trumpets,
>   Proclaim the Salvation of Jesus Christ,
>   Marching on towards the battle cry.

---

56. 楊伯倫，〈願那靈火復興我〉。

2. 在主前同心的禱告，
讓我們忠於十架的呼召，
以讚美在寶座前圍繞，
讓復興的火在我裡面燃燒。

2. With one heart praying for the lost,
Faithful to the calling of the cross,
Let's praise Him and worship in one accord,
The fire of revival burns brighter in my soul.

(副歌)
復興的火， 聖靈的火，在我心中點燃；
復興的火， 聖靈的火，把我燒在主祭壇。

(Chorus)
Revival's fire, Spirit desire, be kindled within my soul;
Revival's fire, Spirit desire, consuming my life, my all.[57]

The first and second stanzas describe the effect of the revival's fire on believers: they become inwardly harmonious and faithful and outwardly proactive in mission, prayer and worship (ENERGY). In the chorus, the parallel "revival's fire" and "Spirit desire" (or "Spirit's fire" in the Mandarin lyrics), make clear that revival is the work of the Holy Spirit. The last line "consuming my life, my all" alludes to the metaphor of sacrifice which combines with the preceding metaphor of the Spirit's fire to express the notion that believers are the sacrifice (Rom 12:1) and that the Holy Spirit is the fire on the altar. The fire of the Holy Spirit provokes so much enthusiasm (HEAT) that believers are willing to offer all that they are and have to God.[58]

"Heaven Opened" 〈天開了〉/Tiffany Wang (施弘美)

The River of Life Christian Church, Santa Clara, CA, published in 2013 the Mandarin Album Heaven Opened, in which the song of the same title "Heaven Opened" employs the vision of heaven opened wide to express the manifestation of God's glory and the Holy Spirit's work. In that vision, the Holy Spirit's works of purification, healing and revival are portrayed in images of water and of fire.

我禱告等候， 禱告等候，
我渴望你榮耀降臨。

57. 劉榮神，〈復興的火〉。
58. Cranfield, *Critical and Exegetical Commentary*, 599–600.

我禱告等候，禱告等候，
我渴望你榮耀降臨。

I'm calling, O Lord, waiting, O Lord.
How I long to see Your glory fall.
I'm calling, O Lord, waiting, O Lord.
How I long to see Your glory fall.

彰顯你同在，伸出你的手，
觸摸我們，醫治這地。
彰顯你同在，紀念你百姓，
恩待憐憫，拯救萬邦。

Show Your presence, Lord, raise Your mighty arm.
Come touch our hearts, and heal our land.
Show Your presence, Lord, please remember us.
Salvation flows to all mankind.

(副歌)
我們看見天開了，神榮光照耀，
你國度降臨，你旨意成全。
我們看見天開了，神榮光照耀，
聖靈江河，從天澆灌，燃燒我熱情，為耶穌。

(Chorus)
We'll see heaven opened wide, God, Your glory shines.
May Your kingdom come, May Your will be done.
We'll see heaven opened wide, God, Your glory shines.
Your Spirit falls afresh on us, my heart burns for You, Jesus Christ.

(橋段)
聖靈火燃燒，煉淨我的生命，
從罪中得釋放，能自由地飛翔。
聖靈火燃燒，醫治恩膏湧流，
使我們得完全，進入神的禧年。

(Bridge)
Burn on, Spirit fire, purify my heart, Lord.
Come set me free from sin, my spirit soars with You.
Burn on, Spirit fire, pour out Your anointing.
Come make us whole again, and bring Your Jubilee.[59]

The first four lines of the lyrics present the believer's words of prayer. The first two lines use the singular "I" to express the individual believer's

---

59. 施弘美，〈天開了〉。

waiting upon and desire for the arrival of God's glory. The next two lines expand to the plural to express the believers' corporate intercession for their land and for all humanity. The chorus depicts a scene of heaven opened wide so that, in answer to the believers' prayer, God's blessings will pour out and they will see the glory of God. "Your Spirit falls afresh on us" likens the Spirit's bestowing of power on the believers to falling water, underscoring the bounty of His provision. That power dwelling in the believers is then depicted by "my heart burns for You, Jesus Christ" in description of the intensity of the believers' passion (HEAT) for the Lord by use of the conceptual metaphor THE HOLY SPIRIT'S REVIVAL IS FIRE. The first phrase of the bridge, "Burn on, Spirit fire," carries the image on by asking that the effect continue and not die down or go out, as fires do (DURATION). The prayers that immediately follow, "purify my heart, Lord" and "come set me free from sin," refer to another quality of fire, namely the power to purify or refine by burning off lesser or unwanted material. The repetition of "Burn on, Spirit fire" is followed by a metaphorical plea for anointing with oil with all the implications of submission, dependence and a conferred status (cf. Luke 4:18; Acts 10:38; Isa 61:1).

"The Holy Spirit's Fire" 〈聖靈的火〉 /Hing-Chai Cheng (曾興才)

The River of Life Christian Church published in 2015 the Mandarin Album So I Will Run, in which the song "The Holy Spirit's Fire" uses the conceptual metaphor THE HOLY SPIRIT IS FIRE to express the believer's prayer to Jesus for transformation through the work of the Holy Spirit.

1. 耶穌，親愛的耶穌，
   歡迎你來，全心歡迎你來，
   用聖靈與火來為我施洗，
   因你是我的智慧、我的公義。

1. Jesus, dear Jesus,
   We welcome your coming wholeheartedly.
   Baptize me with the Holy Spirit and fire,
   for you are my wisdom and righteousness.

2. 耶穌，親愛的耶穌，
   歡迎你來， 全心歡迎你來，
   洗淨我的汙穢和一切罪惡，
   因你是我的聖潔、我的救贖。

2. Jesus, dear Jesus,
   We welcome your coming wholeheartedly.
   Cleanse my filth and all my sins,
   for you are my holiness and salvation.

(副歌)
喔！聖靈的火喔！聖潔的火！
來煉淨我，來復興我，燃燒我對耶穌的熱情。
喔！聖靈的火！喔！聖潔的火！
賜下能力，讓我活出主耶穌的生命，影響這世代。

(Chorus)
O Holy Spirit's fire! O Holy fire!
Refine me, revive me, kindle my passion for Jesus.
Grant me power to live out Jesus' life and influence
this generation.[60]

"Baptize me with the Holy Spirit and fire" in the first stanza echoes Matthew 3:11 and Luke 3:16, reflecting the conceptual metaphor THE HOLY SPIRIT'S JUDGMENT IS FIRE. "Cleanse my filth and all my sins" in the second stanza uses a water metaphor to express Jesus' forgiveness. The chorus returns to the metaphor of fire with "Holy Spirit's fire" and its synonym "Holy fire." The petitions, "purify me" and "revive me," apply the metaphors THE HOLY SPIRIT'S JUDGMENT IS FIRE and THE HOLY SPIRIT'S REVIVAL IS FIRE respectively. In the latter, the heat of fire is the believer's passion for Jesus (HEAT) and the energy of fire is the power to witness for Jesus (ENERGY).

Section Conclusion

Our analysis above shows that the lyrics of those five Mandarin Christian songs generally reflect the biblical metaphor THE HOLY SPIRIT IS FIRE. The sub-metaphor, THE HOLY SPIRIT'S REVIVAL IS FIRE occurs in almost every one of the five. Although "Hymn to the Holy Spirit" and "Heaven Opened" do not include "revival" in their lyrics, both appeal to the image of flaming fire to express a flourishing spiritual state. Regarding the conceptual metaphor THE HOLY SPIRIT'S JUDGMENT IS FIRE, the notions of repentance and forgiveness of sin, prerequisites for revival, are found in "May the Spirit's Fire Revive Me," "Heaven Opened" and "The Holy Spirit's Fire." The last of those connects the baptism of the Spirit and fire.

---

60. 曾興才，〈聖靈的火〉。

The songs skilfully utilize the image of fire to describe the effect of the Holy Spirit on believer's spirituality. They use (1) the STAGES of a fire and the INTENSITY and ENERGY of fire for the influence of and empowerment by the Holy Spirit and (2) the HEAT and DURATION of fire for a believer's strong passion and lasting commitment. "Heaven Opened" and "The Holy Spirit's Fire" contain metaphors of both water and fire. Alternation between the use of those metaphors in the Bible occurs in, e.g., Isaiah 4:3, Jeremiah 7:20, and Malachi 3:1–5, so is not original or inappropriate in the lyrics. "The Fire of Revival" connects the metaphor of the Spirit's fire with the metaphor of sacrifice, so adding a new layer of meaning to the image.

Conclusion

In this chapter, we have investigated the Mandarin Christian term "The Holy Spirit's Fire" ("聖靈的火") /"the Spirit's fire" ("靈火"), by exploring its theological implication through the lens of the conceptual metaphor THE HOLY SPIRIT IS FIRE and by checking whether biblical references support its use. Analysis of the biblical texts establishes the basis for the conceptual metaphor THE HOLY SPIRIT IS FIRE and the two sub-metaphors THE HOLY SPIRIT'S JUDGMENT IS FIRE and THE HOLY SPIRIT'S REVIVAL IS FIRE. That done, we have seen how the selected five Mandarin Christian songs use the two sub-metaphors to portray the characteristics of the Holy Spirit and to describe the influence of the Holy Spirit on the believer's inner state of mind and outward behaviour.

"The Holy Spirit's fire"/"the Spirit's fire" is not esoteric or abstract theological terminology but a concept and an image. The biblical authors referred to the common knowledge of fire's qualities to create vivid images of the lively activity of the Holy Spirit. We, as readers of the Bible, can use the images to understand in greater depth the authors' messages.

I hope that this short chapter will be of help to Christians, when they use the terms or sing songs about the fire of the Spirit, to consciously appreciate the metaphor and to understand the abundant and profound truths conveyed by it.

Bibliography

Aristotle. *The Rhetoric of Aristotle: A Translation*. Edited by John Edwin Sandys. Translated by Richard C. Jebb. Cambridge: Cambridge University Press, 1909.
Bauer, Walter, et al. *Greek-English Lexicon of the New Testament and Other Early Christian Literature*. 3rd ed. Chicago: University of Chicago Press, 2000.

Beougher, Timothy K. "Revival, Revivals." In *Evangelical Dictionary of World Missions*, edited by A. Scott Moreau et al., 831. Baker Reference Library. Grand Rapids: Baker, 2000.

Blenkinsopp, Joseph. *Isaiah 1–39: A New Translation with Introduction and Commentary*. Anchor Bible 19. New York: Doubleday, 2000.

Blomberg, Craig L. *Matthew*. New American Commentary 22. Nashville: Broadman & Holman, 1992.

Bock, Darrell L. *Acts*. Baker Exegetical Commentary on the New Testament. Grand Rapids: Baker Academic, 2007.

Brown, Francis, et al. *Hebrew and English Lexicon of the Old Testament*. New York: Oxford University Press, 2001.

Bruce, F. F. *1 & 2 Thessalonians*. Word Biblical Commentary 45. Nashville: Thomas Nelson, 1982.

Brueggemann, Walter. *Isaiah 1–39*. Westminster Bible Companion. Louisville: Westminster John Knox, 1998.

Cairns, Earle E. *An Endless Line of Splendor: Revivals and Their Leaders from the Great Awakening to the Present*. Wheaton, IL: Tyndale House, 1986.

Chafer, Lewis Sperry. *Systematic Theology*. 8 vols. Grand Rapids: Kregel, 1993.

Cranfield, C. E. B. *A Critical and Exegetical Commentary on the Epistle to the Romans*. Vol. 2. 2 vols. New York: T. & T. Clark, 2004.

Davidson, Donald. "What Metaphors Mean." In *On Metaphor*, edited by Sheldon Sacks, 29–45. Chicago: University of Chicago Press, 1979.

Davies, W. D., and Dale C. Allison. *A Critical and Exegetical Commentary on the Gospel According to Saint Matthew*. Vol. 1. 3 vols. London: T. & T. Clark, 2010.

Davis, Raymond J. 《高山靈火：一個非洲土族集體歸主的當代神蹟，非洲埃塞俄比亞開荒宣教紀實》。楊信成譯。新加坡：KIANOS，1998。

Dunn, James D. G. *The Acts of the Apostles*. Grand Rapids: Eerdmans, 1996.

Finney, Charles G. *Revival Fire*. Albany, OR: AGES Software, 1995. https://www.hopefaithprayer.com/books/RevivalFire.pdf.

Frame, James Everett. *A Critical and Exegetical Commentary on the Epistles of St. Paul to the Thessalonians*. Edinburgh: T. & T. Clark, 1979.

Gibbs, Jeffrey A. *Matthew 1:1—11:1*. Concordia Commentary. St. Louis: Concordia, 2006.

Gundry, Robert H. *Matthew: A Commentary on His Handbook for a Mixed Church under Persecution*. Grand Rapids: Eerdmans, 1994.

Hagner, Donald A. *Matthew 1–13*. Word Biblical Commentary 33A. Dallas: Word, 1993.

Howe, Bonnie. *Because You Bear This Name: Conceptual Metaphor and the Moral Meaning of 1 Peter*. Biblical Interpretation Series 81. Leiden: Brill, 2006.

Hughes, R. Kent. *Acts: The Church Afire*. Preaching the Word. Wheaton, IL: Crossway, 1996.

Kienzler, Jonathan. *The Fiery Holy Spirit: The Spirit's Relationship with Judgment in Luke-Acts*. Journal of Pentecostal Theology, Supplement Series 44. Dorset, UK: Deo, 2015.

Köhler, Ludwig, et al. *Hebrew and Aramaic Lexicon of the Old Testament*. 2 vols. Leiden: Brill, 2001.

Kövecses, Zoltán. *Emotion Concepts*. New York: Springer, 1990.

Kövecses, Zoltán, and George Lakoff. "Anger." In *Emotion Concepts*, by Zoltán Kövecses, 50–68. New York: Springer, 1990.

Lakoff, George. "The Contemporary Theory of Metaphor." In *Metaphor and Thought*, edited by Andrew Ortony, 202–51. Cambridge: Cambridge University Press, 1993.

———. *Women, Fire, and Dangerous Things: What Categories Reveal about the Mind*. Chicago: University of Chicago Press, 1990.

Lakoff, George, and Mark Johnson. *Metaphors We Live By*. Chicago: University of Chicago Press, 1980.

Lakoff, George, and Mark Turner. *More than Cool Reason: A Field Guide to Poetic Metaphor*. Chicago: University of Chicago Press, 1989.

Morris, Leon. *The Gospel According to Matthew*. Pillar New Testament Commentary. Grand Rapids: Eerdmans, 1992.

Mounce, William D. *Pastoral Epistles*. Word Biblical Commentary 46. Nashville: Thomas Nelson, 2000.

Nolland, John. *Luke 1—9:20*. Word Biblical Commentary 35A. Dallas: Word, 1989.

Oepke, Albrecht. "Ζέω, Ζεστός." In *TDNT*, 876–77.

Opperwall-Galluch, Nola J. "Revive/Reviving." In *The International Standard Bible Encyclopedia*, edited by Geoffrey W. Bromiley et al., 4:178. Rev. ed. Grand Rapids: Eerdmans, 1988.

Plummer, Alfred. *An Exegetical Commentary on the Gospel According to Saint Matthew*. Grand Rapids: Eerdmans, 1956.

Richards, Ivor A. *The Philosophy of Rhetoric*. Mary Flexner Lectures on the Humanities 3. London: Oxford University Press, 1981.

Soskice, Janet Martin. *Metaphor and Religious Language*. Oxford: Clarendon, 1985.

Wallace, Daniel B. *Greek Grammar Beyond the Basics: An Exegetical Syntax of the New Testament*. Grand Rapids: Zondervan, 1996.

Zhang, Juan. "A Contrastive Study of Conceptual Metaphors of Fire and Huo." Master's Thesis, Hunan Normal University, 2013.

巴特曼 (Bartleman, Frank)。《火浪湧來：艾蘇薩街復興始末》. 朱東譯。教會復興叢書 9. 台北市：橄欖，1989。

古約翰 (Goforth, Jonathan) et al.《靈火繼焚燒：韓國大復興續》. 吳亞青和鄭夙珺譯。教會復興叢書 8. 台北市：橄欖，1993。

李景雄。〈聖靈頌〉。《華人聖頌》，羅炳良編。香港：福音證主協會，1992。

威廉布雷爾和布魯斯亨特 (Blair, William, and Bruce Hunt)。《野火燎原：韓國大復興報導》. 黃莉莉譯。教會復興叢書 7. 台北：橄欖，1987。

施弘美。〈天開了〉。《天開了》，顧中萍編輯。生命和敬拜讚美系列. Santa Clara, CA：矽谷生命河靈糧堂，2013。

高科爾 (Koch, Kurt E.)。《奔騰之火：拿大復興實錄》. 雅風譯. 教會復興叢書 5. 台北市：橄欖，1986。

曾興才。〈聖靈的火〉。《奔向愛我的神》，顧中萍編輯. 生命和敬拜讚美系列。Santa Clara, CA：矽谷生命河靈糧堂，2015。

楊伯倫。〈願那靈火復興我〉。《華人聖頌》，羅炳良編。香港：福音證主協會，1992。

愛德華·米勒 (Miller, Edward)。《火從天降：阿根廷大復興》. 韓正愷譯。教會復興叢書 3. 台北市：橄欖，1986。

———.《火的延燒：阿根廷大復興續篇》. 劉仰青譯. 台北：橄欖，1986。

蔡麗安(Choy, Leona Frances)。《靈火力源：屬靈偉人對聖靈的探究與體驗，1850-1930》. 邵大衛和譚素敏譯. Petaluma, CA：中信出版社，1993。

劉榮神。〈復興的火〉。《全能的創造主》，游智婷編輯. 讚美之泉敬拜讚美詩歌本 6. Tustin, CA：讚美之泉，2001。

戴理望（Davis, Raymond J.)。《高山靈火：一個非洲土著集體歸主的當代神蹟》. 楊信成譯. 新加坡: KIANOS, 1998。

9

Renewing Global Christianity

An Asian American Pentecostal Perspective on the Way

AMOS YONG[1]

Introduction

IN ABOUT THE MIDDLE of 2013, while I was serving as dean of the School of Divinity of Regent University in Virginia Beach, Virginia, I had the occasion as part of a sabbatical to travel across North America and then, over five weeks, around the world on a six-country tour, speaking at various churches and schools connected to the global renewal movement.[2] Over the course of almost four months, I blogged about my travels, thinking about the renewing work of the Spirit in and from the various contexts I visited.[3] The following re-

1. Amos Yong (PhD Boston University) is, as of July 2014, Professor of Theology & Mission and, as of July 2019, Dean of the School of Theology and the School of Intercultural Studies at Fuller Theological Seminary, Pasadena, California; he is a Pentecostal pastor's- and missionary-kid, and has held ministerial credentials with the Assemblies of God since 1987.

2. The sabbatical and the around-the-world trip was funded by The Luce Foundation; as one of the Henry Luce III Fellows in Theology for 2012–2013, I wrote and published *Renewing Christian Theology*.

3. These blogs appeared in *Renewal Dynamics* (renewaldynamics.com), the official blog of Regent University School of Divinity and the Center for Renewal Studies, founded by Wolfgang Vondey, but are no longer available. Some of these blogs have appeared previously in my essay, "Missional Renewal," albeit deployed therein for missiological purposes specifically (rather than with the Asian American theme that is

produces these blogs more or less as they were originally published, although I have inserted footnotes clarifying and expanding on various points, as well as calling attention to relevant scholarly literature. The final concluding section is a new reflection, two years after these blogs, in which I reconsider these impressions specifically from my Asian American location.

From "Empowered Evangelicals" and "Radical Middlers" to . . . : The Society of Vineyard Scholars and the Renewal of the Vineyard—22 April 2013

These past few days I have been privileged to have been a guest at the fifth annual conference of the Society of Vineyard Scholars (SVS).[4] As a renewal movement in its second generation, the Vineyard as a whole is *both* confronting the various challenges attending to *and* also embracing the many opportunities opened up by charting a way forward that builds and expands on the legacy of its charismatic founder John Wimber.[5] A number of observations stand out for me as someone who is an outsider to the Vineyard but one sympathetic to its quest, at least as played out in the SVS, for a robustly charismatic and renewalist theological identity and self-understanding.

First, the conversations I had with Vineyarders (some within the group prefer Vinyardites) indicate that they are embracing the difficult but important task of ongoing self-discovery and self-identification. Under Wimber's leadership, the dominant projection was of the movement as "empowered evangelicals." This has clearly allowed the Vineyard to influence and contribute to the ongoing charismatization of Evangelicalism in the contemporary North American landscape. However, contemporary Vineyarders looking into the middle of the twenty-first century are not convinced that such a posture will enable the movement to counteract the equally challenging trends that are evangelicalizing their charismatic sensibilities and commitments, often to the detriment of the vision and mission of church renewal that is at the heart of historic Vineyard distinctives.

A few years ago, an initial history of the early Vineyard was published by Bill Jackson as *The Quest for the Radical Middle: A History of the Vineyard*

---

dominant in this essay); I am grateful to Sophia Megallanes and the editors of *Quadrum* for allowing me to use these blogs here also for the purpose of this essay and book.

4. My plenary presentation at the conference was recently published: Yong, "Christological Constants," 19–33.

5. The movement is one of three discussed from a sociological perspective in Miller, *Reinventing American Protestantism*; an engaging anthropological study is Luhrmann, *When God Talks Back*.

(1999).⁶ I confirmed with some at the conference that this still adequately addresses the Vineyard self-understanding. I certainly can see that thoughtful Vineyarders continue to identify with such a "radical middle" path between various binary options as did those in the first generation that preceded them—i.e., between rigidly dispensational and liberal/existential notions of the reign of God (the biblical kingdom of God being a notion that remains central to Vineyard thought and praxis); between merely objective and wildly subjective understandings of the person and work of the Spirit; or between pragmatic or emergent and propositionalist or classical theological and practical orientations. Such trajectories embody not an anti-evangelical attitude but one that seeks a renewed Evangelicalism. Yet the label "radical middlers," while catchy and accurate within the preceding scheme, does not in and of itself indicate the parameters within which Vineyarders are journeying, and as such is clumsy as an adequate theological description.

What I did observe was that the SVS is bringing together both established leaders and younger scholars and scholar-pastors in common quest. This group is looking for a way forward for Vineyard theology *and* practice that does not bifurcate the life of the mind from either the work of the Spirit or the heralding of the reign of God. Many also seem to have worked through to a post-Western, post-modern, and post-Enlightenment set of sensibilities that allows them to embrace their task as an ongoing journey. I applaud this dynamic self-understanding. It not only allows for the ongoing renewal of the Vineyard within and amidst ever-prevalent but necessary institutionalizing impulses, but is also consistent with the legacy of their founder, especially his emphasis (derived from George Eldon Ladd) of the now-and-not-yet character of the coming reign of God.⁷ I would encourage SVS members to be in conversation with those in other (pentecostal/charismatic) renewal movements also seeking to retain a healthy, vital, and invigorated missional presence in the globalizing world of the twenty-first century, not only to learn from them but also to contribute to this important conversation that ought not be shut down.

Global Renewal: A View from (Western) Canadian America—17 May 2013

This past week I have been spending time—courtesy of my friend and current second vice-president of the Society for Pentecostal Studies, Michael

---

6. Jackson, *Quest for the Radical Middle*.

7. See, e.g., Wimber, *Kingdom Ministry*; cf. Ladd, *Gospel of the Kingdom*; Ladd, *Presence of the Future*.

Wilkinson—on the campus of Trinity Western University (TWU) and with its Associated Consortium of Theological Schools (ACTS), including the Canadian Pentecostal Seminary (CPS), lecturing on global renewal theology. To be sure, when the apostles were told that the outpouring of the Spirit was to empower them to bear witness to the gospel to the ends of the earth, they were thinking certainly of Rome rather than of Vancouver, British Columbia, much less Langley, British Columbia, and even Abbottsford, British Columbia (where I preached last Sunday, at Christian Life Community Church). Yet equally to be sure, the winds of the Spirit have blown north, as one scholarly volume is aptly titled,[8] so that Pentecost and the renewing work of the Spirit has also—indeed, even!—occurred above the US border (Americans from the US may find hard to believe).

Yet the renewal movement in Western Canada certainly has its own distinct flavor. British Columbian renewalists see commonalities stretching up and down the Pacific Northwest (PNW) rather than eastward across the vast Canadian expanse, meaning that there may be more in common within PNW renewalism than there is between Canadian Pentecostalism stretching from the central to the Maritime region in the far Eastern shore. But what are some of the characteristics of pentecostal and charismatic renewal Christianity in this area, one that is quite secular but also very cosmopolitan and multicultural?[9]

While there is much to talk about, one feature that stands out is how renewalism can flourish as a minority tradition. By this, I am referring to the demographically minute segment of the population that represents pentecostal, charismatic, and evangelical Christianity in a pluralistic (Western) Canada. Yet even with these constraints, some renewalists are forging new conversations and pathways. The CPS, for instance, realizes that graduate theological education in the (Western) Canadian context can only succeed when intentional and strategic collaboration across evangelical and even ecumenical and traditional lines are forged. ACTS thus includes pentecostal, evangelical, Baptistic, Mennonite, Reformed, and even Roman Catholic partnerships. The future of renewal within this matrix is less an us-versus-them phenomenon but a matrix of more-or-less charismatically oriented or at least informed traditions in which each member or tradition of the theological community (body) has specific gifts that edify the whole for the common good (1 Cor 12:12ff.).

---

8. Wilkinson and Althouse, *Winds from the North*.

9. On religiosity in the secular PNW, see Killen and Silk, *Religion and Public Life*; and Wellman, *Evangelical vs. Liberal*.

So renewal and revival may not be exploding across Western Canada like it is numerically in other parts of the world. However, sometimes being a part of a minority tradition teaches us some important lessons and opens up possibilities that we might not otherwise consider when our numbers are stronger and we are part of or have access to the dominant social order. So while renewal Christianity in (Western) Canada may lack some of the pizzazz of what is occurring in the global South (or even south of their border or eastward across the Canadian landscape),[10] I would not underestimate its potential to demonstrate leadership in certain venues going forward. That is surely a mark of the Spirit, of whom we "do not know where it comes from or where it goes" (John 3:8).

The International Church of the Foursquare Gospel and Global Renewal—5 July 2013

This past weekend, through the invitation of A. J. Swoboda, author of the forthcoming *Tongues and Trees: Toward a Pentecostal Ecology Theology* in the JPT Supplement Series (announced for April 2013, but it is late!)[11] and his friends, I had the privilege of hanging out with the vanguard of the Foursquare gospellers in the Pacific Northwest (PNW) area. Preaching at Faith Center in Eugene, Oregon, and at Theophilus Church in the Hawthorne district of southeast Portland, and then engaging with three dozen of the denomination's ministers from the North Pacific (Oregon and Alaska) and Northwest (Washington and Northern Idaho) districts was a real treat. Although not one of the larger classical pentecostal denominations in North America, it is strongest in the PNW region, with hundreds of churches across Washington, Oregon, Alaska, and Northern Idaho.

But how can I know that the Foursquare in the PNW is at the vanguard of their church when I have not visited them around the rest of the country, much less the world? Two reasons: First, I could tell from the books they are reading,[12] the questions they are asking, and the things they are passionate about, that they are at the forefront of classical pentecostal churches as a whole, about which I do know a little bit, in terms of engaging with present

---

10. Pentecostalism in Eastern Canada is certainly being transformed by migration from the majority world; see Wilkinson, *Spirit Said Go*.

11. Since *Tongues and Trees*, Swoboda has also published (as editor), *Blood Cries Out*, and (with Daniel L. Brunner and Jennifer L. Butler), *Introducing Evangelical Ecotheology*, and thereby established his reputation as *the* leading pentecostal ecotheologian working at the present.

12. Including (of course!) my own, *Hospitality and the Other*, and *Who is the Holy Spirit?*

trends and anticipating future expressions of the coming reign of God. Second, a witness from an unexpected source: over dinner one evening with faculty from George Fox Seminary (where I graduated with a master's degree in Christian history and thought back in 1993), I asked Native theologian Randy Woodley[13] which church was doing exemplary work among Native populations in North America, and he responded without hesitation: the Foursquare, in terms of its empowering indigenous leaders.[14] His response was completely unexpected but confirmed my sense that something important was happening among this relatively small group of Foursquare gospellers here and around the country.

In conversation with their various leaders, I came to discern that in some respects, the more or less adolescent phase of Foursquare development may actually be part of the key to its current vitality. What I mean is that, as they put it, it has only been in the last twenty-five years that the church leadership has transitioned from the McPherson family (since 1988),[15] and this has opened up to myriad conversations about its identity, mission, and vision. What is remarkable is that these discussions are not being prematurely foreclosed; but rather than being debilitating, they have instead invigorated a range of responses, at least in terms of exploratory practices, and it is these latter responses that have revitalized the church, especially in the PNW, even while keeping their discursive negotiations relevant and interesting.

While a sociologically reductionist "explication" of Foursquare PNW is certainly possible, I do not want to discount a theological—better: pneumatological—factor. Perhaps the renewing work of the Spirit is facilitated at least in part through a persisting adolescence that resists all of the suffocating aspects of ecclesial "maturation" (growing up).[16] To be sure, such a "youthful" denominational or even institutional phase can be challenging in some respects, but if not hierarchically predetermined, may leave open conceptual and practical space for pentecostal mission to innovate for the renewal of the

---

13. Woodley, *Shalom and the Community*.

14. See Bear-Barnetson, "Introduction to First Nations Ministry." In addition, Tarango, *Choosing the Jesus Way*, has covered developments among Native Americans within the larger Assemblies of God denomination; see also pentecostal missiologists, Waldrop and Alexander, "Salvation History," 109–24.

15. Remember the church was founded by Aimee Semple McPherson; an informative historical perspective on her achievements that goes a long way in identifying the "DNA" of the movement extending into the present is Sutton, *Aimee Semple McPherson*.

16. Friesen, *Norming the Abnormal*, documents Foursquare's efforts to resist the pressures of institutionalization, at least as compared with the Assemblies of God, a comparative study that itself sheds much light on the flexibility of Foursquare in the present time.

church. Those interested in global renewal may need to take a closer look at what is happening in the International Church of the Foursquare Gospel, especially in this "pagan" region of the PNW.

From Azotus to Auckland: Renewal at the Bottom of the Earth?—5 July 2013

As Philip found himself transported suddenly from the Gaza road to Azotus (Acts 8:40), so also I went to sleep on an airplane out of LAX [Los Angeles International Airport] and awoke in Auckland last weekend. I was here for the "Theology, Disability & the People of God" conference sponsored by Laidlaw and Carey Baptist Colleges, but also preached at Titirangi Baptist Church and then spent half a day meeting with pentecostal scholars, pastors, and leaders here in New Zealand's largest city. My hosts, Andrew Picard and Myk Habets at Carey and Graeme and Linda Flett and Fiona Sherwin at Laidlaw (among many others), were wonderful blessings, all on top of an already incredibly rich conference.[17]

But what about global renewal close to the bottom of the world? Two major trends emerged for me in discussing the state of renewal here in Kiwi-land. First, the charismatic movement which arrived in the late 1960s has permeated much of the church. It is fair to say that there has been a widespread pentecostalization and charismatization of the churches in the last forty plus years, so much so that there are as many bapticostals and baptismatics—for instance (my nomenclature)—as any other type of Christian.[18] One might even talk about a "Hillsong-ization" of the churches, given the adoption of its music and worship genres in many churches on both islands. On the other hand, the palpable presence of megachurches like Hillsong, particularly through the telecommunicative and other exchange networks of globe-trotting apostles, evangelists, and other "superstar" pastors and preachers, has also brought about a homogenization of renewal in this part of the world.[19] So on the one hand, there is a proliferation of renewal among the different churches, but on the other, there is a growing standardization of these streams according to a few megachurch templates.

Yet I also think there is a wild card that might provide a prophetic edge for Kiwi renewalists to lead global renewal from the bottom of the world, and that relates to if and how the hearts of Maori New Zealanders

---

17. See my published presentation, Yong, "Disability and the Renewal," 250–63.
18. See the recent study of Knowles, "Transforming Pentecostalism," 330–48.
19. On Hillsong as a global phenomenon, see Evans, "Hillsong Abroad," 179–96.

can be revitalized by the Holy Spirit.[20] The Maori initially became Christians with the Treaty of Waitangi in 1840 that gave the indigenous islanders rights as British subjects; however, over the next century, more than 90 percent of Maori abandoned their Christian faith in large part because of what they felt were breaches of the Treaty by the European settlers. The issues remain hotly contested, even today. However, the fact is that the Maori constitute up to 15 percent of the Kiwi population and may be in the best position of any indigenous or native groups around the world to not only make a substantive contribution to their own future, but also work toward the common good of their country.

Although I am neither a prophet nor the son of one (cf. Amos 7:14), I would not be surprised if it is but a matter of time before the Maori embrace some form of renewal Christian expression, in part because of the depth of their spirituality. When that happens, they will further transform the religious landscape of New Zealand and, perhaps more importantly, rejuvenate Kiwi Christianity so it can become a prophetic exemplar of a post-Western and post-secular quest for justice and human flourishing along the way of Jesus as Messiah for the middle of the twenty-first century. If renewal continues to expand within and across the majority world, why might it not also be reinvigorated by Spirit-filled Maori at the bottom of the earth?

My friends at Laidlaw and Carey are alert to the possibilities and are working hard along many challenging fronts; but perhaps the Spirit of God has some surprises left even here in a thoroughly secular New Zealand—would it be unimaginable if such unfolded along some of the lines intuited above?[21]

From the Areopagus to Alphacrusis: Down-Under Renewal—13 July 2013

My first visit to the continent of Australia was a memorable one. It included preaching at the Wesley International Congregation in the Central Business District (CBD) of Sydney (underneath the Westfield mall and the Sydney Tower) to a pan-Asian/multicultural, youthful, and charismatic congregation, and being hosted by Alphacrusis College in the Sydney suburbs

20. Some initial gestures in this direction are found in Worford, "Theology of the Holy Spirit," 185–90.

21. Not coincidentally, I note, one of the leading theologians of the Spirit—or more accurately, "pneumatologians" (to coin a neologism) of Third Article theology, as it is becoming more widely known—is from New Zealand: Carey Baptist theologian, Myk Habets. Among his various books on this front are *The Spirit of Truth* and *Third Article Theology*.

first for an Empowered 21 scholars' consultation on Asian Pentecostalism[22] and then for a two-day conference on "Pentecostal Theology & the Marketplace."[23] I also got to visit my auntie (my mother's sister) who I had not seen in over forty years: she had come to Sydney from Malaysia as a teenager in a nursing program in the early 1970s (when Australia had a shortage of nurses and sponsored them in from around the Pacific Rim), and my family emigrated from Malaysia shortly thereafter to the USA. The initial forces of globalization had taken her southeast and me and my family to America. Migration for us both at that time seemed to have taken us to the ends of the earth, although my trip Down Under this time around can be seen also as going from one end to another.[24]

If the Wesley Mission draws its energy from the contemporary currents of globalization (situated as it is within and even under the hub of an internationalized CBD), the E21 consultation explored, among other topics, the Asianization of Australian Pentecostalism even as the conference engaged with what might be called the Hillsong-ization of global Pentecostalism. Worship at the Wesley Mission evidenced the influence of Hillsong, albeit as refracted and reflected through the faces and voices of a pan-Asian youth choir in multicultural Aussie style. Then the consultation highlighted how although pentecostal churches in Australia are among the few that have been growing in the last decade (whilst other denominations and churches have been stagnant or declining, as in the Euro-American West), such growth has been significantly boosted by the world itself coming Down Under. That is the sense in which Australian Pentecostalism has been and is being especially Asianized, even as such Australasian and Oceanian Pentecostalism itself is being charismatized (see the preceding section on Kiwi Pentecostalism), or, more accurately, Hillsong-ized.[25]

There is no doubt that when talking about global renewal Christianity the Hillsong Aussies are leading the way.[26] Sydney is the third most expen-

---

22. Which papers have since been published in Synan and Yong, *Global Renewal Christianity*.

23. I lecture for this conference from my work on pentecostal theology and economics in *In the Days of Caesar*, ch. 7, and in Attanasi and Yong, *Pentecostalism and Prosperity*. The conference organizer and the one who orchestrated my invitation and stay was Shane Clifton, Alphacrusis faculty member and leading pentecostal theologian from Down Under; aside from many other publications, he also has written on the conference theme: Clifton, "Pentecostal Approaches to Economics," 263–81.

24. I reflect on this in my essay, "The Im/Migrant Spirit," 133–53.

25. The chapters in part IV of Synan and Yong, *Global Renewal Christianity*, address these various developments.

26. Aside from his chapter on Hillsong already cited (note 19 above), see also the book-length study by Evans, *Open Up the Doors*.

sive city in the world in part because Australia is also one of the wealthiest nations there is (per capita, that is), and thus the Christianity embodied by the Hillsong brand is one that features professionalism in style, an orientation toward success, and the pursuit of excellence (according to a range of market measures at least). To get underneath (or down under) global renewal, then, is to get or understand renewal Down Under. One cannot comprehend either apart from the other.

Two thousand years ago, St. Paul wandered into discussions at the Areopagus and began interacting with those "telling or hearing something new" (Acts 17:21). I have wondered with my Alphacrusis colleagues this past week about what is really new, and what is not so new under the sun, vis-à-vis the renewing work of the Spirit. With only 22.5 million Aussies, they oftentimes feel as if what is happening Down Under is insignificant against the backdrop of the present global renewal movement. However, like it or not, and whatever else we might say or think about Hillsong ecclesially, theologically, and liturgically, there is no denying that at least for the moment, it is arguable that as they go, so goes global renewal.[27]

My auntie left Muslim Malaysia over forty years ago to come to a country she did not anticipate would be increasingly secularized; today, however, a post-secular Australia is nurturing one of the wellsprings of global renewal. My own migration, part of a reverse missionary trend (from the Malaysian "rest" to the American "West") now interfaces with a global renewal dynamic that comes from Down Under and goes in multiple directions to the ends of the earth. My visit helps me to understand at least one trajectory of the wind of renewal; it remains to be seen where and how the perturbations of this breath will fluctuate . . .

The Future of Renewal: A Malaysian-American Reconnaissance—22 July 2013

I left Malaysia, my place of birth, about thirty-seven years ago, when my parents immigrated to the USA as missionaries to Chinese speaking immigrants in California. I spent this past week in Kuala Lumpur (KL)—only my third trip back to my homeland, all since 2001—enjoying visiting with my family, feasting (practically nonstop—forgive me Jesus!) on the distinctive Malaysian foods, enduring the humidity, and marveling at the incredible urbanization and modernization of this city (there are probably as many

---

27. Thus has Clifton, with Roman Catholic theological colleague Neil Ormerod, written *Globalization and the Mission of the Church*, which addresses these important missiological issues.

skyscrapers per square mile in the KL metropolitan area as anywhere, with many more to come). Having lived in America since 1976, I felt as if I was coming back to the ends of the earth; in reality, I had gone as a 10-year old to the ends of the earth, and now have tasted home again.

While here I had the privilege of visiting some amazing congregations. My first Sunday I ministered at the oldest Assembly of God (AG) church (since 1934!) in the heart of the hustle and bustle of KL, First Assembly of God Church, with my message interpreted into Cantonese and Mandarin in two services. Then in the middle of the week, I got a chance to visit the church my father, Rev. Joseph Yong, pastored from 1969 to 1975, Glad Tidings Church, in Petaling Jaya (a KL suburb), now a megachurch with Cantonese, Mandarin, Tamil, and Indonesian sections and preparing to celebrate its fiftieth anniversary plus dedication of its grand "Vision Center." My second Sunday was at the mega-Calvary Church, at their new and massive Calvary Convention Center (CCC), where wireless-interpretation of the service (and my sermon) was provided into Bahasa Malaysia and Cantonese. The 23rd World Pentecostal Conference will be held at the CCC during the last week of August (next month).[28]

In the midst of all this, I had the privilege of lecturing at the Bible College of Malaysia and then interacting with a number of the principals and leaders of the Malaysian Association of Theological Schools. Although theological education here in this small country is no less challenging than in other parts of the world, yet even amidst the dominant Malay Muslim sociopolitical context and ethos, there is guarded optimism. Malaysia has long been an international crossroads, going back as far as the fourth century when its ports serviced trade routes between India and China. Today, it remains in many ways the hub of Asia, featuring indigenous Malays, East Asians (of all types, predominantly Chinese), and South Indians, among many other nationalities. There is a growing Malaysian diaspora around the world even as this fast developing nation is also the migration destination for those from many other nations, tribes, and tongues.[29]

Renewalists (pentecostals and charismatics) are found across the evangelical-ecumenical spectrum (the lines between these are a bit fuzzy in this context) even as classical pentecostal churches continue to thrive. While overt evangelization of Muslims remains legally prohibited, this does not hinder believers from praying and believing for the renewal of

---

28. An overview of renewal in Malaysia is in Lim, "Pentecostalism in Singapore and Malaysia," 213–32; see also Tan, "Pentecostal and Charismatic Origins," 281–306.

29. For an overview of Christianity in Malaysia, see Chia, "Malaysia and Singapore," 77–94.

the land.³⁰ Observations about renewal happening in the East Malaysian context are encouraging toward these ends. There is a sense that just as the ends of the earth came to Jerusalem for the first century Pentecost, followed by the apostolic sending back toward those same ends, so also is the Malaysian church a multi-cultural fellowship of the Spirit poised for further and more palpable international impact. OK, so Malaysian Christians are not as numerous as South Korean ones, and they are certainly outnumbered by many other nations; but the Hebrew renewalist prophet cautioned against despising the day of small things (Zech 4:10), so I would not count out the possibility of a global renewal catalyzed or precipitated through a new Pentecost across the Malay peninsula. Perhaps the tropical heat here prefigures fresh tongues of fire that will alight on KL and go from here to the (other) ends of the earth.

From the Clash to the Renewal of Civilizations: A View from Jakarta—29 July 2013

That the "clash of civilizations" thesis regarding the coming Armageddon between Islam and the West, including Christianity in the most apocalyptic scenarios, remains an ominous possibility is felt no less in Indonesia than it is in various pockets around the world. Yet my recent visit to Jakarta, including stops at International English Service, Harvest Theological Seminary, Seminari Bethel (affiliated with the Church of God, Cleveland), and Gereja Bethel Indonesia GLOW Fellowship (in the Serpong suburb), suggests to me that the church in Indonesia may be poised to make a substantive contribution to the next generation of renewal theology. Here are two major reasons for my cautious optimism.

First, the postcolonial democratic philosophy of "pancasila"—literally, the "five principles" [framing a harmonious co-existence between citizens of many faiths]—puts Indonesian theologians in a unique position to contribute to theologies of interfaith encounter and relations, political theologies, public theologies, theologies of culture, theologies of contextualization, and theologies of mission in the context of twenty-first-century globalization.³¹ The many languages of the many people groups may potentially become a resource for an authentic Indonesian theological contribution to these various theological discourses. If so, Indonesian theologians would not have to

---

30. See, e.g., Rowan, *Proclaiming the Peacemaker*.

31. Thus, Joas Adiprasetya, my co-host, professor of theology, and President of Jakarta Theological Seminary, has published *An Imaginative Glimpse*, to which I contributed the foreword.

repeat what western theologians have been or are saying on these matters but can interject their own constructive models and approaches. I believe that renewal theologies grounded in the "many tongues of Pentecost" narrative of Acts 2 are in as good a position as any to facilitate such contributions.[32] The fact that renewal theologies note and even emphasize how the various languages of the world can be instruments of declaring the wondrous works of God (Acts 2:11) is arguably an optimal foundation for the next generation of Indonesians engaged in the constructive theological task.

This is because, second, the contemporary Indonesian state remains what might be called a "mediating" context, perhaps *par excellence*.[33] What I mean is not only that "pancasila" might mediate between Islam (the dominant religious majority of the country) and a religiously pluralistic world, but also that the history of this country has itself has been constituted through a series of mediations—for instance, between the colonial Dutch and Germans on the Western end (Sumatra) to the colonial Americans on the Eastern end (bordering the Filipino islands); between the indigenous Malay on the Northern side to the aboriginal Melanesians and Australians on the South/eastern side; between South Asian (Indian) and East Asian traders and their legacies and presences; between island-sharing with East Malaysians (in Borneo) on the one hand and with Pacific Islanders (Papua New Guineans) on the other hand; etc. Indonesian theologians who take their own histories, contexts, and geographies seriously are primed to think about a range of "islandic" theologies given the thousands of islands that make up the nation.[34] Such efforts will foreground the distinctive particularities comprising the peoples' lives amidst the criss-crossing trends that have marked the Indonesian experience over the last few millennia, and which modernization, urbanization, and globalization have accelerated.

Again, it seems to me, renewal theological sensibilities and intuitions are suitable for such an important and yet dynamic present task. Here, the ancient and yet future orientation of faith in the historic and also coming Christ can only be forged and articulated if there is a robust pneumatological theology that inspires Christian confession in a multi-lingual, cultural, and religious domain. Indonesia, in this sense, is a microcosm of what the world

---

32. See my *Spirit Poured Out on All Flesh*, ch. 4.

33. Since I wrote this blog, Cartledge, *Mediation of the Spirit*, has appeared, urging that we consider the mediatorial potential of pentecostal spirituality and theology in this context.

34. See the classic study of Tetsuro, *Climate and Culture*, which explores how topography, geography, and weather patterns impact religious belief and practice. A pneumatological theology of geography is applied analytically to the Aotearoan aquascape (as opposed to landscape) in Birgin, "Waters of Aotearoa" 165–84.

of the twenty-first century is increasingly becoming. Is it too much to hope that a homegrown Indonesian theology will be relevant not only for its people but for the global church, perhaps even sparking the renewal of the Christian theological tradition? I hope that its theologians will emerge, renewalists and otherwise, to take up the challenge of fulfilling the promise of a faithful and yet relevant Christian theology for the third millennium.[35]

Renewal in Stereo—The Sounds of Renewal: What Hath Cambridge to Do with Azusa Street?—3 August 2013

I have just spent this past week at Oxford, first at the Oxford Center for Mission Studies (OCMS) and then at the second Congregational Music & Worship conference (CMWC) at Ripon College, Cuddesdon. A mere ten miles apart, yet my experiences this week have provided for me a stereophonic perspective on global renewal. I mean this in the following two respects.

First, the CMWC opened up a new set of windows into global Christianity. Here for the first time, I was surrounded not by religious studies scholars or theologians (my usual colleagues and conversation partners), but musicologists, ethnomusicologists, and worship studies scholars and practitioners, among others. The field of congregational music and worship is rather heterogeneous, with many working in this arena deploying interdisciplinary tools. Besides this interdisciplinary ferment, the conversation was rich precisely because of the global scope of existing scholarship. Research on music and worship practices around the world—not only the Euro-American West but also across Australasia, Africa, and Latin America—will always stimulate wide-ranging conversation, and certainly did so this week.[36] Further, by my unscientific count, about one third of all presentations focused on or interfaced with renewal movements directly or took up issues related to such movements. As a scholar of global renewal, this is an educational heaven! More importantly, since I have always known how central music is to renewal spirituality and have in the last few years begun working on an edited book on global pentecostal and charismatic music and worship, participation in this conference confirmed for me how untapped this field of inquiry is for renewal (pentecostal and charismatic) studies. If scholarship on global renewal has missed opportunities so far to explore these aspects of renewal Christianity, I am more convinced than ever that a musicological lens will sound out new trajectories of understanding of renewal praxis, mission, and lived realities, even while facilitating the kind of oral, aural,

---

35. See my *Renewing Christian Theology*.
36. See my brief article, "Worship in Many Tongues," 14–17.

kinesthetic, aesthetic, affective, and sonic reflections that are desperately needed for renewal theology in its second century.[37]

If the CMWC shone a musicological sound-scope on the global renewal movement, then work being done through the OCMS highlights how renewal is never far from the surface of global Christianity. The OCMS has brought together a diverse faculty to serve students especially from the majority world. Its holistic missiological approach recognizes that the gospel meets not just abstract souls but people embodied in various historical, social, cultural, geographical, and material contexts. Thus any relevant theology of mission will have to take into account and be able to engage incarnationally and pentecostally with global realities and local particularities, simultaneously. Again, while the OCMS does not limit its research and scholarly initiatives to renewal movements specifically, there is also no denying that given the ongoing pentecostalizing and charismatizing of world Christianity, renewal movements and issues are intertwined in OCMS projects and discourses at many levels, not the least of which are the work of its students and the publications of OCMS's Regnum Books imprint.[38]

My OCMS-CMWC conversations press home a fact that most of us realize but often forget: that global renewal is diverse, not only because of the shift of the center of Christianity to the global South, but also (even especially) because it has to be felt, heard, and experienced, not just read about. If OCMS emphasizes that the landscape of renewal crosses continental divides, then CMWC accentuates that the soundscape of renewal spans a wider range of instruments, genres, styles, and repertoires—among other musical dimensions—than its waspel (a new word I learned referring to white intonations of black gospel music) or even Hillsong versions might grant. CMWC may not return to Oxford in the future (its third conference may be held elsewhere); but OCMS will continue to expand our understanding of global renewal even as it will continue to provide fodder for its students and researchers. Hence either temporarily (in CMWC) or even in the short-to-longer term (OCMS), Oxford will remain a site for snap- and sound-shots of renewal trends unleashed in part through Azusa Street a century ago, at least to video- and audio-graph as well as document its trajectories, if not also to be caught up in the winds of renewal.

---

37. My presentation at the conference, "Improvisation, Indigenization, and Inspiration," 279–88; I have further discussed the orality and affectivity of pentecostal spirituality in my "Spirit and Proclamation."

38. My contribution is Im and Yong, *Global Diasporas and Mission*.

Global Pedagogies: Renewing Theological Education Today—10 August 2013

I have recently finished a five-week, six-country whirlwind trip around the world. It was an honor to have preached in small and mega-churches during my trip, a privilege to have lectured in diverse venues ranging from Bible institute and established college settings to scholarly conference environments, and a blessing to have had the chance to renew old friendships while gaining many new ones. My travels have prompted reflection on many aspects of global renewal . . . but as I return to my regular "day job" as dean of a theological school, I want to pause to briefly focus on theological education amidst the dynamics of contemporary globalization. Against this latter horizon, a number of considerations deserve mention.

First, there is a groundswell of theological education around the world. Bible institutes, leadership colleges, and other church-, network-, and megachurch-based training centers and programs are proliferating. On the one hand this is exciting, reflecting the fact that there is one body of Christ and one fellowship of the Spirit constituted by many members (not only globally or internationally but even within any country or region); but on the other hand, this is itself one manifestation of wider trends related to ecclesial fragmentation. So if a post-denominational church-scape opens up to these various possibilities, those institutions of theological education will emerge out of the pack that can engage the broadest spectrum of churches and point the way forward in the twenty-first century. In this pluralistic ecclesial context, seminaries and divinity and theological schools that are resolutely Bible-based, Christ-centered, and Spirit-empowered will speak the language of the churches more clearly than those who are not as triadically oriented.[39] Curricular innovations, pedagogical sensibilities, and scholarly initiatives attuned to these developments across the global church are in the best position to lead the discussion moving forward.[40]

Second, however, institutions of theological education not only serve the church and empower Christian mission but also have one foot always in the academy. The fact that ecclesial interfaces with culture, society, and globalization are complicated in turn requires interdisciplinary understanding, without which the church's mission will be comprised either because of accommodation or irrelevance to the world. Such understanding must be

---

39. See my essay, "Finding the Holy Spirit at the Christian University," 455–76 and 577–87.

40. The communications revolution will continue to transform theological education; see for instance my "Incarnation, Pentecost, and Virtual Spiritual Formation," 27–38.

informed by academic expertise across many fields of knowledge, precisely what theological faculties ought to provide as communities of (faithful) inquiry. The challenge of course is that such faculties have to be at least bilingual, interpreting scholarly discourses to the churches (and their students) while also translating ecclesial tongues to the academy. Perhaps this is in part why those who can embrace the multiplicity of tongues as declaring the wondrous works of God (Acts 2:11) are in a better position to facilitate theological education for the present global context.[41]

This means, third, that the future of theological education will need to be evangelical and yet ecumenical (in serving churches across the Protestant, Catholic, and Orthodox spectrum), be relevant in interfaith matters (given that most Christians around the world find themselves as part of a minority tradition), and be adept across disciplinary lines. Can the center hold amidst the various particularities and constituencies that have to be navigated? Perhaps it is naïve to think that renewal pedagogies are in as good a position as any to accomplish such expansive tasks. Theological education that is undertaken in the Holy Spirit is precisely for that reason also Christ-centered and biblically founded, although the reverse is not always the case. The opportunities are legion—may renewalists working in the arena of theological education ride the winds of the Spirit in order to be effective shapers of hearts, minds, and hands to make a difference in their churches, the academy, and the world.[42]

Updated (Second) Impressions from the Perspective of the Asian American Diaspora—August 2015

In the years since I recorded the preceding reflections, I published *The Future of Evangelical Theology: Soundings from the Asian American Diaspora*.[43] Let me venture three retrospective comments in light of this book and the theological program it charted.

First, as should be clear from the proceeding, the Asian world is constituted by multiplicity and plurality, not only many cultures but also many ethnicities, languages, and religions. The Asian American world is therefore no less pluralistic, albeit now refracted through the pluralism that is also "America." While evangelical and renewal theologians particularly might be

---

41. I make some initial suggestions in this direction in "Holy Spirit and the Christian University," 163–80.

42. Coulter and Yong, *Finding the Holy Spirit at the Christian University*, documents historical trends and charts next steps.

43. Yong, *Future of Evangelical Theology*.

threatened by such plurality, a Day of Pentecost perspective attentive to the Spirit's redemption of the many tongues of the Mediterranean world—the known "global" in the first century—might be a catalyst instead of dialogical mission in a pluralistic world, one that is attentive to the "testimonies" of the other and yet also able to bear adequate witness to the risen Christ simultaneously.[44] This may also be why there is one body with many members so that the spiritual gifts of each may build up the diversity of the body (1 Cor 12) to bear witness in a pluralistic world.[45]

Second, as already noted, the "worlds" of Asia and America are in flux, each now informing and shaping the other even as both are being transformed by the forces of globalization. Transnational and transcontinental migration means not only that Asians and Asian Americans are caught up in the ebbs and flows of the global political economy but that their identities are changing. If before "Asian" needed to be qualified by nationality, ethnicity, geography, etc., and then "Asian American" already denoted hybridity, these are surely less static in the present global ferment. A renewal perspective, however, insists that even the hybridity of the God-man Jesus of Nazareth was brought about by the Holy Spirit,[46] and thus also will the Spirit who is being "poured out upon all flesh" (Acts 2:17a) constitute dynamic human creatures in relationship to the saving work of the triune God. If this is the case, then, the shifting sands of creaturely identity are caught up and redeemed by the power of the Spirit of Christ. What emerges is thereby a unity-in-multiplicity declaring the wonders of God and "speaking about God's deeds of power" (Acts 2:11b).[47]

But in the end, on this side of the eschaton, we see through a glass dimly (1 Cor 13:12a), and hence have to continuously discern the Holy Spirit from the other spirits. In a pluralistic cosmos,[48] distinguishing the Spirit of God in Christ from other powers is essential, even if not always easy.[49]

---

44. I have also published two companion volumes toward this end: Yong, *Dialogical Spirit* and *Missiological Spirit*.

45. I expand on this Pauline charismatic ecclesiology in *Bible, Disability, and the Church*, ch. 3.

46. See here the insightful work of Bantum, *Redeeming Mulatto*.

47. See also my *Spirit of Love*, esp. ch. 9.

48. E.g., Kärkkäinen et al., *Interdisciplinary and Religio-Cultural Discourses*.

49. From an Asian perspective, for instance, theologians are beginning to ask about the relationship of the life-giving Holy Spirit to the life-force *qi* in the Chinese context. Leading the way here is my fellow pentecostal theologian and friend, Yun, *Holy Spirit and Ch'i (Qi)*; that this is not an aberrant trajectory is evidenced by the work of others, including but not limited to Kim, *Holy Spirit, Chi, and the Other*, and Lee, *Spirit, Qi, and the Multitude*. I support such inquiries, but have heretofore adopted a more cautious comparative approach—e.g., *The Cosmic Breath*, and *Pneumatology and the*

Hence we find ourselves all the more, and always, reliant on the Holy Spirit, who leads us into all truth. We also discover afresh what it means to say that we are dependent on the guidance of the Spirit as manifest in the Christian tradition, and in the church ecumenical, so that discernment emerges from out of ongoing participation in the body of Christ and the fellowship of the Spirit as she (and we) interact with our fellow human creatures along the way.[50] Only on this journey betwixt-and-between do we identify the presence and activity of the Spirit of the living God who is *not of* but yet also *in* the world. Come, Holy Spirit, once again . . .[51]

Bibliography

Adiprasetya, Joas. *An Imaginative Glimpse: The Trinity and Multiple Religious Participation*. Eugene, OR: Pickwick, 2013.

Attanasi, Katherine, and Amos Yong, eds. *Pentecostalism and Prosperity: The Socioeconomics of the Global Charismatic Movement*. Christianities of the World 1. New York: Palgrave Macmillan, 2012.

Bantum, Brian. *Redeeming Mulatto: A Theology of Race and Christian Hybridity*. Waco, TX: Baylor University Press, 2010.

Bear-Barnetson, Cheryl. "Introduction to First Nations Ministry: Everything One Wants to Know about Indigenous Ministry in Canada and the United States but is Afraid They are Too White to Ask." DMin thesis, The King's Seminary, 2009.

Birgin, Helen. "The Waters of Aotearoa: Experience of the Holy Spirit?" In *Land and Place—He Whenua, He Wāhi: Spiritualities from Aotearoa New Zealand*, edited by Helen Birgin and Susan Smith, 165–84. Auckland: Accent, 2004.

Brunner, Daniel L., et al. *Introducing Evangelical Ecotheology: Foundations in Scripture, Theology, History, and Praxis*. Grand Rapids: Baker Academic, 2014.

Cartledge, Mark J. *The Mediation of the Spirit: Interventions in Practical Theology*. Pentecostal Manifestos Series. Grand Rapids: Eerdmans, 2015.

Chia, Edmund Kee-Fook. "Malaysia and Singapore." In *Christianities in Asia*, edited by Peter C. Phan, 77–94. Malden, MA: Wiley-Blackwell, 2011.

Christian-Buddhist Dialogue.

50. As I unpack in my *Spirit-Word-Community*.

51. I am grateful to Peter Tie for inviting my contribution to this project, and to Ryan Seow, my graduate assistant, for proofreading the article (although I remain fully responsible for any errors of fact or interpretation). Because I did not have time to write a fresh article for this volume when I was approached by Peter in 2015, I volunteered to string together these previously posted blogs and pose them as an "essay"; and then, I appended footnotes to my own work to give readers some idea of what I might have contributed to the book if I had started from scratch (this explains why the citations, one excepted, all derive from 2014 and earlier). In 2018, the editors of the journal *Quadrum* (of the Foursquare Scholars Fellowship) approached me to write an article for their theme issue on missiology, and I used some of the blogs to address missiological themes for them (see note 3 above).

Clifton, Shane. "Pentecostal Approaches to Economics." In *The Oxford Handbook of Christianity and Economics*, edited by Paul Oslington, 263–81. Oxford: Oxford University Press, 2014.

Coulter, Dale, and Amos Yong. *Finding the Holy Spirit at the Christian University: Renewing Christian Higher Education*. Grand Rapids: Eerdmans, 2018.

Evans, Mark. "Hillsong Abroad: Tracing the Songlines of Contemporary Pentecostal Music." In *The Spirit of Praise: Music and Worship in Global Pentecostal-Charismatic Christianity*, edited by Monique Ingalls and Amos Yong, 179–96. University Park: Pennsylvania State University Press, 2015.

———. *Open Up the Doors: Music in the Modern Church*. London: Equinox, 2006.

Friesen, Aaron T. *Norming the Abnormal: The Development and Function of the Doctrine of Initial Evidence in Classical Pentecostalism*. Eugene, OR: Pickwick, 2013.

Habets, Myk. *The Spirit of Truth: Reading Scripture and Constructing Theology with the Holy Spirit*. Eugene, OR: Pickwick, 2010.

———. *Third Article Theology: A Pneumatological Dogmatics*. Minneapolis: Fortress, 2016.

Im, Chandler H., and Amos Yong, *Global Diasporas and Mission*. Regnum Edinburgh Centenary Series 23. Oxford: Regnum, 2014.

Jackson, Bill. *The Quest for the Radical Middle: A History of the Vineyard*. Kenilworth, South Africa: Vineyard International, 1999.

Kärkkäinen, Veli-Matti, et al., eds. *Interdisciplinary and Religio-cultural Discourses on a Spirit-Filled World: Loosing the Spirits*. New York: Palgrave Macmillan, 2013.

Killen, Patricia O'Connell, and Mark Silk, eds. *Religion and Public Life in the Pacific Northwest: The None Zone*. Walnut Creek, CA: AltaMira, 2004.

Kim, Grace Ji-Sun. *The Holy Spirit, Chi, and the Other: A Model of Global and Intercultural Pneumatology*. New York: Palgrave Macmillan, 2011.

Knowles, Brett. "Transforming Pentecostalism: Some Reflections on the Changing Shape of Pentecostalism in Aotearoa-New Zealand." In *Global Renewal Christianity: Spirit-Empowered Movements Past, Present, and Future*. Vol. 1, *Asia and Oceania*, edited by Vinson Synan and Amos Yong, 330–48. 4 vols. Lake Mary, FL: Charisma, 2015.

Ladd, George Eldon. *Gospel of the Kingdom: Scriptural Studies in the Kingdom of God*. Grand Rapids: Eerdmans, 1990.

———. *The Presence of the Future: The Eschatology of Biblical Realism*. Rev. ed. Grand Rapids: Eerdmans, 1996.

Lee, Hyo-Dong. *Spirit, Qi, and the Multitude: A Comparative Theology for the Democracy of Creation*. New York: Fordham University Press, 2013.

Lim, Timothy T. N. "Pentecostalism in Singapore and Malaysia: Past, Present, and Future." In *Global Renewal Christianity: Spirit-Empowered Movements Past, Present, and Future*. Vol. 1, *Asia and Oceania*, edited by Vinson Synan and Amos Yong, 213–32. 4 vols. Lake Mary, FL: Charisma, 2015.

Luhrmann, Tanya M. *When God Talks Back: Understanding the American Evangelical Relationship with God*. New York: Vintage, 2012.

Miller, Donald E. *Reinventing American Protestantism: Christianity in the New Millennium*. Berkeley: University of California Press, 1997.

Ormerod, Neil, and Shane Clifton. *Globalization and the Mission of the Church*. Ecclesiological Investigations 6. New York: T. & T. Clark, 2011.

Rowan, Peter. *Proclaiming the Peacemaker: The Malaysian Church as an Agent of Reconciliation in a Multicultural Society*. Oxford: Regnum, 2012.

Sutton, Matthew Avery. *Aimee Semple McPherson and the Resurrection of Christian America*. Cambridge: Harvard University Press, 2007.

Swoboda, A. J., ed. *Blood Cries Out: Pentecostals, Ecology, and the Groans of Creation*. Eugene, OR: Pickwick, 2014.

———. *Tongues and Trees: Toward a Pentecostal Ecological Theology*. Journal of Pentecostal Theology Supplement Series 40. Blandford Forum, UK: Deo, 2014.

Synan, Vinson, and Amos Yong, eds. *Global Renewal Christianity: Spirit-Empowered Movements Past, Present, and Future*. Vol. 1, *Asia and Oceania*. 4 vols. Lake Mary, FL: Charisma, 2015.

Tan, Jin Huat. "Pentecostal and Charismatic Origins in Malaysia and Singapore." In *Asian and Pentecostal: The Charismatic Face of Christianity in Asia*, edited by Allan Anderson and Edmond Tang, 281–306. Baguio City, The Philippines: Asia Pacific Theological Seminary Press, 2005.

Tarango, Angela. *Choosing the Jesus Way: American Indian Pentecostals and the Fight for the Indigenous Principle*. Chapel Hill: University of North Carolina Press, 2014.

Tetsuro, Watsuji. *Climate and Culture: A Philosophical Study*. Translated by Geofffrey Bownas. New York: Greenwood, 1988.

Waldrop, Richard E., and J. L. Corky Alexander Jr. "Salvation History and the Mission of God: Implications for the Mission of the Church among Native Americans." In *Remembering Jamestown: Hard Questions about Christian Mission*, edited by Barbara Brown Zikmund and Amos Yong, 109–24. Eugene, OR: Pickwick, 2010.

Wellman, James K., Jr. *Evangelical vs. Liberal: The Clash of Christian Cultures in the Pacific Northwest*. Oxford: Oxford University Press, 2008.

Wilkinson, Michael. *The Spirit Said Go: Pentecostal Immigrants in Canada*. New York: Peter Lang, 2006.

Wilkinson, Michael, and Peter Althouse, eds. *Winds from the North: Canadian Contributions to the Pentecostal Movement*. Religion in the Americas 10. Leiden: Brill, 2010.

Wimber, John. *Kingdom Ministry, Kingdom Service*. Ann Arbor, MI: Servant, 1987.

Woodley, Randy. *Shalom and the Community of Creation: An Indigenous Vision*. Grand Rapids: Eerdmans, 2012.

Worford, J. E. "A Theology of the Holy Spirit." In *Religious Studies in the Pacific*, edited by John Hinchcliff et al., 185–90. Auckland: Colloquium, 1978.

Yong, Amos. *The Bible, Disability, and the Church: A New Vision of the People of God*. Grand Rapids: Eerdmans, 2011.

———. "Christological Constants in Shifting Contexts: Jesus Christ, Prophetic Dialogue, and the *Missio Spiritus* in a Pluralistic World." In *Mission on the Road to Emmaus: Constants, Context, and Prophetic Dialogue*, edited by Cathy Ross and Stephen B. Bevans, 19–33. Maryknoll, NY: Orbis, 2015.

———. *The Cosmic Breath: Spirit and Nature in the Christianity-Buddhism-Science Trialogue*. Philosophical Studies in Science & Religion 4. Leiden: Brill, 2012.

———. *The Dialogical Spirit: Christian Reason and Theological Method for the Third Millennium*. Eugene, OR: Cascade, 2014.

———. "Disability and the Renewal of Theological Education: Beyond Ableism." In *Theology and the Experience of Disability: Interdisciplinary Perspectives from Voices Down Under*, edited by Andrew Picard and Myk Habets, 250–63. New York: Routledge, 2016.

———. "Finding the Holy Spirit at the Christian University: Renewal and the Future of Higher Education in the Pentecostal-Charismatic Tradition." In *Spirit-Empowered Christianity in the 21st Century: Insights, Analyses, and Future Trends*, edited by Vinson Synan, 455–76. Lake Mary, FL: Charisma, 2011.

———. *The Future of Evangelical Theology: Soundings from the Asian American Diaspora*. Downers Grove, IL: IVP Academic, 2014.

———. "The Holy Spirit and the Christian University: The Renewal of Evangelical Higher Education." In *Christian Scholarship in the Twenty-First Century: Prospects and Perils*, edited by Thomas M. Crisp et al., 163–80. Grand Rapids: Eerdmans, 2014.

———. *Hospitality and the Other: Pentecost, Christian Practices, and the Neighbor*. Faith Meets Faith. Maryknoll, NY: Orbis, 2008.

———. "The Im/Migrant Spirit: De/Constructing a Pentecostal Theology of Migration." In *Theology of Migration in the Abrahamic Religions*, edited by Peter C. Phan and Elaine Padilla, 133–53. Christianities of the World. New York: Palgrave Macmillan, 2014.

———. "Improvisation, Indigenization, and Inspiration: Theological Reflections on the Sound and Spirit of Global Renewal." In *The Spirit of Praise: Music and Worship in Global Pentecostal-Charismatic Christianity*, edited by Monique Ingalls and Amos Yong, 279–88. University Park: Pennsylvania State University Press, 2015.

———. "Incarnation, Pentecost, and Virtual Spiritual Formation: Renewing Theological Education in Global Context." In *A Theology of the Spirit in Doctrine and Demonstration: Essays in Honor of Wonsuk and Julie Ma*, edited by Teresa Chai, 27–38. Baguio City, The Philippines: Asia Pacific Theological Seminary Press, 2014.

———. *In the Days of Caesar: Pentecostalism and Political Theology—the Cadbury Lectures 2009*. Sacra Doctrina. Grand Rapids: Eerdmans, 2010.

———. *The Missiological Spirit: Christian Mission Theology for the Third Millennium Global Context*. Eugene, OR: Cascade, 2014.

———. "Missional Renewal: Pentecostal Perspectives to and from the Ends of the Earth." *Quadrum* 1 (2018) 133–56.

———. *Pneumatology and the Christian-Buddhist Dialogue: Does the Spirit Blow through the Middle Way?* Studies in Systematic Theology 11. Leiden: Brill, 2012.

———. *Renewing Christian Theology: Systematics for a Global Christianity*. Waco, TX: Baylor University Press, 2014.

———. "The Spirit and Proclamation: A Pneumatological Theology of Preaching." *The Living Pulpit* (May 2015). http://www.pulpit.org/2015/05/.

———. *Spirit of Love: A Trinitarian Theology of Grace*. Waco, TX: Baylor University Press, 2012.

———. *The Spirit Poured Out on All Flesh: Pentecostalism and the Possibility of Global Theology*. Grand Rapids: Baker Academic, 2005.

———. *Spirit-Word-Community: Theological Hermeneutics in Trinitarian Perspective*. New Critical Thinking in Religion, Theology and Biblical Studies. Aldershot, UK: Ashgate, 2002.

———. *Who is the Holy Spirit? A Walk with the Apostles*. Brewster, MA: Paraclete, 2011.

———. "Worship in Many Tongues: The Power of Praise in the Vernacular." *Worship Leader* 122 (2015) 14–17.

Yun, Koo Dong. *The Holy Spirit and Ch'i (Qi): A Chiological Approach to Pneumatology*. Eugene, OR: Pickwick, 2012.